I0083933

Kindling of an Insurrection

Kindling of an Insurrection

Notes from Junglemahals

CHANDAN SINHA

Routledge
Taylor & Francis Group
LONDON NEW YORK NEW DELHI

First published 2013 in India
by Routledge
912 Tolstoy House, 15–17 Tolstoy Marg, Connaught Place, New Delhi 110 001

Simultaneously published in the UK
by Routledge
2 Park Square, Milton Park, Abingdon, Oxon OX14 4RN

Routledge is an imprint of the Taylor & Francis Group, an informa business

© 2013 Chandan Sinha

Paperback edition published 2015

Typeset by
Star Compugraphics Private Limited
5, CSC, Near City Apartments
Vasundhara Enclave
Delhi 110 096

All rights reserved. No part of this book may be reproduced or utilised in any
form or by any electronic, mechanical or other means, now known or hereafter
invented, including photocopying and recording, or in any information storage
and retrieval system without permission in writing from the publishers.

British Library Cataloguing-in-Publication Data
A catalogue record of this book is available from the British Library

ISBN 978-1-138-84744-6

But play no tricks upon thy soul, O man;
Let fact be fact, and life the thing it can.

ARTHUR HUGH CLOUGH
(*Dipsychus*, 1850)

Everything has been said before, but since nobody listens we have to
keep going back and beginning all over again.

ANDRÉ GIDE
(*Le traite du Narcisse*, 1891)

You may not be interested in war, but war is interested in you.

ATTRIBUTED TO LEON TROTSKY
(Quoted in Michael Walzer,
Just and Unjust Wars, 2006)

To

The people of Junglemahals
for their infinite fortitude and resilience

&

B.N. Yugandhar
for his infectious, undying enthusiasm
for public service

Contents

◎

PART I: CHARTING PERILOUS SEAS

List of Plates

◎

All photographs © Chandan Sinha

List of Abbreviations

◎

ACMOH	Assistant Chief Medical Officer of Health
ADM	Additional District Magistrate
ADO	Agriculture Development Officer
AEO	Additional Executive Officer
ARD	Animal Resource Development
AWC	Anganwadi Centre
BCW	Backward Classes Welfare
BDO	Block Development Officer
BEUP	Bidhyak Elaka Unnayan Prakalpa
BL&LRO	Block Land and Land Reforms Officer
BLDO	Block Livestock Development Officers
BMOH	Block Medical Officer of Health
BPHC	Block Primary Health Centre
BWO	Block Welfare Officer
CADC	Comprehensive Area Development Corporation
CDPO	Child Development Project Officer
CEC	Chief Election Commissioner
CEO	Chief Electoral Officer
CMOH	Chief Medical Officer of Health
CPM	Communist Party of India (Marxist)
CRPF	Central Reserve Police Force
DCF&S	District Controller of Food & Supplies
DFO	Divisional Forest Officer
DLLRO	District Land and Land Reforms Officer
DM	District Magistrate
DO	District Officer
DPLO	District Planning Officer
DPO	District Project Officer
EFR	Eastern Frontier Rifles
FCI	Food Corporation of India
FPC	Forest Protection Committee
GDA	General Duty Assistant
GI	Galvanised Iron

GoI	Government of India
HMIS	Health Management Information System
IAY	Indira Awaas Yojana
ICDS	Integrated Child Development Scheme
ITDP	Integrated Tribal Development Project
LAMPS	Large and Multipurpose Societies
LWE	Left Wing Extremist
MHU	Mobile Health Unit
MLA	Member of Legislative Assembly
MPLADS	Member of Parliament Local Areas Development Scheme
MSK	Madhyamik Siksha Kendra
NFBS	National Family Benefit Scheme
NFFWP	National Food for Work Programme
NGO	Non-Governmental Organisation
NOAPS	National Old Age Pension Scheme
NRDMS	National Resource Development and Management System
OCs	Officers-in-Charge
P&RD	Panchayat and Rural Development
PCAPO	Peoples' Committee Against Police Oppression
PHE	Public Health Engineering
PMGY	Pradhan Mantri Gramodaya Yojana
PMGSY	Pradhan Mantri Grameen Sadak Yojana
PRA	Participatory Rural Appraisal
PWD	Public Works Department
PHC	Primary Health Centre
RSVY	Rashtriya Sama Vikas Yojana
SAE	Sub-Assistant Engineer
SCP	Special Component Plan
SDL&LRO	Sub-Divisional Land and Land Reforms Officer
SDO	Sub-Divisional Officer
SDRO	Sub-Divisional Relief Officer
SGRY	Sampoorna Grameen Rozgar Yojna
SGSY	Swarnajayanti Gram Sammriddhi Yojana
SHC	Sub-Health Centre
SHG	Self-Help Group
SP	Superintendent of Police
SSA	Sarva Shiksha Abhayan
SSK	Shishu Shiksha Kendra

TDC	Tribal Development Corporation
TLM	Total Literacy Mission
TSC	Total Sanitation Campaign
TSP	Tribal Sub-Plan
VVI	Village Vulnerability Index
VEC	Village Education Committee
WBLR	West Bengal Land Reforms (Act)

Glossary

◎

aal	Raised earthen divider demarcating plots of land, especially cultivated fields
adivasi	Tribal
Agrahanya	Ninth month in the Hindu calendar, beginning around 22 November and ending around 21 December
Alchiki	Santhali script
alta	Red water-based colorant used by women in India to paint the borders of their feet
Aman	Paddy crop cultivated during the monsoon
amin	A surveyor
amlas	Bureaucrats
arhar	A type of pulse
ashirwadi	A gift given on an auspicious occasion as a mark of blessing
atang	A forest creeper
Aush	First paddy crop harvested by early October
babu	A term that may connote respect, or indicate a well-off person or a superior
babui	A variety of long grass used for making strings and ropes
Badhna	A festival celebrated by various tribes in Central India, including Santals, Bhumij and Lodhas
Baisakh	The first month in the Bengali calendar, beginning normally on 14 April and ending on 13 May
basti	Habitation
ber	Indian plum or jujube fruit, *Ziziphus mauritiana*
bhajan	Devotional song sung by Hindus, often in groups
bheri	A shallow lake used for fish cultivation
bhushir dokan	Cattle-feed shop
bidi	A thin, short cigarette made by wrapping tobacco in *kendu* leaves

bindi	A decoration in the centre of the forehead worn by women in India; usually in the shape of a small dot
boro	Paddy crop cultivated in the spring
Buddha Purnima	The full moon day in April–May celebrated by Buddhists as the birthday of Gautam Buddha
chaar chala	A roof sloping on four sides
chaddar	A sheet of cloth
chak	Crossroad; also called *chowk*
chala	Section of a roof
charpoy	A cot
chiku	Sapodilla, *Manilkara zapota*
cholai	Illegal liquor
chourasta	Crossroads; where four roads meet
dal	Soup of pulses/lentils
danga	Raised area or upland
Deepawali	Festival of lights celebrated in October/November
dhal bundh	A dam on a slope to arrest drainage of surface water
dhappabaji	Chicanery
dholak	A two-sided drum played by beating with both hands
dhoti	An article of traditional male attire in India, known as *veshti* in South India; a long, usually about 5m, piece of cloth that is wound around the lower body
dhuna	Resin of the Sal tree
dhup dani	Incense holder
diya	Small fire-baked clay lamp
Durga puja	The ten-day long festival of Goddess Durga, usually in the months of September or October
gamcha	A thin towel
garvagriha	The *sanctum sanctorum* of a (usually South Indian) Hindu temple
ghara	A clay pot
ghat	A paved landing place, including a set of stairs, on the bank of a river or a pond
gherao	Protest in the form of encirclement of an official or an office building
ghugni	A dish made of Bengal gram or dried peas

gola	Storage container for grain
Gram Panchayat	The lowest local self-government body at the rural level in India, comprising one large or several small villages
gunin	An astrologer-cum-priest
gunthe	Cow dung cakes used as fuel
haat	A weekly market in rural areas
handi	Deep cooking vessel
hanria	An alcoholic beverage prepared by adivasis by fermenting rice in a clay pot, which gives the beverage its name
harikirtan pandal	A shed where devotional songs are routinely sung by people of a community
Hati thakur	Elephant God
jaffrey	Cement/concrete screen
jamai	Son-in-law
jawan	Soldier
jelebis	A fried sweet
jhamela	Trouble, agitation
jhinga	A vegetable
jhola	Cloth bag
jhora	Stream
kabiraj	Practitioner of traditional medicine, doctor
kachu	A vegetable — root-tuber of Colocasia
kal-baishaki	Thunderstorms
Kali puja	Festival of Goddess Kali
katha	A traditional measure of land
kendu patta	Leaf of the *kendu* tree, *Diospyros melanoxion*; used to make *bidis*
khal	Stream, brook or a canal
khas	Of the government
khat	A cot
khichdi	A simple dish made of rice and lentils cooked together
kirtan	Devotional song or singing
kodal	Local spade
kuchcha	Earthen
kuon	Dug well
kurkut	Red ants
lathi	Stick
lau	Bottle gourd or calabash, *Lagenaria siceraria*

lep	A paste
machan	Temporary raised platform erected for safety or for keeping a watch
Madhyamik	The tenth standard examination in West Bengal
Magh	Tenth month of the Bengali calendar
Mahajan	Moneylender
mahua	A tree, *Madhuca longifolia*, found in central and northern India, bearing edible flowers and fruit; distilled by the adivasis to make an alcoholic beverage of the same name
Makarsankranti/ Makar/Choto Makar	A major harvest festival celebrated all over India, signifying the transition of sun from one sign of the zodiac, Sagittarius, to another, Capricorn; usually falls on 14/15 January
mandir	Temple
mansik	A vow
mashari	Mosquito net
mela	Fair
moksha	Salvation
moong	A type of pulse
morrum	Gravel
mouza	Village
murgi	Chicken
muri	Puffed rice
nagara	Large, traditional adivasi drum
nala	Stream or channel
natyamancha	Stage in a temple for devotional dance performances
ojha	Traditional medicine man
ole	A local root vegetable
paan	Betel leaf
pacca	Permanent, made of durable material
pakouri	A fried, salty savoury
pallu	Loose end of a sari
palon	A vegetable
Panchayat Samiti	Intermediate local self-government body at the block-level
pantabhat	Leftover rice soaked in water overnight
paschim	West
Patta	Deed of ownership of land
pitha	A traditional cake
pon	A measure, two handfuls, of straw

Poush	Ninth month of the Bengali calendar
Pradhan	Chairperson of a Gram Panchayat
Pranibandhu	A trained worker utilised by the Animal Resource Development Department in West Bengal to provide basic services to people in far-flung rural areas for the upkeep of their livestock
puja	Religious ceremony
pujari	Priest
pukur	Pond
purab	East
Rajbari	Palace
rasogolla	A Bengali sweet
ryoti	Belonging to ryots or owner-cultivators of land
Sabhadhipati	Chairperson of the local self-government body at the district level
Sabhapati	Chairperson of the local self government body at the block-level
sahayak/sahayika	Helper
sajne	Drumsticks, *Moringa Oleifera*
samadhi	Memorial of a saint
sansad	General governing body
sech bundh	Irrigation dam
shradh	Religious ceremony performed by Hindus for the dead
sishya	Student
tali	Terracotta tiles
Taluka Mandal	Name for Panchayat Samiti in other states of India
tand	Sloping land
tangi	Axe
tassar	A fabric akin to silk
than	Shrine
thana	Police station
til	Flax plant or seed; the edible seed yields cooking oil
Tusu	A regional goddess worshipped only by girls during the festival of *Makarsankranti* in the western region of West Bengal
Zamindar	Landlord
zari	A thread traditionally/originally made of gold or silver, but now of other materials also, for brocade work on silk saris and other garments

Acknowledgements

◎

For the writing of this book, I owe thanks to a number of persons.

Dr Suraj Kumar, who was associated with this project from the beginning, first read some of the original tour notes and encouraged me to turn the account into a book. In the later stages, he also read the subsequent drafts and was a constant source of support and advice. Likewise, Prof. M.L. Das and Shri Alapan Bandhopadhyay also looked through the tour notes and, later, the first draft enriching me with their candid and constructive criticism. Shri Samar Ghosh was gracious enough to find time from his frenetic schedule to read the manuscript and make several useful suggestions.

To Shri Randhir Arora and Dr Sugata Ghosh I owe thanks for not only reading a large segment of the manuscript but also for excellent advice about its structure and layout. In the final stages of its preparation, Prof. Satyajit Singh played a key role in guiding the manuscript towards publication. Many thanks are due to the team at Routledge for the meticulous editing and production of the book.

Two individuals upon whom I forced parts of the manuscript at different stages are my wife, Nandita, and son, Neilabh. Their frank assessment was invaluable. They, along with Vedushi — our daughter, were as supportive as ever of my lonely venture.

Paschim Medinipur District
(Map showing Blocks)

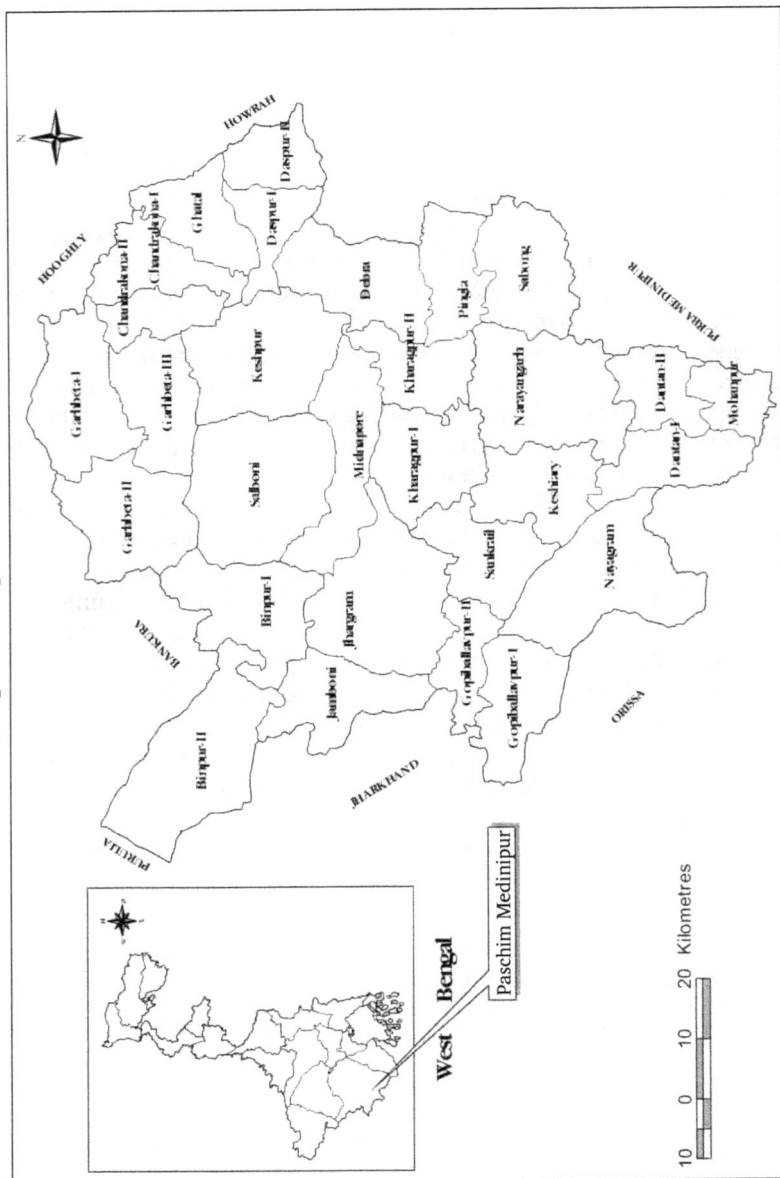

Source: National Resource Development and Management System, Paschim Medinipur, West Bengal

Prologue

◎

It all began because of an acute distrust of my memory, the fear of forgetting facts observed during my visits to remote parts of the districts where I served. And it started with my assignment as the District Magistrate (DM) and Collector of Cooch Behar.

Mindful from the beginning that a District Officer (DO) is fundamentally a field officer, I spent several days each week roaming the villages in the flat, green countryside. At the end of the day I would find that unless I recorded my perceptions during my visits and put them together the same evening, I would miss out on a number of interesting facts, insights and impressions. More importantly, actions suggested by these observations on-site were then in the danger of floating in my head as half-remembered pious intentions and blurred but taunting regrets. Therefore, I had fallen into the habit of writing longish records of my tours much before I joined my new assignment as DO of Paschim Medinipur on 3 March 2004.

While in Cooch Behar I was sure that it was the poorest district in the State of West Bengal. As I began visiting the deeper reaches of the western and the north-western parts of Paschim Medinipur, the conviction steadily grew that these were perhaps some of the most underdeveloped areas in the state — a conviction borne out later by hard facts and statistics. By this time my habit of writing tour notes in detail had become deep-rooted; especially, because I found the minutiae helpful in seeking information on specific points, in making decisions, and issuing unambiguous instructions that conveyed a credible familiarity with ground reality. Given the magnitude of the task at hand in the limited time available to me, I was convinced that to make even a dent in the cast-iron grip in which poverty held a large number of people in the Junglemahals I needed to direct the efforts of the district administration with precision, pointedly. For the first six months my tour notes were meant for me alone. Soon things changed.

Towards the third week of September the Chief Minister of West Bengal visited Paschim Medinipur district to attend some public functions. On the same day the Chief Secretary held a video conference with all DMs to monitor development programmes. Since I was to spend the entire day engaged with the Chief Minister's visit, I had deputed the Additional District Magistrate (ADM), Zilla Parishad, to attend the video conference. After the Chief Minister left for Kolkata the ADM briefed me about the issues raised and discussed by the Chief Secretary at the conference, but he forgot to mention one important instruction: the Chief Secretary had directed that the DMs visit the backward villages identified in each district by the Panchayat and Rural Development (P&RD) Department, the list for which had been circulated to all DMs, and should then prepare a development plan for each village visited. *The DMs were also directed to send their records of these tours to the Chief Secretary.*

A couple of weeks later I called on the Chief Secretary to brief him about the on-going programmes. Towards the end of the meeting, he said, 'I have seen the formats you have developed for the monthly progress reports you have asked your Sub-Divisional Officers (SDOs) and Block Development Officers (BDOs) to submit in the first week of every month, including their inspection visits. What about your tour notes? Have you written anything? Or do you only ask your officers to submit reports?' He smiled, and added, 'If you have written anything send it to me. I would like to go through it and the CM would also like to read it.'

Unaware of his instructions issued during the video conference, I was stung by the question. It seemed that the Chief Secretary was wondering whether I practised what I preached. I merely said, 'I shall send my tour notes immediately, sir.' I would show him!

Upon returning to Midnapore I selected a set of four notes of tours in the *early* part of my tenure — to underline that I did what I expected from my colleagues. And having brushed them up to erase grammatical and typographical errors, I forwarded them to the Chief Secretary 'for his kind perusal'.

Approximately three weeks later I received a call from one of the officials in the Chief Minister's office. He started by asking excitedly, 'Sir, what have you written in your tour notes?' A little alarmed, I asked, 'Why? What's happened?' 'No, the CM liked them very much. He has read them word by word, line by line and is fascinated by them'. I heaved a sigh of relief.

A few weeks later, prompted by the Chief Secretary, I sent another set of four tour notes to him. A couple of weeks later the same officer from the Chief Minister's office called me again. This time, apparently, the tour notes had moved the Chief Minister to tears. He had liked the tour notes sufficiently to instruct that the notes be published in *West Bengal*, a monthly journal brought out by the Information & the Cultural Affairs Department, and that a copy of these be sent to the Governor, Shri Gopalkrishna Gandhi. I thanked my stars that we had a Chief Minister who could stomach harsh truths presented to him by junior officers like me. I am not sure to what extent my tour notes would have drawn the appreciation in the highest executive office in other states.

Even before joining my charge in Paschim Medinipur district I knew that my tenure would be short-lived. Not because I apprehended being evicted from the district for some premeditated contretemps, nor because I anticipated local political obstructions, which I did face, but because I was due for promotion in January 2005. Hence, I knew that my days in the district were numbered. However, to enable me to complete a few of the developmental programmes that I had initiated, I was allowed to continue serving in Paschim Medinipur district until the middle of April 2005.

Early one morning, a few days after handing over charge, I re-ceived a text message from one of my former colleagues in the district. It read, '*Ganashakti* has published translation of your tour notes today. Second part to follow.'

To say that I was surprised would be putting it mildly. *Ganashakti*, as everyone in West Bengal knows, is the mouthpiece of the Communist Party of India (Marxist) or CPM. The daily newspaper is read religiously by the party faithful. I managed to get hold of a copy of the day's *Ganashakti* and went through the article which was titled 'Kothay daridro, kibhabe mokabila, pratibedan-e janachen jelashashak', — 'Where is poverty, how it is being combated, reports district magistrate'. The article, on the front page of the paper, was a translation and summarisation of some of my tour notes, by and large a faithful reproduction. The tour notes published in *West Bengal* were thus serialised in *Ganashakti* on 22, 23 and 24 April 2005. What astonished me was that although they had highlighted the efforts by the district administration to develop in the *adivasi* populated areas of Paschim Medinipur, the CPM party newspaper had chosen to publish the less than complimentary observations made by me and, indeed, gave me, credit for doing so. This was quite unprecedented, especially so, because by and large *amlas*, or bureaucrats, are usually at the receiving end of the newspaper's opprobrium. This indicated that the tour notes had touched a chord somewhere. However, that did not inspire me enough to consider publication of these records.

Introduction

◎

In the afternoon of 2 November 2008, while returning from the inauguration of the proposed Jindal Steel Plant in Salboni, Paschim Medinipur, the convoy of the Chief Minister of West Bengal had a narrow escape. Although it succeeded in injuring six security personnel, a landmine exploded by Maoist extremists missed its mark. Feverish police action followed initial consternation and several interior villages were combed in search of the culprits. One such village was Choto Pelia near Lalgarh, where late in the night of 6 November a police team raided poor adivasi huts and arrested some school boys and women. Reportedly, some policemen also kicked and beat them up, as a consequence of which one frail, 55-year-old woman, named Chintamani Murmu, lost the use of an eye.

The incident was like a flaming arrow shot into a haystack; it lit a conflagration. The red land, knee-deep in parched grass and tinder dry groves, burst into flames; fanned by angry local winds, the blaze swept through the Junglemahal region of the district. Nurtured by years of discontentment, and stirred over the last decade by Left Wing Extremists (LWEs) operating in the quiet forests, rage against the alleged police atrocities burst into open. In the months that followed, the world, perhaps for the first time, witnessed live on the television screen the 'liberation' of a large piece of territory by Maoist guerrillas.

On the same night of 6 November hundreds of adivasis surrounded the Lalgarh *thana* and cut off its electricity supply and telephones lines. By morning thousands of Santals, armed with bows and arrows and *tangis* had blocked all roads leading to Lalgarh. The blockade was firmed up by digging trenches across the roads and felling tree trunks over them, effectively cutting off the block headquarter from the rest of Midnapore. By the evening of the same day, as anger grew and more adivasi men and women joined the spontaneous protest, the electricity and telephone lines to Lalgarh were also snapped. The struggle was supported by smaller tribal organisations, initially by the Bharat Jakat Majhi Madwa Jan Gaonta. Therefore, at the start adivasi elders purportedly guided the swiftly intensifying movement, which was characterised by a largely democratic, consultative process of decision-making. The principal demands that rose from this growing, seething mass of rage was a traditional one: the Police Superintendent of Paschim Midnapore should apologise to the wronged adivasi women by doing sit-ups holding his ears and the other policemen involved in the rampage should crawl along the street rubbing their nose on the ground.

The demand was not met.

The agitation spread from Lalgarh, its epicentre, to other parts of Jhargram sub-divisions including the Jhargram and Binpur-II blocks. Initial meetings and processions transformed into *gheraos*, and culminated in the reverse siege of a large swathe of forest land of which, if not the geographic, the strategic heart was Lalgarh — for which the movement and the area came to be known. Daily agitations by hundreds of people, mostly women, armed with *lathis*, bows, arrows, and axes, and the blockading of roads leading into the area with felled trees alternated with nightly killings by Maoists.

Almost within a week since the *gherao* of the Lalgarh Police Station, the Peoples' Committee against the Police Oppression (PCAPO) emerged as the body leading and organising the rising. Although PCAPO has consistently claimed that it has no connection with the Maoists, the police have maintained that the Maoists not only inspired the leadership of the Organisation but also provided strategic support and guidance. The PCAPO, led by people younger than those in the traditional adivasi organisation, framed an 11-point charter of demands which, including public apologies by the police officials, also encompassed several related to the provision of basic services, such as health, education and food security. The PCAPO also expanded the area of the movement. By 20 November the forest fires had spread to the adjoining blocks of Salboni, Jambani, Garhbeta, and then to Nayagram, Gopiballavpur and Sankrail. In parts of these areas too roads were blockaded by digging them up or by felling trees across them, and police stations and police outposts were pointedly cut off. Protests, mass meetings, motor cycle processions, and unyielding adherence to the demands raised by the PCAPO swept across the Junglemahals. Borne by strong winds of hurt sentiment, the flames leapt across to light new conflagrations in other districts of Bengal with sizeable tribal populations or pockets. In Bankura, Purulia, Birbhum, Burdwan, and Murshidabad, fuming rallies and processions in support of the Lalgarh movement burned indeterminate trails.

Given the unexpected and unprecedented nature of the Lalgarh backlash, initially the Government appeared to be too taken aback for any action. Nevertheless, soon the negotiations were started; continued over a protracted period, they bore few fruit. A curious reaction followed, which may only be termed as the withdrawal of the State from the affected area that, although it included more than merely the Lalgarh or Binpur-I Block, in general came to be called Lalgarh. On 27 November 2008, under pressure of the PCAPO the first police camp was withdrawn from Ramgarh, a few kilometres away from Lalgarh. Soon other police camps also folded up their tents. Gradually, the majority of police camps, including several armed police and Central Reserve Police Force (CRPF) units, which had been located strategically to counter Maoist militants, were withdrawn from the area. Most other wings of government and the panchayat system, which were in any case poorly staffed in the area, could neither move nor function and, therefore, administration and the delivery of services came to a standstill.

This reverse seize, and, hence, the 'liberation' of the Lalgarh area continued for over eight months. The incidents leading up to the 'recapture' of Lalgarh by the police on 21 June 2009, and the events that have followed have received sufficient attention in the media, not to bear repetition. Even after all this, life can hardly be said to have returned to normal for people of the Junglemahals. Although over 4,000 security personnel have been deployed in the area, the adivasis demand for basic amenities such as health, services, nutrition, food security, education, and basic physical infrastructure such as electricity, roads and even provision of drinking water remain in a limbo. For the moment the forest fires may have subsided, but the embers remain.

Why this book?

The events of the past four or five years, during which left wing extremism spread and bloomed across more than 150 districts of the country, have focussed sharp attention on the conflict between the Maoists and the State. The entire country is now alive to the internal crisis posed by left wing extremism, principally in the tribal areas of central and eastern India. Newspapers and magazines daily and periodically bring out articles on the clashes between the security forces and Maoists. Journalists and academics have published several reports and studies on the conflict and its causes. A few have even highlighted the resultant plight of the people in the conflict-afflicted backward areas, especially of the adivasis. Yet I feel that from this cacophonous discussion on Maoism versus the State, an awareness of the living conditions of the people who are caught between the two is missing. The roots of the upheaval largely remain out of sight.

To a limited extent this book may assist in creating at least a marginally better appreciation of the 'Maoist problem' and may offer cues for response with understanding; it comprises my tour notes, written while serving as the DM of Paschim Medinipur in 2004–2005, presented chronologically and woven into a narrative that recounts the tangled situation on the uneven ground and also the response of the government. This work may, thus, serve to expose the fundamental causes of the multi-faceted alienation of this marginalised group spread across several states and, albeit indirectly, focus on the objective conditions that have given rise to this insurrection within the nation's heartland. Concerned citizens of our country and the State need to recognise these conditions — my reason for writing this account.

At this juncture I must clarify that this work does not pretend to be an in-depth sociological or ethnographic study of the people in the Junglemahal. It is also not a methodical examination of the political-economy of rural-forest society. It is most vehemently *neither* an apologia for the vulnerability of people of the region, nor a justification for the lack of development of the area. Yet it *is* offered as a record of a field administrator's experiences, of his efforts to understand the intricacies of the immediate society so that he may serve it better. Facts seen, insights gathered and perceptions formed have been recorded and offered for the little all they are worth.

At times it is possible that the reader may feel the tone and tenor of the writing to be rather official-centric, even officious. Particularly, this may occur either when the narrative focuses on mundane administrative work or on official interactions. While trying to avoid this pitfall, I must confess that I consciously have diluted neither the dry description of routine work nor the nature of the discourse between my colleagues and me. The first, simply because the routine, the ordinary, the day-to-day processes are what make up administration: checking registers and estimates, examining the construction of a building or a road, talking to field workers, measuring grain or kerosene during inspection, marking attendance and sometimes even selection test answers, and such like. These routines comprise most of a civil servant's work in the field; they are unglamorous but essential.

The second, because, after all, these notes are a factual record of his work by an administrator; and, administrators must administer. Governance is about making decisions, communicating them and ensuring implementation of the decisions. Although, as may be seen in the course of the book, consultation when dealing with various actors — state and non-state — remained the norm, finally decisions were made and given for compliance. They may be couched in a request or cushioned in an appeal, but within the machinery of government a decision is a command; it is meant to direct and instruct action, not to underscore hierarchy. Possibly, this statement may displease the collegially minded, especially the votaries of absolute egalitarianism, but in the interest of truth I am inclined to take the risk.

Nevertheless, let me add, only in Part I of the book the original format of the tour notes has been kept almost intact — essentially to convey to the reader how these notes were used by me for administrative ends. In the remaining two parts of the book, in the interest of the readers' convenience, I have tried to rub off the rough edges and make the narrative smoother without detracting from its integrity.

Despite my conscientious attempt to keep a record of my tours, I could not make extended notes of all the tours that I undertook during my 14-month-long tenure in Paschim Medinipur. I visited the field for various periods, more often than not without notice, and at all times of the day and night; the shorter forays frequently were left undocumented. In a large number of instances my observations were cryptic, disjointed, and often consisting only of the points of action to be taken. In several other cases the tours related to other administrative, particularly regulatory, functions which may not be of much relevance or interest in the present context; the numerous visits to different blocks preparatory to the elections, inspection of blocks and panchayat samitis, supervision of field functions such as motor vehicle and excise raids, and land related appraisals would fall in this category, and have been omitted. The tour notes that do feature here reflect the human condition in rural areas of Paschim Medinipur district, particularly in the Junglemahals. Although tempted to do so, I have not included all the tour records of this type in this book. Rather, I have selected those that were coherent and substantive enough to interest the reader by offering in each case a slightly different facet of rural life. For these reasons, although chronologically arranged, the tour notes are not evenly spaced in time. Yet they do reflect obvious issues and challenges faced routinely by the inhabitants of Junglemahals and the attempts of the district administration to grapple with these.

To assist in understanding the narratives better they are interspersed with short segments that help construct the context as the narrative moves on. Several significant events stand out as timemarks in the course of the 14 months. Some of these were cyclical administrative events — such as the general elections to the Lok Sabha in May 2004; others were seasonal — floods in Ghatal in August of the same year; some others — such as the report on starvation deaths in Amlasole — were catalytic; while still others were administrative interventions undertaken for development — such as the survey of villages and the Village Vulnerability Index (VVI) or the housing scheme for the Lodhas. Since all these events had a bearing on administrative response and often determined them, brief accounts of these are included in the intervening segments; shorter ones, in italics, are appended at the beginning and sometimes at the end of a tour note. The Appendix consists of additional information about the district and the events covered and may be referred to by readers so inclined.[1]

Structurally, I have grouped the chapters into three parts. Each part encompasses a few months of my 14-month tenure as Collector of Paschim Medinipur and highlights the nature of our preoccupations in each period. They mark gradual transitions that may not be obvious if the narrative were presented in an uninterrupted series. The focus of each part has been explained in a short introduction before the section begins.

Paschim Medinipur

Hearsay has it that the proposal to bifurcate 24 Parganas district, at one point of time the largest in the country, was first mooted in 1886. It finally came about in 1986 when the district was carved into two, North and South 24 Parganas (although after division how either could still encompass 24 Parganas remains a matter of conjecture!). The demand to divide the erstwhile Midnapore district into two was apparently raised in the 1970s. It was, therefore, surmised that the separation would be effected by the 2070s. Yet times change, as does the pace of change itself; Midnapore district was split into two, Paschim (West) and Purba (East) Medinipur, on the first day of the 21st century.

The new district, Purba Medinipur, was formed of the southern and south-eastern sub-divisions of Contai, Haldia and Tamluk, while the old district — 'old' because Midnapore, the historic district town, continued to be its headquarters — renamed as Paschim Medinipur included the four sub-divisions of Midnapore Sadar, Kharagpur, Ghatal, and Jhargram. In the bargain, the fertile and relatively more developed coastal areas of the former district as well as the port town of Haldia went to the new district.

Before proceeding further, perhaps it may be useful to examine what the term 'Junglemahal' connotes. In common parlance it refers to the hilly, forested areas of the districts of Paschim Medinipur, Bankura, Purulia, and Birbhum. According to L.S.S. O'Malley,[2] early in the 19th century it was thus designated by the British and marked out as a separate area for purposes of administration, i.e., revenue collection, and included adjoining portions of present day Jharkhand. Especially due to the writings of such eminent Bengali authors as Bibhutibhushan Bandopadhyay, this entire area has held a special space in the popular Bengali imagination.

Junglemahal has also been a popular tourist destination among most sections of Bengal, particularly the well-off and the adventurous. While the wealthy built bungalows, sometimes even mansions in these forested lands where they spent a few weeks each year, the middle class, fired by the writings of the authors, chose to visit various parts of the Junglemahal in autumn or spring. Hence, to say that the area does not find place in Bengali consciousness is not true. But this Junglemahal did not quite recognise the reality underlying the familiar collage of images of the region in the popular mind.

Located to the south-west side of the state, Paschim Medinipur is bordered by Mayurbhanj and Balasore districts of Odisha in the west and south-west, Purba Midnapore in south and south-east, Hooghly in the north-east, Bankura and Purulia districts in the north and north-west. Geographically it is the south-eastern extension of the Chotanagpur plateau with which it shares many characteristics.

As in neighbouring Chotanagpur, large sal forests occur in the lateritic upland areas in the north-western and western parts of Paschim Midnapore where forests occupy about 1 per cent of the total area. Indeed, more than half the forests comprise sal trees while a good portion of the rest is mixed — including bamboo — and almost 20 per cent of forest area is dry, bushy scrub land. Located at the highest point in the watersheds, the forests do not occupy a wide, unbroken area but protrude into flat and cultivable areas or wasteland-like fingers. Water from these forested areas flows down into the valley or to the bottom of the watersheds to be drained away into the rivers flowing through this district, thus, depleting both precious top soil and water. Kangsabati, Silabati, Subarnarekha, Keleghai, and their tributaries are the principal rivers of the district. Although in certain areas in the forest divisions some measures have been taken in the past for soil and water conservation, no overall master plan is available to indicate areas in which interventions are required.

Before its bifurcation on 1 January 2001, Midnapore district with an area of over 16,000 sq. km and a population of about 10 million was the most populous district in the country. Even after its division the Paschim Medinipur district encompasses 9295.28 sq. km and a population of 5,218,399 people,[3] spread across four administrative sub-divisions, 29 development blocks and eight municipalities. The Midnapore Sadar, Jhargram and Kharagpur sub-divisions have one municipality each — Midnapore, Jhargram and Kharagpur respectively. The other five municipalities are clustered in the Ghatal sub-division. Paradoxically, three of these, Khirpai, Kharar and Ramjivanpur municipalities, are classified as 'Rural Municipalities'. Corresponding to the 29 blocks there are an equal number of panchayat samitis which consist of 290 gram panchayats.

Out of the total population of more than 5.2 million in Paschim Medinipur, the rural population numbers 4,575,651 or 87.68 per cent. This great mass of population lives distributed over 7498 census villages spread across the district. Overall, 18.07 per cent of the population belongs to the scheduled castes and 14.89 per cent to the scheduled tribes; the state aggregates for each are 23 per cent and 5.5 per cent, respectively. The vast majority of the tribal population lives in 19 of the 29 blocks of the district. Although 16 different tribes make up the adivasi population in the district, the Santals are by far the most numerous. The Lodha-Sabars are the smallest and most backward of the tribal groups.

Identified by the Planning Commission of India as one of the 150 most backward districts in the country, Paschim Medinipur district has two distinct agro-climatic and geographical zones. The western and north-western parts of the district — the dry, uneven and forested laterite zone — comprise some of the most vulnerable areas of the district; they include all of Jhargram sub-division, more than half the area in Midnapore Sadar sub-division, and a portion of Kharagpur sub-division. This hard land is home to a majority of the adivasi population in Paschim Medinipur, and is a part of the Junglemahals encompassing the forested regions of two neighbouring districts, Bankura and Purulia.

On the basis of the figures provided by the 2001 Census it can be ascertained that 414 or 5.46 per cent of the total villages in Paschim Medinipur had a population size of less than 50 persons! And 776 villages (10.24 per cent) had a population of less than 125 persons. On examining the data-set village-wise we find there were some villages which had a population size of less than five persons. If a village is to be defined as a legally delineated territory with a resident population, then we cannot but help treat these miniscule settlements as villages. From the available data it is evident that a vast majority of the villages in this district have very small populations. Indeed, 4721 villages, or 62.28 per cent of all the villages in this district, have a population of less than 500 persons, while 34.50 per cent of villages have a population of less than 250 persons!

It may be of interest to the reader that of a total of 7498 villages in Paschim Medinipur, 505 or 6 per cent, villages are populated *entirely* by scheduled tribes. Of these only eight villages, all in Binpur-II block, have a population of more than 500 persons; the largest is Bhimarjun with a population of 637. Binpur-I (95 villages), Binpur-II (70), Nayagram (47), and Jhargram and Jamboni (44 each) together account for 60 per cent of the villages where all inhabitants are tribals. Overall, 14 per cent of the villages in Paschim Medinipur have a tribal population exceeding 75 per cent and the vast majority of these fall under the Jhargram sub-division also referred to as the Junglemahal. It may make one wonder if it is a coincidence that left wing extremism has found a firm foothold in these blocks. And why?

◎

Notes

1. Readers unfamiliar with the structure of field administration in India may perhaps need an introduction to a 'district' and 'district administration'. The district is the territorial unit for planning, implementation and evaluation of diverse federal and state programmes in regulatory and developmental administration. Its origins may be traced back to the Mauryan Empire; its shape was firmed up during the Mughal period; and it crystallised into its present form during British rule. Nevertheless, naming a typical district in India is a difficult proposition; the size and population vary from state to state and even within a state. Districts may be as small as a few square kilometres or as large as 40,000 sq. km; the population of a district may range from 150,000 to 8 million, and in one district may be heard more than half-a-dozen languages and a dozen dialects. Over the years the number of districts in India has increased and until date there are 604 districts in the country. However, a common feature of districts across the country is its system of administration.

Each district has a machinery of administration headed by the office of the Collector also known as the District Magistrate and in some parts as Deputy Commissioner. He/she is the district officer (DO) who is a representative of Government and is the integrating force in district administration. Apart from the extensive office of the DO, a district may have up to 35 offices of departments of the State Government and even ten of the Central Government. A district is administratively apportioned into sub-divisions comprising blocks which are made of villages. After the 73rd amendment three-tier Panchayat Raj institutions have also come into existence in almost all districts as units of local self government. Therefore, at the district level are Zilla Parishad, at the block level the Panchayat Samitis or Taluka Mandals, and below that the gram panchayat. Not all departments of the State or Central Government are represented at all levels in a district. The most extensive presence is that of the revenue and development administration headed by the district officer, the police and health department. In most states, the Gram Panchayats include more than one village. A village, and in India there are over 600,000, is the smallest territorial unit. Of all the units of administration mentioned, the village is the only 'real' unit, where concept merges into reality, were people are born, live and die. For all meaningful purposes villages, and municipalities, are where the impact of governance or the lack of it may be visible.

Perhaps it is just as well to keep in mind that administration at the district level and below is affected by a variety of factors. The cycle of seasons, administrative events such as elections and census operations, administrative deadlines such as the beginning and the end of the financial year, natural and man-made calamities, and festival and fairs — all exert their peculiar pressure, and press for their different imperatives upon the administrative machinery. Planning for programme implementation must take into account the role of these various factors, and there can be no uniform description for the entire country or the entire state. Sometimes, in the case of very large districts, as in West Bengal, the same description and the same schedule may not hold good throughout the district itself. The topography and vegetation of an area determine not only the priorities of people inhabiting it but also where and when certain types of programmes can or cannot be implemented. Therefore, if in the course of this book the reader comes across reference to dissimilar administrative priorities pursued in different parts of the district she need not be surprised.

For a more elaborate description of the district and district administration see my work, *Public Sector Reforms in India: New Role of the District Officer*, New Delhi: Sage Publications, 2007.

2. L. S. S. O'Malley, *Bengal District Gazeteers: Bankura*, 1995, reprinted by the Government of West Bengal (first published 1908).

3. Unless otherwise mentioned, all demographic data in the book have been drawn from the 2001 Census, Government of India.

Part I: Charting Perilous Seas

Although coming from another district I hit the ground running in Paschim Medinipur district and despite my experience as a District Collector — in geographic, demographic, socio-economic, and political terms — large parts of the new district were unfamiliar territory. Therefore, the first few months in Paschim Medinipur I spent exploring the waters that I had been assigned to sail, mapping out the reefs and shoals, the deeps and the shallows.

Much time was spent not just in poring over data and maps and periodic reports pulled off dusty shelves, but also touring around the remoter parts of the district and meeting people. To be able to serve, to do anything useful, I had to know who and what I was dealing with. It was also necessary to strengthen the administrative machinery and re-establish or institute effective routines. That the general elections to the Lok Sabha fell in these same months did not make matters easy. And then, of course, Amlasole happened — a shot fired across the bow!

The First Weeks

◎

In the afternoon of 3 March 2004 I took charge as the DM and Collector, Paschim Medinipur. Having just concluded a tenure of little less than three years as the DO in Cooch Behaar, in the north-eastern corner of the state, this was my second such charge. Earlier I had spent two tenures in the undivided Midnapore district: first, as an SDO of Contai for less than a year in 1991–1992, and then again for a little more than a year as ADM and District Land and Land Reforms Officer (DLLRO), Tamluk in 1995–1996. In the first posting I had been ejected from the district against my will, while the second time round I had steered myself out after a satisfying 14 months. Yet here I was again, and likely to stay for at least a year, since I was due for a promotion in January 2004. I knew that my time in the new district was limited. Nevertheless a year is a long stretch and there was much to do in the district — how much I would learn within a couple of days.

That afternoon, after taking charge as I sat alone for a little while in the high-ceilinged hall-like office chamber of the DM in the Collectorate, my thoughts veered towards the irony of my familiarity with the district. Perhaps I had been posted here by the Government because I was an 'old Midnapore hand'. However, almost the entire area under my jurisdiction during these two tenures now fell in the new district of Purba Medinipur. My acquaintance with Midnapore, the district headquarters, had been limited to periodical day-long visits to the Collectorate or the Zilla Parishad office for meetings or the occasional social visit to a colleague's residence. Midnapore town itself had little to offer by way of attraction, either in terms of shopping, recreation or entertainment for the family. Ghatal was familiar ground because it had been part of the earlier Tamluk land district when I was ADM and DLLRO, Tamluk. But, the rest of the new district of Paschim Medinipur I hardly knew. As they had not been within my area of responsibility earlier, Midnapore Sadar, Kharagpur and Jhargram sub-divisions I had never toured. My imme-diate task would be to familiarise myself with the Collectorate and its officers and then with the area and its inhabitants. Hence, soon after signing the joining report I had asked the ADM to convene a meeting in my chamber of all available officers in the Collectorate at 4.30 p.m.

About a dozen officers were present in the meeting, including the three ADMs. After a round of introductions, I passed around a short feedback form to each officer. I had designed the form first when I had joined as SDO, Contai and had used it in all my field postings so far to get some basic information from new colleagues: What were their duties and responsibilities in their current position? Which of their programmes were doing well? What were some constraints that they faced? What were their suggestions for improvement? I asked them to return the form the following morning after giving the questions some thought and recording their responses. I concluded the meeting by sharing my expectations with them, and these were simple enough.

I expected punctuality in office and the field, emphasised public service orientation and promptness in dealing with work, and a proactive approach to responding to the requests and requirements of the poor and the weaker sections — among which I specified children, women, the scheduled castes and scheduled tribes. I also hoped that among the officers there would be regular and quick communication because that was essential for our functioning as a team. As the meeting dispersed I thought wryly to myself that the officers must have heard similar exhortations many times before. Yet I had spent enough years in government service to put my faith in André Gide's words.

The next morning I left early for Kolkata. The Chief Secretary had convened a meeting at 11 a.m. of all DMs and Superintendents of Police (SPs) to review preparations for the forthcoming general elections to the Lok Sabha. The meeting lasted about two hours. As it was about to end, the Chief Secretary asked me to see him in his room after the meeting.

In his office, the Chief Secretary told me that the Government was very concerned about the situation in the forested areas of Paschim Medinipur district where left wing extremism has surfaced from time to time. He himself had visited the area earlier and was convinced that the main reason for the unrest was inadequate development of the region and the shortage of basic amenities. Therefore, he wanted me to ensure, especially in view of the approaching summer, that there were sufficient numbers of sources of drinking water in each village. Diarrhoea and malaria were common killers in this area; therefore, the district administration was to see to it that basic health facilities function properly and regularly. The previous year the Midday Meal Scheme for primary school students had been started across the state, but coverage in the schools of Junglemahal was reported to be very erratic. The Chief Secretary wanted that Self-Help Groups (SHGs) and village-level committees should be involved in the scheme to stabilise it. Another major problem of the area was the shortage of irrigation facilities. Due to this the laterite belt was entirely dependent for the monsoon for the single *kharif* crop, paddy. He had discussed this with other departments and was of the view that surface water conservation schemes should be undertaken through the panchayats as well as through the line departments. The Public Distribution System (PDS) was another area of concern and needed attention. The Chief Secretary assured me that in pursuit of these priorities I would receive all possible support from the Government and that I had a completely 'free hand' in dealing with obstacles that I may face.

The same afternoon I attended another meeting in the Chief Secretary's office along with a few other DMs and senior officials of the Backward Classes Welfare (BCW) Department. The meeting focussed on tribal development, specifically on enhancing the traditional sources of income of the adivasis. Through the entire Junglemahal the adivasis are dependent on minor forest produce for their livelihood during a significant period of the year. The three main products collected and sold by them are *kendu patta*, or leaf used to make *bidis*; *sal patta*, of which disposable plates and bowls are stitched; and *babui* grass from which strings and ropes are woven. *Sal* seeds are also pressed for oil. *Kendu patta* is by far the most valuable minor product extracted from the forest and constitutes a multi-crore market. The tribals who collect the leaves are by law expected to sell them through the Large and Multipurpose Societies (LAMPS) constituted under the Tribal Development Corporation (TDC). However, problems in disbursement of remuneration by the LAMPS often force the indigent adivasi to sell the *kendu patta* collected to middlemen. Although low, the returns are quick; a subsistence livelihood has few options. If we could ensure that the tribals were not forced to carry out distress sale of their collected stocks of leaves to middlemen but sold all the produce through the TDC network we could ensure that they got a fair price for their labours. Apart from estimating the probable production in a year, for gathering *babui* grass, storage godowns managed by SHGs could also be built in remote areas. Sal leaf plate-making machines run by electricity have come into the market now. We must explore potential for introducing it in those parts of the Junglemahals where electricity has reached; this would serve to augment the earnings of those engaged in this occupation. Finally, *tassar* is also produced in the area and needed expansion. An assessment was to be made to this end.

I returned to Midnapore in a thoughtful mood. The Chief Secretary had placed a very large responsibility on my shoulders.

The next few days passed in receiving visitors, whether officials of Panchayats and Municipalities, or representatives of staff associations who came to register their presence. I also visited various sections of the Collectorate, not just to meet the workers but also to check attendance. On Monday, 8 March, I visited the Zilla Parishad and called on the Sabhadhipati with whom I discussed the various schemes that were under implementation.

As the first few days passed I gradually became more acquainted with the Collectorate and the district. A few disturbing aspects of my office became clear. Twelve years ago when I had joined as SDO, Contai sub-division, the Midnapore Collectorate was a fine-tuned machine where procedures, practices and norms were well established and worked smoothly. Files were immaculately maintained and the numerous registers were kept up-to-date. Things had now changed for the worse. The old *dhoti*-clad babus who had the rules at their ink-stained fingertips had all retired and the newer ball-point bearing generation had not quite picked up enough knowledge nor seemed to take pride in the work of their office. Consequently practices and procedures had been short changed and norms and conventions given the go by. There was an acute shortage of officers and also of staff, especially due to the distribution of officers and staffs between the two districts, the old and the new. Information channels from the field had also become clogged and one was often at a loss for facts and figures.

I knew that I had my work cut out for me.

1
Where Extremes Meet
◎

To reach Jhargram from Midnapore the most direct way is to take the National Highway until you reach Lodhasuli where you turn right onto the State Highway. And as you turn right, in stages you drive back almost 15 to 20 years in time. The feeling grows in force as you move towards Jhargram; while for me beyond Jhargram, especially in Belpahari, it was déjà vu. Then I remembered that I had been born and raised in the heart of Jharkhand, where while growing up my friends and I had roamed its vales and forests, and also that I had traveled extensively in the 'unspoilt' tribal areas of Odisha. These areas also appeared to be 'unspoilt' by development!

Known commonly by the name of its headquarters, Belpahari, Binpur-II block is located in the north-western extremity of the district. An elongated area covering 576 sq. km, it thrusts out from the main body of Paschim Medinipur as an arm raised in challenge. With 42 per cent of its population belonging to the Schedued Tribes, it is the block with the highest concentration of tribal population in the district. On 25 February a landmine explosion set off purportedly by the People's War near Badiam hill, between Bhulabeda and Kankrajhore, had blasted a police vehicle; eight persons, two police officers, five Eastern Frontier Rifles (EFR) jawans, and the driver, had died in the attack; four others had been seriously injured.

For my first tour in the district, I had consciously chosen reportedly the most backward area in the district, with a large tribal population and grievously affected by left wing extremism. I wanted to know how bad 'worst' was and what we were up against.

Upon reaching the block headquarters at about noon with the SDO, Jhargram, I examined the cash book and other registers, collected some basic figures of the block and then drove on to Banspahari, the north-western extremity of the district. En route, we visited Belpahari Prathamik Vidyalaya, situated at the side of the road, where 96 students have been enrolled. Today about 60 children had their meals under the cooked Midday Meal Programme. I found that the school was being let off at 1.30 p.m. — two and a half hours before closing time. The school is housed in a *pacca*, two-room structure 30 ft long by 10 ft wide; a slender verandah running the length of the building serves also as a classroom. Nearby, an unfinished one-room building, constructed up to the lintels, stands separate, alone. I asked the BDO to find out why it had not been finished and to take steps to complete it at the earliest. I also requested the two teachers present to take classes until 4.00 p.m. regularly.

Our next stop was at Neguria Prathamik Vidyalaya, village Neguria, Banspahari Gram Panchayat. A hundred children were enrolled here — 16 in class-III, 42 in class-IV, 41 in class-I, and 21 in class-II. There is no water source adjacent to the school; neither is there a latrine nor a urinal for the children. As the old building, with mud walls and a straw roof, was unusable, students of class-III and class-IV were sitting outside, on the ground beneath a tree. There was one room where children of class-I and II were sitting together. Only 47 students were present. Under the Midday Meal Scheme, 8.3 quintals of rice comprised the balance stock in the school. A new school building and a hand pump were required here.

Housed in a hut, about 50 m down the road is located the Neguria Anganwadi Centre (AWC). Next to it is the hand pump that supplies most of the drinking water to this village, including the primary school. According to nearby residents, the Anganwadi worker, Rajlakshmi Mandal, who lives in Banspahari, does not run the centre regularly. On the days she does open the centre, *khichdi* is provided to the 40–50 children who come here. Today the AWC did not open its doors at all. And yesterday was pay day, hence Rajlakshmi Mandal, away to collect her honorarium, failed to turn up! The helper, Mandira Pal, told me that there were some medicines in stock but I was unable to verify the position because the tiny store room was locked. We learnt that there was actually no helper in this centre; Mandira Pal was working without appointment!

At 2.50 p.m. we reached the Chakadoba Gram Panchayat office. A lone brass Godrej lock dangling on the door duly greeted me. A Revenue Inspector's (RI) office is also located here; that too was closed. I instructed the SDO to issue a show cause notice to the executive assistant and other employees of the Gram Panchayat as to why disciplinary action should not be taken against them for dereliction of duty. Some people living nearby told us that the Gram Panchayat office opened only thrice a week. The RI office had not functioned in a long time. The DLLRO should issue show cause notices to the RI and his staff.

A strong signal needs to be sent to all field officers that they must attend office and provide their duty-bound services to the people of the area. I asked the SDO to convene a meeting at the sub-divisional level and impress upon all officers that any laxity in this matter will not be tolerated.

Banspahari, Bhulaveda and Simulpal are the three disturbed Gram Panchayats of this block; LWEs are known to be active here. I instructed the SDO to visit all the three Gram Panchayats, inspect their accounts and keep a close watch on their functioning.

Strings made of *babui* grass appear to be a major source of income for the people here. At various places along the roads, I found people under trees, especially women, working on rolls of thin rope by looping them around the branch or trunk of the tree, pulling alternately on each end to rub them to stringy smoothness. Could a mechanical device not be created for this purpose? One of the main problems faced by the tribals engaged in making of *babui* grass rope is of storage; first, of the grass and, second, of the finished products. Under the allocation plan of the Swarnajayanti Gram Sammriddhi Yojana (SGSY), storage godowns for this purpose need to be constructed in several villages where people are dependent on this cottage industry.[1] The BDO also has an interesting idea about setting up a storage and marketing centre at Belpahari: to ensure that the indigent producers get a fair rate for their products, and the *babui* rope, or string, can be collected and stored by an SHG and sold to one or two traders from Belpahari itself.

At several points all along the route I noticed a number of Mark-II tube wells standing dry and unusable. Upon inquiring I learnt that only minor repairs were needed to make them functional again. I asked the BDO to give this task the highest priority and chalk out a schedule for his Sub-assistant Engineers (SAEs) to repair and restore the tube wells.

We reached the Bhulabeda Gram Panchayat office at 3.10 p.m., and there too were greeted by locks on the doors of three of the four rooms. Tarachand Soren, *sahayak*, was present and sitting with not even a scrap of paper on his empty desk, obviously without work. The Gram Panchayat secretary, he informed us, had been transferred to Kanko Gram Panchayat; the executive assistant from Kanko was supposed to replace him. The secretary from this gram panchayat had promptly moved to Kanko but his replacement was yet to make an appearance in remote Bhulabeda!

We returned to Belpahari at 4.30 p.m. and went directly to the Block Primary Health Centre (BPHC). Dr Bishui, the Block Medical Officer of Health (BMOH) was in the Centre. From the ensuing discussion it emerged that the Mobile Health Unit (MHU) that was supposed to visit six places in the three affected Gram Panchayats had become irregular; the principal reason for this was the absence of a doctor. The doctor who had been assigned from Midnapore had not been coming for the past two to three months. In his absence the medical support and care, supposed to be provided by the unit, had also vanished. One Dr Samanta had been deputed for the mobile unit from the District Sadar Hospital, but his visits were not always predictable. Initially two persons were deputed for this service. One, a lady doctor, never joined. This arrangement needs to be revamped quickly.

There are also three Primary Health Centres (PHCs) in this block: one at Silda, another at Odolchua, and the third at Raghunathpur. The ones at Odolchua and Silda are not manned; no staff member is posted there. In Silda and Raghunathpur no medical officers are posted. One doctor had been posted in each PHC, but they were withdrawn some time back. At present, there are four doctors in this BPHC. They take turns to visit Raghunathpur and Silda to attend to the outdoor patients. No water supply system is in place at the BPHC. I asked the BDO and BMOH to prepare an estimate for a deep tube well and submit it by Monday, 15 March 2004. Funds for such interventions are available under the Pradhan Mantri Gramodaya Yojana (PMGY); we may as well utilise them.[2] According to the BMOH, the stock of medicines in the BPHC, is satisfactory; except for tetanus toxin (which is in short supply throughout the state), and, from time to time, saline and some antibiotics. However, there is sufficient Septran (an antibiotic) in stock. I have asked the BMOH to ensure that the mobile unit goes to different locations every day as scheduled, and that each location is covered, if not every week but at least every alternate week, by the doctor. On other days the

General Duty Assistants (GDAs) and other health assistants may attend to the problems of the people to the best of their ability.

There is a Krishi Bikash Kendra at Kapgari in Jamboni Block which is also quite well staffed and can be utilised for training and extension purposes in the area. These issues must be taken up with various officials immediately.

◎

Notes

1. Swarnajayanti Gram Sammridhi Yojana (SGSY) is the flagship poverty alleviation programme of the Ministry of Rural Development, Government of India. It was introduced in 1999 by merging all previous poverty alleviation schemes. Although individuals are not excluded, emphasis of SGSY is upon formation of SHGs, particularly of women, for development of micro-enterprises in the rural areas. The programme involves district administration, Panchayat bodies, banks, NGOs, and local technical institutions to ensure that backward and forward linkages, including training, infrastructure, and marketing support may be provided to the SHGs. Families below the poverty line and those belonging to the weaker sections are especially targeted.
2. Pradhan Mantri Gramodaya Yojana (PMGY), launched in 2000–2001, aimed at village-level development in five key areas, i.e., primary health, primary education, housing, rural roads, and drinking water and nutrition with the objective of improving the quality of life of rural citizens. Funding was provided for interventions in each of the five sectors by the Central Government. It has since been merged with the Bharat Nirman programme.

General Elections 2004

◎

On 17 March 2004 the Chief Electoral Officer (CEO) of West Bengal had convened a meeting of all DMs and SPs of the state. The meeting was held in the Council Chamber of the imposing Raj Bhavan in Kolkata. All three Election Commissioners of India, including the Chief Election Commissioner (CEC), were present apart from the CEO, the Home Secretary and other State Government officials. This was a routine, preliminary meeting in the context of the Lok Sabha Elections scheduled to be held in May.

The CEC set the tone of the meeting by underlining the need for neutrality and impartiality in the conduct of elections. A number of serious complaints had been received by the Election Commission regarding the manner in which elections were conducted in the state; due to employment of 'subtle methods' to corner votes in elections by various political parties, freedom of voters to vote was in doubt. He reminded us that during the conduct of the elections all State Government officers and other employees engaged in the election process were on deputation to the Election Commission of India. Therefore, it was all the more important that the prevailing impression, which detracted from the neutrality and impartiality of administration, should be dispelled. By turn the other Election Commissioners also spoke, and while adding layers to the central message went over different aspects of the conduct of elections. Emphasis was given on the need to publicise the deployment of electronic voting machines and to popularise it by ensuring that the voters knew how to use them. The entire process should be transparent and by the book. The DMs and SPs should be easily available and the administration should be 'voter friendly and freely accessible'.

After dealing with each aspect of the elections one of the Election Commissioners, Shri Gopalaswami, focussed upon Paschim Medinipur district. The SP and I were asked to stand up and introduce ourselves. Whereupon he began by saying that elections in Paschim Medinipur have been reported neither to be free nor fair.

In some cases even the candidates were not allowed to enter the polling booths or to move around freely. He asked us what we proposed to do about it. I replied that we would take all necessary steps to ensure that no voter was prevented from exercising his or her franchise; for this purpose we would chalk out a new programme to educate the suffrage and sensitise all Government officials engaged in carrying out elections. Shri Gopalaswami then directed the SP, Paschim Medinipur to send him daily reports regarding election complaints through me to the Election Commission of India. Taking up a few other districts he warned, 'If anyone strays from the rules, grievous punishment will be visited upon him'. With these ominous words ringing in our ears the SP and I returned to Midnapore.

Within a week, on 23 March 2004, I held a district level election meeting in preparation of the forthcoming elections. By that time, the SP and I had also discussed the steps we needed to take to at least attempt to assure the Election Commission about our neutrality and impartiality. Almost by routine, before the Lok Sabha elections the District Election Officer and District Collector/DM holds at least two rounds of meetings with representatives of all major political parties. These meetings are attended by the SP and other senior officials of the district. The election schedule is discussed, and problems and issues on either side are addressed. We decided that for these elections the SDOs would also hold a sub-divisional level meeting with the representatives of the political parties, and the SP and I would hold meetings with block level representatives of political parties in selected block headquarters where trouble of any kind had been reported in the past. Thereafter, we could even consider asking the concerned BDOs and the officers-in-charge (OCs), police stations, to hold meetings in gram panchayats with a history of violence or of inter-party clashes.

I planned to go one step further. One of the primary concerns expressed by the Election Commission was that the election should not only be peaceful but also free and fair, particularly because the voters in certain areas specified by them, such as Keshpur and Panskura blocks, were allegedly living and voting in a reign of 'silent terror'. The law and order machinery was geared to ensure that the smallest incidence of violence, including threats, would be dealt with promptly and severely. However, it was necessary to once again convey to the voters in general that the district administration meant to be extremely strict and fair, to inform them about the steps they could take if they wished to report something, and to whom. Overall, we should ensure that the electorate is aware that the administration is there with them, and also how it proposed to help them. In sum, I proposed that we should run an election campaign of our own; if political parties could exhort people to vote for their candidates, we could certainly inform the people about their rights and their responsibilities, and assure them of our demonstrable unstinted support.

When I first mentioned this to some of our senior officers there were some smiles, because no one thought I could be serious. Nothing of the kind had been done earlier and they could not see how this would serve any purpose. However, when I made it clear that I was completely serious about the campaign they all fell in with the scheme, especially when I reminded them of the Election Commission's sword of Damocles hanging over all our heads. I also explained to them that instead of just two meetings with political parties and district level officers, this time round we shall meetings with block representatives of political parties in 17 identified blocks, and some meetings even below that level, because we wanted to convey both information and reassurance to the political parties. It was also necessary to simultaneously communicate these two messages to the voting population. As far as elections in Paschim Medinipur were concerned, it was not enough to convince political parties unless we could reach the voters through a mass contact programme. Hence, our campaign.

Once the Collector had made it clear that he was in earnest about the 'election campaign', things rapidly fell in place. Soon messages were finalised, posters and leaflets were designed and given out for printing, carrying the names of selected control rooms and telephone numbers. We also went through an intricate exercise to identify places to put up posters and distribute leaflets. Further, having learnt from experience that, because of uneven proficiency in literacy, the best method to disseminate information in the rural areas is not wall-writing or posters, but, as in cinema advertisements of yore, by broadcasting over the microphone; thus the SP and I also recorded messages on audio cassettes and on video compact discs (VCDs).

The preparation of publicity material took little time. The greater test was ensuring that they were used and that the message reached the suffrage of Paschim Medinipur. An interesting administrative exercise by itself, it necessitated energising the existing sub-divisional, block and gram panchayat machinery and intense supervision. The audio cassettes were distributed among the blocks, to be played in every habitation by a hired operator on a van-rickshaw twice in the intervening period. The VCDs were distributed among the network of cable operators across the district with the request to play the short recordings during prime time. And the posters and handbills were, respectively, put up and distributed in carefully selected public places throughout the district. Like all other election activities this campaign was also rigorously monitored.

According to the election law, campaigning by political parties must cease 48 hours prior to the date of the poll. This rule is applicable to political campaigning, but not to our campaign for a free and fair election. Therefore, in the two days before 10 May 2004, the day of poll, while political voices fell silent, loudspeakers on van-rickshaws hired by the district administration repeated the appeal to voters across the district to vote fearlessly!

I am not sure what the impact of our 'election campaign' was, but we certainly did not rely upon publicity alone for ensuring a free and fair election. Police arrangements were firm, and monitoring of action on election-related complaints a nightly affair. Fortunately for the SP and me the elections ended without any major incidence of violence; not even one re-poll had to be conducted in any of the 2870 polling booths in Paschim Medinipur.

Despite the evidently fair and peaceful completion of the election, I wish I could say with certainty that all voters cast their vote without fear.

2

In Pursuit of *Kendu patta*

◎

Located on the south-western side of the district, Gopiballavpur-I block borders Odisha to the south and Jharkhand to the west. Almost one-fifth of the area of the block is under forests, a source of livelihood to the population, of which 35 per cent are tribals. The valuable kendu *leaf, used for rolling* bidis, *and sal leaf are the two most important raw materials collected by the people.* Kendu *leaf, which commands a premium, was purchased through government agencies set up by the TDC, and a support price was provided so that the* kendu *leaf gatherers were not exploited by private traders. The delay in disbursement of the price encouraged people, mostly tribals to sell the leaves to illegal private traders who would despatch them onwards to Odisha. While arranging with the Government to provide funds in advance to the LAMPS, so that timely payment could be made to the* kendu *leaf collectors in the district, I also decided to strengthen the monitoring of the regulatory mechanism by curbing illegal trade in* kendu *leaf.*

I had arranged to carry out a joint raid with the Divisional Forest Officer (DFO), Jhargram against the private traders of *kendu* leaf to send a strong signal to the traders who were carrying on their illegal and exploitative business in various parts of the *kendu* leaf producing areas. Early in the morning, our meeting point was the Gopiballavpur-I Block Office. On the way, I was joined by the SDO, Jhargram, Ganesh Chaudhary. There were two sets of issues that I wished to discuss with him. The first set concerned the problems of coordination, to be taken up with the DM, Bankura, for the conduct of elections in Jhargram and adjoining areas. The second related to the mobile health check-up camps that had been revived recently in the more far-flung clusters of villages of Jhargram sub-division.

As confirmed yesterday by Dr Soren, the Assistant Chief Medical Officer of Health (ACMOH), Jhargram, the MHU functioning from

1 April 2004 was visiting six different locations through the week. He had drawn up a schedule for the visits, which needed wide publicity, especially in the villages visited by the MHU and the surrounding areas which it will be visiting. Notices in Santhali and Bengali needed to be put up in these areas. I also told the SDO that I would expect a weekly report, particularly from the the the BMOH, Belpahari, about the number of patients served in each village by the MHU during the week. The drug position, i.e., medicine availability, for the MHU should also be monitored weekly.

SDO, Jhargram, suggested that one person from the block, an extension officer, may accompany the MHU staff from time to time so that other services or the position of the services may also be verified. In this manner local problems concerning basic amenities, such as drinking water, irrigation, etc., may also be explored. This is an excellent idea and needs to be taken up immediately. I asked the SDO to accordingly tie up with the ACMOH, Jhargram.

Another concern is the shortage in the supply of medicines to *swasthya sahayikas*, local female health workers, engaged largely for family welfare through panchayats. The Additional Executive Officer (AEO), Zilla Parishad, has already asked for a status report in this matter. Apparently there is, on the one hand, no shortage of medicines; on the other, the supply of medicines to the *swasthya sahayikas* is quite irregular! The original arrangement was that the *swasthya sahayikas* would obtain their medicine supply from the health sub-centres. As it is, we find that a large number of medicines expire unused in these centres. Why cannot some of these medicines be handed over to the *swasthya sahayikas* for distribution among the needy? Paracetamol, Metrogyl, folic acid, and iron tablets can certainly be supplied in this manner.

At 10.15 a.m. we reached Gopiballavpur-I block office. On the way, at the Sathaniamara *mouza*, we crossed a bridge over the Gourikhal River. This is a very important bridge because it connects Gopiballavpur-I, Gopiballavpur-II and Nayagram. Regardless of its importance, the bridge is in a state of disrepair; it is also very narrow. It may be a good idea to propose the construction of a new bridge on this site. This should be taken up under the Rural Infrastructure Development Fund.

As we approached our destination — the depots of, Upendranath Mahato, a trader reported to be located in Saria — we stopped at

Amjuri Beat office to take along someone from the forest office to identify the village. After we turned from the Gopiballavpur road towards Saria, we found that although it was a *pacca* road, not many trucks or transport vehicles were plying on it. A few trekkers crossed us but they were heavily, I repeat heavily, over-loaded. Perhaps, we need to issue more route permits on this stretch of road. The question is, would there be takers for these permits willing to invest in vehicles?

The Saria LAMPS comprise three long godown-cum-worksheds enclosing a central yard. A large stock of *kendu patta* had already been collected by the members of this LAMPS. Swollen mounds of dried brown leaves lay in the godowns while more recently collected leaves, the green giving way to a drained tan, lay spread in neat rows in the courtyard. A large group of women were busy tying dry leaves into bundles. The overseer of the LAMPS showed us the way towards Mahato's depots, which was actually a little further along the road.

One depot, a long low brick and Galvanised Iron (GI) sheet-covered building, was located next to the main road — the godown was locked. Outside, bundles of *kendu* leaves, 20 leaves to a bundle, lay scattered all around. The place was deserted. Not a soul was present to talk to or unlock the door of the godown. The LAMPS overseer informed us that another godown was located about half a kilometre away.

To get to the second godown we turned off the state highway and moved across the open ground dotted with bushes and a few low trees. The sun was out in full force and as we drove across the rolling red landscape fringed with the weathered green of the persistent scrub, I wondered how this remoteness bred exploitation. Mahato's second depot was an area surrounded by a rude fence vwith a small hut in the middle. Around the hut, again bundles of *kendu* leaves lay drying in the open. We had been walking about the small compound, when suddenly one of the BDO's staff members exclaimed, 'There he is'! At a little distance, breaking the serenity of the bush-line, a man had leapt onto a bicycle and was pedaling away furiously. The police jeep in front of us had also sighted him. The cyclist was given chase and finally apprehended. This man turned out to be Upendranath Mahato! We questioned him for some time about his activities. I left a little while later, instructing the DFO and the other officers to make a water-tight case against the offender.

As we were leaving the village of Saria, I noticed a few houses by the roadside and some earthen-ware laid outside. There were a few rows of little terracotta horses and a rude elephant. In this hamlet, Banyachara, there are two houses of potters, one of the craftsmen there is Bankim Bera. He was a graying man in his mid-forties. The little horses are, of course, used as offerings at places of worship; their sale is mostly seasonal, coinciding with festivals for placating local deities. The elephant is also worshipped, especially to ensure that during their movement elephant herds do not trample upon the villages. The potter families farm small portions of land and make earthen pots and other vessels for the local markets, but the demand for their wares has declined over the years. Now they are neither full-time potters, nor full-time farmers.

On the way back I passed fields of *babui* grass that had already been harvested. The thick clumps had been neatly trimmed about 4–6 inches from the ground giving the spot a crew cut. The entire region appeared to be extremely dry, without any source of irrigation. Large sections of the straggling forest lie degraded. According to the DFO, Nayagram, the forest is very thick, as it is in Jhargram, Belpahari, etc. However, the open land populated by scraggy clumps of struggling trees insinuates past splendour rather than present abundance. We need to explore how, and if, we can provide irrigation in this area; perhaps the watershed approach would be the best way forward.

As we drove along I noticed giant ant-hills dotting the thin forest. One can see them from afar: tall, pyramidesque mounts of red earth that have grown loftier over the years as generations of ants pile their labours, layer upon layer. It struck me that it may not be a coincidence that in areas where ant-hills are found human beings also construct durable mud houses. I recall noticing several years ago the presence of both ant-hills and solidly built, 'eco-friendly' and comfortable houses of red earth in the southern parts of Bankura, and even in my own Chotanagpur. If ants can make ant-hills that will survive the rain and wind and hail over succeeding years, human dwellings made of earth would certainly be at least as strong and enduring. Fittingly, the houses in these areas of the district are mostly built of earth with straw roofs supported by bamboo or sal frames.

Along the route are large patches of groundnut, which has been recently introduced in this area — a most welcome development.

Maize as well as *arhar*, a pulse, can also be introduced here. Upon my return I must ask the principal agriculture officer to explore the possibilities of growing both these crops in the area within this year.

As we passed Topsia, I noticed some small girls working on the *aal*, raised dividers, of the paddy fields that had long been harvested and its stubble stood brittle and dry. They were digging at the base of the *aal* with their sickles. I could not understand why, and the SDO and the BDO also could not enlighten me. Stopping to find out, I got out of the car and called out to them. They looked up, gathered their small bags and sickles and fled, perhaps, thinking that the security guards were going to harass them. Puzzled, I went alone for a closer examination of the *aal*. Although the girls had vanished, I met a boy walking home towards the cluster of houses among the trees beyond the fields. Upon gentle persuasion he informed me that the girls had been digging up the snails hibernating in the *aals*. Normally they would emerge from their sleep only after the arrival of rains. But sleeping snails are an easy catch, and provide some variety, and protein, to the frugal diet of the poor.

◎

3
Public Meeting in Bansberh: Small Expectations
◎

Binpur-I block forms the north-west shoulder of Paschim Medinipur district. Lalgarh, another name for the block, is the Gram Panchayat where the headquarters of the block are located. The river Kangsabati, meandering from north to south, bifurcates the block. Five Gram Panchayats fall on the eastern side while the remaining five, including Lalgarh, on the western side. Of the total population of 139, 148 (Census 2001) 29 per cent are Scheduled Tribes and 25 per cent belong to Scheduled Castes.

The road from Lalgarh to Sijua wound through an area that appeared to be one of the poorest I had yet visited in Midnapore. The mud houses and the service delivery centres, such as primary schools and health centres, seemed to be particularly vulnerable. Most of the latter are housed in either *kuchcha* huts or sheds. Shortage of water seems to be the principal problem in this area — cattle and humans share ponds for bathing and drinking water.

From Kantapahari we turned towards Bansberh and onto the recently sanctioned road being built under Sampoorna Grameen Rozgar Yojna (SGRY).[1] Bansberh, Eshabandh, Sitaram are the three villages that are being connected by a 3.5 km-long road being built, the top constituted of compacted morum.

A meeting to assess local needs had been called under a banyan tree at the edge of a parched football field, a point where Bansberh and Eshabandh villages meet. It was attended by about 50 men and 70 women and children. Badal Hansda, a teacher at Kantapahari High School, conducted the affairs of the meeting. As usual the meeting started with a ceremonial welcome, followed by a short dance by tribal girls to the accompaniment of *dholaks*, then a speech

by the teacher who spoke on behalf of the people. He thanked the
administration for the construction of the road. However, he pointed
out that education, health, drinking water, and irrigation facilities
in the area required urgent attention of the administration. Some
others also rose to make short speeches and requests. One of the
demands that came up was the extension of the road, under construction right now, by about 200 m so that it can cover the entire
village; there was also a request for more roads.

The teacher-in-charge of Nama Bansberh Prathamik Vidyalaya,
Dol Govinda Mahato, lamented the shortage of space. I requested
him to get an estimate prepared with the help of the block office
for a two-room primary school building that may be constructed
with the available funds. Drinking water is the most serious problem in this area. There are but three wells in the three hamlets of
Upar Bansberh, Madhya Bansberh and Nicha Bansberh. According
to the people present, especially the women, Sitaramdahi village
needs a well and also a check dam. A Shishu Shiksha Kendra (SSK)
Centre is running in that village. The nearest High School is located
about 4 km from there, in Kantapahari. The representative from

Plate 3.1 Anganwadi in a Santal village

Sitaramdahi, Rani Murmu, is articulate and was clearly able to convey the demands of her village.

In Bansberh I visited AWC No. 108, that runs in the primary school; there is no separate building for it. The food materials are stored in a nearby house. This year no medicines have been supplied here. The AWC is not being utilised for the routine immunisation programme, although this can be easily arranged on outreach days. Sombari Mandi is the helper and Samita Murmu is the absent Anganwadi worker here. The condition of the AWC is not particularly inspiring. According to the people of the area, which even the helper admitted hesitantly, the Anganwadi worker made an appearance at the AWC, maybe, once a week. Besides the food materials nothing else can be seen: no medicines, teaching/learning materials, or play things for the children — all of which are supplied from time to time to the AWCs. The District Project Officer (DPO), Integrated Child Development Scheme (ICDS) should issue a show cause notice to the Anganwadi worker, and the Child Development Project Officer (CDPO) should also visit the Centre and make an assessment of the situation there.[2] The helper also did not know where the registers were kept or whether they had been maintained regularly. An independent building for the AWC could also be proposed and constructed from either the SGRY fund or some other fund.

Bleaching powder (for purification of wells) has also not been supplied in this area for a long time. The Chief Medical Officer of Health (CMOH) must be advised to provide the powder, before the onset of monsoon, to all gram panchayats and Sub-Health Centres (SHCs) in the block.

Electricity is available in only two houses in Bansberh. This facility needs to be extended to the rest of the village and to the two nearby villages. Rural Electricity Development Corporation should be the source of funding as well as implementation of the scheme.

On the way back we stopped at the *haat* in Lalgarh. The vegetable market in Lalgarh appears to be quite large. Small and large bitter gourds were being sold at ₹3 and ₹4 a kg, respectively. Other vegetables such as *patal*, *danta* (drum stick) and *nimbu* (lemon) were also being sold. The price of 100 Sal leaf plates was about ₹10 but could probably be bought for ₹8 if one bargained. The rate was the same for Sal leaf bowls. Bundles of Sal leaf, green or dry, were being sold for one rupee. Each bundle contained about 50 leaves. A handful of *babui* rope was available for ₹12 apparently, *babui* rope is not sold by the length. The rate of the *babui* rope used for making *charpoys* is even less, about ₹9 per handful. The rate of rice, and not of very good quality either, is ₹9–10 a kg.

The problem in Sijua Gram Panchayat appears to be related to the improper functioning of panchayat, and the divide between the panchayat and the people. There is no shortage of money for development purposes. Yet, the panchayat bodies and the various committees at the village levels such as Village Education Committees (VECs), mother and teacher committees, etc., are not functioning properly. All BDOs must be asked to verify the regularity of VEC meetings, if necessary by examining the resolution books of the committees. It is expected that the VECs should meet once a month while the school is in session. The utilisation of maintenance and Total Literacy Mission (TLM) grants received by the schools also needs to be reviewed and verified.[3]

On the road back to Midnapore I could not help wondering about the fundamental nature of the demands made on the administration by the people of Bansberh: a few dug wells or basically holes in the ground, some check dams, a building for the primary school, a functioning ICDS, and basic health care. In all these years the government has not been able to ensure even these. It is remarkable that despite the monumental failure of the government in the area, people have such high expectations from it.

◎

Notes

1. Launched in September 2001, the Sampoorna Grameen Rozgar Yojana (SGRY) merged two existing employment generation schemes, the Jawahar Gram Samridhi Yojana (JGSY) and the Employment Assurance Scheme (EAS). The scheme sought to provide additional wage employment and food security in the rural areas through the creation of lasting community, social and economic infrastructure. Special emphasis was given upon wage employment to women, Scheduled Castes, Scheduled Tribes and parents of children withdrawn from hazardous occupations. Since 2008 the SGRY has been entirely merged with the Mahatma Gandhi National Rural Employment Guarantee Scheme (MGNREGS).
2. Integrated Child Development Services (ICDS) Scheme was launched in 1975 on Mahatma Gandhi's birth anniversary, 2 October. It is designed as a comprehensive childhood development scheme that aims to improve

the nutritional and health status of children in the age group of 0–6 years, take care of proper psychological, physical and social development of the child, and reduce the incidence of mortality, morbidity, malnutrition, and school dropouts. It seeks to achieve these objectives by setting up ICDS centres called Anganwadis, covering all habitations in rural areas, run by two female personnel known as the Anganwadi worker and the helper. Cooked meals are provided to the children and to pregnant and lactating mothers enrolled in the Anganwadi on a daily basis. The regular health check-up and immunization of the children and the women is also coordinated through the centre. The children are also imparted pre-school education.

3. Total Literacy Mission (TLM) was initiated under the National Literacy Mission, Government of India, in 1988. The aim of the campaign is to raise literacy levels across the country by ensuring functional literacy of non-literates in the age group of 15–35 years in both rural and urban areas. The campaign was implemented through the engagement of local volunteers who took the responsibility to impart the three 'R's — Reading, Writing, and Arithmetic — to an identified group of persons in their locality, usually late in the evening after working hours. The Continuing Education Scheme aims to provide support to neo-literates in the post-literacy phase.

4

Amlasole

◎

Within a few days of joining the district, on the basis of a preliminary assessment, I had decided to prepare a plan for the focussed development of eight predominantly tribal blocks, namely, Binpur-I, Binpur-II, Jamboni, Gopiballavpur-I, Gopiballavpur-II, Nayagram, Garhbeta-II, and Salboni. On 15 March, I held a meeting with the SDOs of Medinipur Sadar and Jhargram sub-divisions and the BDOs of the eight blocks. It was explained to them that a comprehensive plan was to be prepared for these areas to accelerate improvement of crucial infrastructure and improve the delivery of essential services. They were asked to submit a list of schemes within 15 days, that may be taken up speedily in the areas of drinking water, irrigation, healthcare and infrastructure development in the social sector. The BDOs were also instructed to take up the repair and re-sinking of defunct hand pumps, the cleaning up and disinfection of wells and provision of new wells in villages without any source of drinking water in the interim period.

The lists of schemes were received in due time. Nonetheless, on 24 March the Election Commission of India notified the schedule of the General Elections to the Lok Sabha; the consequent coming into force of the Model Code of Conduct forestalled implementation of most of the schemes. The election process finally ended with the counting of votes and declaration of results on 13 May 2004. In the interim period developmental activities almost came to a standstill.

Even so, during this phase efforts were made to ensure the upgrading of delivery facilities, improvement in the availability of drinking water, and involvement of LAMPS for the purchase of kendu leaves at enhanced rates. The Chief Secretary, whom I sent progress reports fortnightly, was personally monitoring these initiatives.

Early on the morning of 10 June 2004, while sipping tea, I picked up a Bengali daily from the table, the headlines screamed at me, 'Anahar o Apushtite Pnach Janer Mrityu Belpaharir Grame!':

'Five Persons Die of Starvation and Malnutrition in a Belpahari Village'. It proceeded to state that five persons had died in the last three months in the village of Amlasole. This had been certified by the CPM panchayat representative of the village, Kailash Mura. The relatives of the deceased had also testified that the five persons, four men and one woman, had all died because they had nothing to eat and no means to earn a decent living. The news story went on to describe the conditions of the people in the village, its remoteness and the lack of any attempt by the panchayats or the administration to develop the area. Apart from the shocking news of the five deaths, I was also a little surprised to find that I had been quoted as stating, 'If this has happened it is certainly most serious. We have not received any such reports. We shall enquire and find out.' I could not recall that any journalist had called me with such news.

In view of the seriousness of the report, I decided to enquire into the alleged starvation deaths that same day. I also directed the BDO, Binpur-II block, to proceed to Amlasole village for a preliminary inquiry, provide whatever immediate relief was possible and to ascertain what measures could be taken immediately. I instructed the SDO, Jhargram, to send a medical team from Jhargram to Amlasole and its neighbouring villages if they had not visited these villages in the last week. At 8.30 a.m I proceeded to Jhargram to attend a pre-scheduled meeting pertaining to the establishment of the Eklavya School for Adivasi children. During the course of the meeting I received a telephone call from the Chief Secretary, who enquired after the newspaper reports and instructed me to proceed to Amlasole to conduct an inquiry. Hurrying through the meeting, I set off for Belpahari enroute to Amlasole.

Accompanied by the SDO, Jhargram, the BDO, Binpur-II, and a Gram Panchayat job assistant, I reached Amlasole at about 4 p.m. Earlier in the day the BDO had conducted a preliminary inquiry and the medical team had also been sent to the villages of Amlasole and Amjharna. Enroute we met the ACMOH, Jhargram sub-division, and his medical team who were on their way back. The ACMOH reported that there were a number of cases of high fever in Kankrajhore, Amlasole and Amjharna, and slides of blood samples had also been taken for tests. In the meantime, the ill had been given medicines for suspected malaria and other ailments. The disinfection of drinking water sources, especially wells, had also been carried out in the three villages.

Even before I reached Kankrajhore and then Amlasole, it was apparent that the living conditions of the people there were exceptionally poor; there was little that met the eye to suggest that efforts had been made to reduce indigence. The road leading to the village was in a very poor condition. Indeed, after crossing Simulpal Gram Panchayat headquarters the condition of the road deteriorated steadily until in places it became merely a muddy, rock-strewn track.

Nestling in a picturesque valley, Amlasole village is at the extreme corner of the north-westernmost block of the district, Binpur-II. The narrow valley between two ranges of well-forested hills in which the village lies is part of the Banspahari Gram Panchayat on the state border with Jharkhand. The village was populated by 16 Sabar families and about 25 Mura (Munda) families. Four wells provided drinking water to the people. There was one primary school and one ICDS centre. The surrounding forest comprises mainly sal and some teak trees, and is quite thick; the hill slopes are also covered with *babui* grass. In Amlasole I did not notice any privately owned *pacca* building. Almost all houses are made of mud and have tiled or straw roofs. Houses of the poorer Sabar adivasis are made of bamboo matting and rough-hewn wooden staves and poles.

Although sparsely populated, the village of Amlasole stretches over a length of about a kilometre along the valley. From afar we could make out a number of vehicles parked along the road at the very first cluster. A significant number of journalists of both the print and the electronic media had reached Amlasole. Spotting the journalists busy at work in the initial clutch of houses, which belonged to the Lodha-Sabars, I decided not to stop at the first house. Instead, having ascertained the location of the houses of the deceased from the local panchayat official accompanying us, I decided to drive to the other end of the village.

The first house we visited was of the late Sanatan Mura (who was about 45–50 years old). His wife Shakuntala, son Pradip and two daughters were present, with whom I spoke at some length. Shakuntala Mura, although uncertain about the date, stated that her husband died about three months ago, sometime in early March 2004. Mura had been suffering from jaundice for some time and was being treated by a *kabiraj*, a traditional physician. The Mura family owns 5 *bighas* (a little less than 2 acres) of land, a dozen goats and a few chickens. The mother and son also made rope out of *babui* grass, which they sold in the nearby *haats* at about ₹9 per kg. They were able to make about 25 kg of *babui* rope in a week. The Muras live in a house made of mud walls with tiled roof, about 40 ft long and 10 ft wide, with a small enclosed verandah. The elder brother of late Sanatan Mura and his family also reside in the same house. Shakuntala Mura told me that there were about 40–45 kg of rice in the house. At the time of Sanatan Mura's death they had about 4–5 *maunds* (about 200 kg) of rice. However, much of the rice had been used up in the *shradh* ceremony that followed the unfortunate death.

I next visited the homestead of late Sambhu Sabar (50 years old). Sambhu Sabar died in March after a period of illness. His wife and son were not in the house. However, I was able to speak to Parvati Sabar, daughter-in-law of the deceased, and some neighbours. Parvati Sabar informed me that her father-in-law had been ill for some time and was also coughing blood. During his last few days he was unable to swallow any food offered to him. Abud Murmu, a neighbour who was present, told me that Sambhu Sabar was receiving treatment for tuberculosis at the Bharat Sebashram Clinic in Ghatsila. He claimed that he had taken the deceased to that clinic. However, when I asked them to produce any prescription from the clinic, Parvati Sabar told me that the prescriptions had been burned with the body of Sambhu Sabar. Sambhu Sabar's family lives in two low huts built of mud and thatch, both about 20 ft in length and 8 ft in width. The family owns no land but rears a few goats and chickens. They also make rope out of *babui* grass and bamboo brooms. In one week they are able to make about 7–8 brooms, which are sold at the rate of ₹10–12 per broom. Other than this, the family depends on the few wage opportunities brought by the sowing and the harvesting season. As some land had been brought under *boro* cultivation, the number of days of wage employment had slightly increased off late. However, work for daily wage was not available on a regular basis. The two huts of this family were built on the slopes of a hill on the fringe of the forest. Most likely they live on forest land; this is but natural, since they have no land of their own.

The house of late Samay Sabar (55 years old) and Sombari Sabar (35 years old) was just about 10 m from the main track. A small hutment of about 15 ft by 8 ft, is occupied at present by his widow, Kokila Sabar, his daughter, his son and daughter-in-law and their infant. I spoke with Kokila and her son Budhu Sabar. Although the mother and son could not give the exact date of the death of the father and the daughter, who died within one month of each other, it appears that Samay Sabar died sometime during the last week of March, while Sombari Sabar passed away towards the end of April. Both father and daughter had been suffering from fever. They did not receive any medical treatment because they had no money, and Kankrajhore, where the SHC is situated, is about 4 km away. In their last days both of them were unable to swallow the mash they were being fed, sometimes made of chira and sometimes of rice. They had also been coughing out globules of blood. From the description given, of the ailment, it appears that tuberculosis was the cause of the death. The family owns no land, and like the families of Sambhu Sabar is dependent upon wage employment and making *babui* rope, of bamboo brooms and sal plates.

The late Nathu Sabar's family comprises his wife, two grown-up sons, the elder aged 35 years and the younger about 30 years, their wives and children. Nathu Sabar was found dead one morning on a hillock on the other side of the valley. According to his sons, he was not suffering from any ailment. However, it was learnt from others in the village that Nathu Sabar was a practising *ojha*. On the night of his death, sometime in the last week of April, Nathu Sabar had gone to practice his calling in a cluster of houses on the other side of the valley. After having concluded his work late in the evening, he had consumed food and the local alcoholic brew with some people in that *para*. Shortly after he left his hosts' home, a heavy hailstorm hit the area. In the morning his wife discovered her husband's dead body. Nathu Sabar had been about 55–60 years of age. The family does not own any land. They have a few goats and chickens of their own. The two brothers tend cattle for those who own livestock in the village. Each of them received about 350 gm of rice per day for their labour. Apart from this, along with the women folk, they also make *babui* rope. The house that they were living in got burnt in a jungle fire about a month back. I visited the site of their erstwhile house and found only a few wooden poles standing. At present, the family is living in the houses of their neighbours.

My findings indicated that the deaths of the first four of the five above named deceased persons were caused by jaundice and tuberculosis, respectively; the cause of death of Nathu Sabar could not be ascertained. However, there is no doubt that all the four families are very poor. Only the family of late Sanatan Mura owned any land. The other families, all belonging to the Sabar tribe, earn their living through daily wage labour or by making rope out of *babui* grass, plates out of Sal leaves and brooms out of bamboo. Indeed, all the 16 Sabar families in Amlasole village were landless and impoverished, with acute dependence on the forest and its produce. Their remoteness from the block and district headquarters, the poor communication infrastructure and uncertainty about regular income made them particularly vulnerable.

Amlasole dominated the headlines for several weeks, even months. Reporters of the print and the electronic media beat a passage through the jungles to the tiny village to cover all aspects of the deaths and the lives of the living in the till-then forgotten village. Political parties and Non-governmental Organisations (NGOs) in hordes followed, providing relief — rice, puffed rice, beaten rice, clothes, medicines, and so on. They came, distributed the materials, made statements to the attendant media and returned. Like Kalahandi in the previous decade, Amlasole became a metaphor for starvation deaths in rural India, of extreme deprivation, of neglect. Yet, most of those who trained their cameras or pens on Amlasole or distributed 'relief' to the people, did not attempt to explore the causes underlying the predicament of the people of the area.

◎

5
Hungry in an *Ashram*
◉

Late in the evening of 11 June, after despatching the report of my inquiry at Amlasole and following up on the relief measures undertaken in Belpahari, I drove off to Jhargram. I had decided that an overall development plan for the eight blocks was not enough; to reach those most in need of assistance from the government, it was necessary to target the weakest of the weak, the most vulnerable villages. The first task was to identify such villages; this could only be done by carrying out a survey of the villages. In the morning I had instructed the SDO, Jhargram, to convene a meeting of the BDOs of Binpur-I, Binpur-II and Jamboni blocks so that we may plan and begin a preliminary survey immediately.

Upon reaching the SDO's bunglow office at about 8 p.m., I explained my aim and intention to the officers. Together we then developed a structured, largely close-ended questionnaire and also decided upon the criteria for selection of villages to be surveyed: known to be poor, remote and largely populated by adivasis. Two to three teams were to be formed by the BDOs for each block, comprising the best officers and staff available in the block. Other block level officers, such as Agriculture Development Officer (ADO), Block Livestock Development Officer (BLDO), (CDPO), and Block Land and Land Reforms Officer (BL & LRO) could also be included in the survey team. The aim was to identify the present condition of the physical and public service infrastructure and also to guage the felt needs of the people.

The BDOs were asked to submit the outputs of the survey by the evening of 16 June 2004. The survey started in the three blocks of the Jhargram sub-division on 13 June 2004 and in two blocks of the Sadar sub-division on 14 June 2004. During this period the survey work was supervised by the SDO, Jhargram, the AEO, Zilla Parishad, and by me.

Upon reaching the Nayagram block office at about noon, I first reviewed the progress of the survey with the SDO and BDO — a rapid survey of the poorest villages in the block. The list obtained from the P&RD Department had been handed over to the BDO and he had also been instructed how to conduct the survey. Earlier the block had identified 27 Lodha villages for the survey. It transpired that only three out of these 27 villages figured in the list of 50 poorest villages in the block identified by the P&RD Department. I instructed the BDO to complete the survey of the remaining 24 Lodha villages which, according to him, were exceedingly poor. He could then proceed to survey the 50 villages identified by P&RD department. Some of these identified villages are, in fact, quite well-off. One of these villages in Nayagram is where the block headquarters is situated — Baligeria, the relatively developed village where the block headquarters are located! Such villages in the supplied list need to be dropped.

I also examined the list of Old Age Pension beneficiaries. Of the quota of 42 beneficiaries, at present only two slots are vacant. Yet in the list of 40 beneficiaries receiving pension I could not detect a single Lodha name; only one belonged to a Scheduled Tribe — Mugli Murmu, wife of late Lobe Murmu of village Patharbundh, Baligeria. The Panchayat Samiti has identified nine more potential beneficiaries of the Old Age Pension Schemes, among which the name of not a single Lodha–Sabar features; only one Scheduled Tribe person has been identified. Two factors may be at play here. First, the Panchayat Samiti in being partial towards certain groups is overlooking the needs of the poorest of the tribals; and second, tribals themselves are totally unaware of the schemes. Possibly both these factors are at work. Therefore, both problems need to be taken up at different levels. There is also a shortage of Antyodaya cards in the blocks.[1] The District Controller of Food & Supplies (DCF&S) needs to be reminded to immediately supply sufficient number of Antyodaya cards to different blocks, especially to Nayagram and Binpur-I so that we may start the writing of cards and take up their distribution quickly.

At 3.15 p.m. we reached Ambisole village — a collection of mostly mud houses topped with straw roofs. We made our way to the Lodha *para* where some houses built under the Indira Awaas Yojana (IAY) are located.[2] They were constructed about four years ago. I examined the house of one of the residents, Gopinath Digar, in detail. The IAY

Plate 5.1 A peep into emptiness

house has not been provided with any windows and doors; gaps in the walls proclaim this neglect. Walls are plastered on the inside but not from the outside. The roof is made of corrugated iron sheet. The single room tenement is about 8 ft wide and 18 ft long. Like in most adivasi houses, a string had been stretched across the room. On this slender line were slung the sum total of their belongings, i.e., all the clothes they had. In a corner lay a few utensils. Apart from a small plastic box for grain there is no storage space in the house. Perhaps the opportunity has not arisen.

Drinking water sources are mostly dug wells with blocks of laterite imperfectly lining the edges. These wells have been not constructed to protect against contamination. What is required here is a special programme to cement the openings and make a platform around the mouth of the wells.

Marko Digar is a leprosy patient in this village. He receives medicines from the health centre and takes them regularly; however, his left hand and arm were not improving. The nearest ration shop is at Sialia, 1 km away.

About 35 Lodha families live in this village with 22 Santal families. A Forest Protection Committee (FPC) consisting of 39 families is functioning here. Though the health sub-centre is located 3 km away at Nangiam, the immunisation of the infants has not been done on a regular basis, since most of them do not go to the sub-centre. The Pulse Polio programme, however, reaches them regularly.

Jiten Digar, a wispy-bearded 40-year-old, bought three goats last year for ₹2800 from Kalmapukuria in Malam Gram Panchayat; his herd has grown to six. Most of the families appear to be interested in rearing goats. A few such as Jiten Digar have profited from this. The mostly landless Lodhas' and other adivasis' preference for goat-keeping is their proximity to the forest: fodder is plentiful, free and, literally, within arms reach.

The people in Ambisole had deposited money for solar lights. However, according to the BDO, the subsidy amount was exhausted; therefore, they were not being able to distribute any further solar light units.

Two old women approached me for help. One was Panomoni Soren who is above 65 years of age. The BDO has been instructed to examine if the Annapurna card[3] may be issued to them immediately, and also to issue the Antyodaya card by next week to the 35 Lodha families living here. One SSK is running just outside the village. The SSK building, if it can be called a building, is a one-room structure about 16 ft long by 8 ft wide — smaller than an IAY house. Both the doors have been stolen. The people here want an additional classroom. This may be built with Sarva Shiksha Abhiyan (SSA) funds.[4]

We reached Poovan village at about 4.20 p.m. and first visited Mangali Pahari's IAY house. Unlike most such houses it is double-storeyed because the house owner has contributed labour and also some money. Mangali Pahari has also received two solar lamps, which are working well I checked the lights; they lit up the bare interior.

Next stop was Pathardoha village where we stopped at the Ashram Hostel for Scheduled Tribe boys. Out of the 20 students enrolled only 12 were present. Aged 10–14, apparently most of them were from this village itself — a consequence of either faulty selection or flawed intention. In one of the four rooms of the hostel, paddy belonging to the local Panchayat member had been spread out to dry. The boys had use of only five cots arranged against the walls in the main central room. A few other cots, in various stages of decreptitude, lay piled on top of each other on one side of the room, unused. If all the enrolled students are staying in the hostel as claimed, then undoubtedly many of them are sleeping on the floor; instead, some of the damaged cots could easily be repaired.

Tonight, in the hostel, there is only rice for dinner. The superintendent claims that he is providing them with four meals: *pantabhat* (rice left in water) in the morning, rice and *dal* at 10 a.m., *pantabhat* again at 4 p.m. and then rice, *dal* and vegetables at night. Not quite convinced, I separately asked some of the boys and found what I feared — they lived on two meals a day. And although there is a small sack of rice in the office, they are out of *dal*. A solitary pumpkin is the only vegetable in sight. Chittaranjan Patra, the supplier of food to the hostel, who walked in just then, appeared to be in control of the situation. When I asked about the used up stock of *dal*, the superintendent energetically assured me that he had been planning to buy some today.

At the root of the shortages faced by this and other Ashram Hostels for Scheduled Tribe and Scheduled Caste children is the inordinate delay in the release of maintenance grants by the BCW Department, and the further delay in transferring them downwards at the district level. Many hostels have not received grants for the last six months. Such a system leaves the poor tribal students in the hostel at the mercy of suppliers such as Chittaranjan Patra!

◎

Notes

1. A food security scheme was initiated by the Government of India in December 2000 for the poorest of the poor families subsisting Below Poverty Line (BPL). Antyodaya Anna Yojana (AAY) envisages identification of this lowest segment from among the BPL families in the states, issuing them an identity card — Antyodaya card — and providing food grains at a highly subsidised rate of ₹2 per kg for wheat and ₹3 per kg for rice. Each family thus identified is eligible to receive a total of 35 kg of grains in a month.

2. IAY is a scheme for provision of low-cost houses to some of the weakest sections of the population in rural areas. Launched in 1985, it aims to provide financial assistance to identified sections of the population to construct a *pacca* house, which is also to be equipped with a smokeless stove and a sanitary latrine. During the selection of beneficiaries, priority is given to sections such as the Scheduled Castes and Scheduled

Tribes, minorities, physically handicapped, and others existing BPL. The recipients are also expected to participate in the con-struction of their own house.

3. Initiated by the Ministry of Rural Development, Government of India, in 2000–2001, the aim of the Annapurna Scheme is to ensure food security for senior citizens living BPL. The scheme provides free grains at the rate of 10 kg per head every month to persons above the age of 65 years of age, who are eligible to receive pension under the National Old Age Pension Scheme but do not receive it. Each beneficiary is issued an identity card which is known as the Annapurna Card.

4. The 86th Amendment to the Constitution of India made education for children of 6–14 years of age free and compulsory, and also a Funda-mental Right. The SSA is the main programme of the Ministry of Human Resource Development, Government of India, being implemented in collaboration with State governments to implement the Universalising of Elementary Education. It aims to establish new schools in habitations without them and build additional classrooms and facilities in existing schools. It also seeks to provide teachers to understaffed schools and build teachers' capacity through training programmes.

6
Nuts and Bolts
◎

*In December 2000 the Prime Minister had announced the introduction
of two programmes to ensure a fundamental degree of food security to
the poorest: the Annapurna Anna Yojana and the AAY. The Annapurna
programme was aimed at the destitute over 65 years of age, not covered
by any Central or State pension scheme. Identified and selected by the
Gram Panchayats, they were given a green ration card that entitled
them to receive 10 kg of food grain per month for free. Antyodaya
was also aimed at the poorest of the poor in rural or urban areas.
The selected families were entitled to 35 kg of food grain against their
yellow card, at the rate of ₹2 per kg for rice or ₹3 per kg for wheat. Both
these programmes were administered through the PDS.*

*Unfortunately, after more than three years even the selection of
the individuals or families, respectively, for the two programmes was
incomplete.*

Driving through Jamboni block enroute to Belpahari it was evident that *aush* paddy had already been planted in a majority of the
plots, while transplantation of Aman paddy is underway. Perhaps
rainfall in this forested, undulating region has not been heavy, but
it appears to be sufficient. Along the road I noticed bare-bodied
men in fields engaged in the second plowing, while in other fields
women, with saris tucked above their knees and bent doubled over,
transplanting paddy.

As we moved towards the forested Belpahari it grew apparent
that most fields had been claimed from the forest; large tracts of
once forested land, denuded over the last 50–60 years, had been
converted into paddy fields and was now under the plough. Other
than paddy I found small patches of *til*, and also maize. The quality
of cattle in this area is poor. Short in stature, the cows yield little
milk. However, bullocks are being widely used for ploughing the

fields in this block. Indeed, I have yet to come across a single power tiller or tractor in this area. There are some water buffaloes — large, lugubrious creatures, also engaged for tilling the land. Almost 95 per cent of the houses in this area are made of mud. The older dwellings still have tan and brown straw roofs while newer ones are covered with GI sheets.

The distant gleam of GI sheets atop a few mud houses is characteristically the first sign of a little prosperity in rural parts — whether in North or South Bengal. If a farmer is able to save a little extra money in a given year he usually chooses to invest it to improve his dwelling. Again, whether in the north or the south, since the roof is the weakest part of the traditional hut, which makes its inhabitants most vulnerable to the vagaries of the elements, it claims attention first. After all, 'roof over the head' is not just a handy metaphor; it encapsulates the primordial human yearning for security. The winter harvest signals not only the coming of spring but also of a period of rejuvenation in human habitations. This is the time when new houses are built and old ones repaired, especially, the time to repair or replace roofs. In the hiatus between two sowing seasons, straw is abundantly available and so is labour.

At about 11.00 a.m. we reached the block office. The first task was to review the action taken on the decisions in the meeting conducted by the SDO, Jhargram, on 19 July 2004.

According to the BDO, Binpur-II, Kanko Gram Panchayat had already lifted their share of rice for the Midday Meal scheme from the distributor. Simulpal Gram Panchayat, however, had not done so. Since the schools are reopening on 13 August 2004, the Gram Panchayat officials should directly lift the rice from the distributor and place it with the schools by 12 July 2004. The Midday Meal Scheme has to be started in 30 additional schools in this block. According to the BDO the Pradhans had been asked to recommend the names of the SHGs who would be responsible for cooking the Midday Meal; the selection process was on. The purchase of utensils would also be taken up and should be completed by 4 August 2004. In one school, Palashboni Primary School, Bhelaria, provision of cooked meals started before the commencement of the monsoon vacation.

Several SGRY schemes had been selected in the Artho Sthayee Samiti[1] meeting yesterday, i.e., 28 July 2004, decided that rice will now be sub-allotted. According to the BDO rice provided under the SGRY-II had been sub-allotted already and would be lifted by 4 August 2004. Under SGRY-I 10 SSKs are to be constructed. The work order was issued on 19 July 2004. According to the BDO the layout of the building is being done. Although the work order for construction of 10 SSKs in 10 Gram Panchayats, one in each, has been issued — except for the formation of a committee at one village, Koriadanga — no work on the ground has been initiated yet. The pace of work is too slow and unless quickened the entire programme will be mired in problems related to delay, including cost escalation.

Although scheduled to be sent on 23 July 2004, proposals from the BCW Department, under the first provision of Article 275/1, were sent on 28 July 2004. I reviewed the manner of processing estimates and plans with the SAEs. The estimates prepared at the block are not according to a standardised format, despite a uniform design being used. This leads to re-writing and re-preparation of each estimate from the beginning leading to duplication of work and loss of precious time. I have instructed the SAEs to standardise the format and save it on their computers so that their work could be simplified; preparation of estimates should become limited to a matter of changing certain parameters only in deference to local variations. If the format is standardised the time taken in grounding and completing the scheme may be considerably reduced. Another matter that needs to be taken up is that new buildings, additional classrooms in high schools and other such buildings often have reinforced concrete roofs. This costs about 30–35 per cent extra and may well be avoided. A general instruction in this regard also needs to be issued. No details regarding the schedule of activity are included in the work order; this should also be standardised for different items of work in all blocks.

The layout of the 10 SSKs will be completed by Thursday next week, i.e., 5 August 2004. By the end of the week the work should also be started by the contractors.

The block *sansad* meeting was also scheduled to be held today from 12 p.m. onwards. I attended the meeting with the Pradhans, Upa-Pradhans and other Panchayat and Panchayat Samiti representatives. The meeting began on time, but I joined it at about 12.45 p.m. Immediately complaints and demands for various schemes were placed. The complaint about the faulty identification of the poor in the BPL list was repeatedly at the top of the list. The

Pradhans wanted funds for development work and for activities that would generate employment. The Zilla Parishad member from Binpur-II, Monilal Hembram, was also present and he spoke about the need for better coordination between the elected representatives and the officials in Binpur-II Panchayat Samiti. He also informed that every time he asked for more funds from the Zilla Parishad he was told that two crores of rupees are lying unused in Binpur-II Panchayat Samiti. He demanded that there should be a programme for taking up various activities quickly in the block.

Towards the end, I addressed the gathering. First I spoke about the food security programme and the schemes such as Annapurna, Antyodaya, and SGRY food for work programme. After updating the members present about the steps being taken regarding distribution of Annapurna and Antyodaya cards, I also requested the Panchayat Samiti and the Gram Panchayat members to monitor the off-take of food grains and its disbursement to the public in general, and the primitive tribal groups in particular. The variety of pensions available was also mentioned, along with the details regarding the criteria and mode of selection. Then I asked the Pradhans of various Gram Panchayats about the progress of the implementation of various schemes in their panchayat. I was very unhappy to learn that almost all Gram Panchayats were still holding on to the SGRY funds. Many of them had not disbursed the IAY funds to the beneficiaries either. I could not help pointing out the irony of the situation to them: on the one hand they were complaining about paucity of funds, and on the other they were unwilling to spend the funds received, when during this season — the lean months of the year — there was a crying need for creating employment. We decided it was necessary to hold a meeting not only with all Pradhans and Upa-Pradhans and Executive Assistants of Binpur-II Panchayat Samiti, but also of all other Panchayat Samitis of the district to discuss the different schemes being conducted by the panchayat bodies, their provisions, the responsibility of panchayat members, and the system of monitoring that needed to be put in place. I have also requested the Sabhapati and BDO to select various schemes from the list of schemes thrown up by the Baseline Survey, for both the SGRY and Rashtriya Sama Vikas Yojana (RSVY) programme.[2] We left Belpahari at about 4.30 p.m. for Jhargram.

◎

Notes

1. Standing Committee on Finance of the Panchayat Samiti Government of India.
2. Initiated in 2003, the RSVY was a backward area development scheme that in the first phase included 150 selected backward districts, including 50 districts affected by left wing extremism. The chief aims of the programme were to increase agricultural productivity, combat unemployment and develop physical and social infrastructure as per local needs to accelerate growth and improve the quality of life of the people in the target districts. It was fully funded by the Central Government.

7

Living with Diarrhoea

◎

At 10.00 a.m I left Midnapore for Lalgarh, about 45 km from the district headquarters, and reached there at about 11 a.m. There has been an outbreak of diarrhoea in some villages of this block, and the BDO was away with the medical team that had come to visit these villages from the district headquarters. The Joint BDO was present. I discussed the progress of the different development schemes with him. It appears that in three Gram Panchayats the IAY funds have not been received because the block had inadvertently supplied wrong account numbers. This seems to be a problem in other blocks too. All BDOs should be asked to report on action taken recently in this regard. The decision for the selection of schemes under SGRY has apparently been taken in the Artha Sthayee Samiti meeting. However, work does not seem to have begun yet. Member of Parliament Local Areas Development Scheme (MPLADS)[1] and Bidhyak Elaka Unnayan Prakalpa (BEUP)[2] schemes are also being 'processed'.

After discussing the schemes with the Joint BDO I left for Bamul *mouza* in Dharampur Gram Panchayat. On the way I met the BDO, and together we went to Bamul where the ACMOH and his team had already been treating the eight patients who had been reported ill. The source of the problem appeared to be, as usual, drinking water. Apparently the Public Health Engineering (PHE) pipeline that lay beneath the road had been damaged because when the road was built, under the Pradhan Mantri Grameen Sadak Yojana (PMGSY), the pipeline was not removed before the work began; and the road rollers had wreaked the damage.[3] The BDO proposed to set up two tube wells in the village. We next went to the Goaldanga where only two diarrhoea cases had been reported. We met the patients and found that they had returned from the PHC in Lalgarh after their treatment over the past 3–4 days. Although there are two tube wells here that supply drinking water, there is ample scope for contamination because the protective platforms around the base of the hand pumps are missing.

Sanitation work has also not taken off in this Gram Panchayat and I could see a number of concrete plates lying unused in courtyards. There is a crying need to take up a Total Sanitation Campaign (TSC) in this area on a priority basis.[4] The BDO acknowledged that this is a problem area in his block. Even the people who are reasonably well-off are not interested in constructing latrines. Another problem, leading to easy infection, is that women folk wash kitchen utensils in the nearest pond or canal. Life-giving monsoon also multiplies the sources of infection, especially due to widespread ignorance of basic hygiene.

The area is undulating and was probably under a thick forest earlier. To me it appears to be similar to what in Chotanagpur is known as *tand*, stretches of gently sloping ground succeeding slope after slope. Although rainfall had not been adequate, the pale green overspreading the paddy field told me that paddy transplantation had taken place in a majority of the area — chiefly because of the large number of shallow tube wells available here. This stretch of villages lies on the banks of, or not very far from, the River Kangsabati and, therefore, the level of ground water is quite high. However, I wonder if this area is really fit for bodo paddy cultivation. There are a number of canals that are supposed to be fed by the Kangsabati canal system. Yet irrigation water does not reach this area even when it is released. At this point of time these canals are serving as water storage facilities. In a number of places shallow pump-sets are being used to draw water from them.

A good proportion of inhabitants in these areas belong to the Schedule Castes and some to the Schedule Tribes as well, including the Lodha-Sabar, Santal and Kheria Sabar. Given the large number of goats that wandered across the roads, goat-keeping seems to be a popular occupation. The quality of cattle is not very good and this area is a fit case for artificial insemination. Houses here, built of mud, are of poor quality. GI sheets cover the roofs and there are a number of double-storey mud houses. There is normally a narrow ledge running along the fronts of the larger dwellings. The floors of these houses are made of beaten earth and there appears to be little that the people use by way of furniture. Most of their belongings lie about on the floor; as in most houses, clothes are flung across a string slung between the two furthest walls of the main room. The problem of hygiene in this area cannot be solved very easily as long as people insist on co-habiting with cattle, goats and poultry. There is no drainage anywhere and water and garbage accumulate within the dwellings during the rainy season.

The houses are grouped together and villages are marked with the presence of large trees. Bamboo is found all over.

The following action points need to be pursued:

(a) A general direction needs to be issued to all BDOs to take up the construction of platforms around wells, from the SGRY funds, especially in the Scheduled Caste and Scheduled Tribe *paras*, where the condition of the wells is worst and they are under the severest threat from the dirt around them.

(b) The use of galvanised iron tubes in hand pumps should be discouraged. Even the Department should be asked to revise their estimates and specifications because they use iron pipes even today.

(c) A system of receiving information about outbreaks of diarrhoea or other epidemics needs to be put in place. Such in-cidents are reported to the health authorities only after a large number of people are affected, when word reaches the block or even the district health officials. How can this be changed, and how can we get information of even the first case, are questions that need to be answered — quickly.

Driving back from Goaldanga, instead of going back to Lalgarh, I decided to go back via the alternate route driving south-west on the road near Dherua, where villages jostle up to the Kangsabati.

In Belpahari it is noticeable that minimum attention and effort is given to preparation of the fields for paddy cultivation, as opposed to the intensive labour invested in the task in the arable eastern and south-eastern parts of Paschim Medinipur and other paddy growing regions of West Bengal. Two reasons are conjointly offered for this: first, these lateritic areas fetch poorer returns to the adivasi cultivators who are not willing to spend or invest too much in preparing the fields for the meagre returns; and, second, the technology used by the adivasis, who have taken to agriculture over the past 100–150 years, for paddy cultivation in the tribal belts, is not as well developed as in the traditionally paddy growing areas of the state. One heartening feature of this area was the presence of a large number of water buffaloes being used extensively for purposes related to cultivation. However, as in Binpur-II block, I did not find much evidence of cattle dung being used as fuel. The availability of fire-wood from the nearby forests may be a deterrent in this regard. However, as time passes, I feel that this would be an area where some extension work will be necessary.

As we passed the Gurguripal High School, rain began lashing the earth. This did not seem to deter the workers in the field who continued with the transplantation of paddy. The amount of labour that goes into paddy transplantation and its cultivation is quite remarkable, and I am not sure that the returns are commensurate, especially in these semi-hilly areas.

◎

Notes

1. Launched on 23 December 1993 by the Ministry of Rural Development, MPLADS enables Members of Parliament (MPs) to suggest and implement development projects through the District Collector in their respective constituencies in response to locally felt needs. Elected members of the Rajya Sabha, the Upper House, may take up development projects from the sum allotted to them in any part of the state from which they have been returned, while nominated members of the Rajya Sabha may do so in any part of the country. Initially, a sum of ₹10 million per annum was allotted to each MP, with which they could allocate necessary sums for different projects to be implemented in their constituency by the District Collector of the area. In 1994 the Ministry of Statistics and Programme Implementation became the supervisory ministry for the scheme, while the allotted sum has been raised twice — to ₹20 million in 1998–1999 and ₹50 million in 2011.

2. BEUP is a counterpart of the MPLADs scheme in the state, and was initiated in West Bengal in 2000–2001. Starting with an allocation of ₹1.5 million per MLA each year, it enables each member to suggest and implement development schemes through the District Collector in his or her constituency. The allocation has since been raised to ₹5 million in 2008–2009.

3. Initiated by the Ministry of Rural Development, Government of India on 25 December 2000, the PMGSY aims to provide all weather road connectivity in rural areas. All habitations with a population of

500 persons and above in the plain areas and 250 persons and above in hill states, tribal populated regions and desert areas are sought to be connected by all weather roads. The scheme is fully funded by the Central Government.

4. Launched in 1999, the main objective of the TSC is to eliminate the practice of open defecation by the year 2017. It seeks to achieve this by generating demand in the rural areas through public awareness, hygiene education, creation of Rural Sanitation Marts for supply of toilet plates, and offering nominal subsidy to poor households. Panchayat Raj Insitutions, government agencies and NGOs are jointly engaged in this endeavour.

Supervision and Monitoring
◎

Those readers who have enjoyed perambulating through Philip Woodruff's delightful *The Men who Ruled India*, and have acquired from it sepia impressions about a Collector's life in the mofussil, are likely to be a trifle disappointed at the present state of affairs. Even today touring is prescribed as the primary means of monitoring and supervision in the field. Yet the District Officer of this age, along with other district and sub-district level functionaries, is severely constrained due to the explosion in the office work, on the one hand, and the sporadic creation along the years of a variety of statutory and administrative bodies for the supervision of the multiplying tasks in the field. For instance, the District Collector heads or is a member of approximately 120 committees in the district alone; additionally, there are other meetings to be attended at the divisional or the state level. The time devoured by meetings of these committees, if so allowed, is prodigious. Hence, when I joined my first charge as Collector in Cooch Behar, a firm believer in the merits of touring, I accepted meetings for most part as a necessary evil and determined to minimise them.

To do so I identified the meetings that I deemed essential for the working of the office of the District Officer and the discharge of his fundamental responsibilities. Even so I was merely able to bring the number down to about a dozen each month. To ensure that these meetings were not just talking shops but effective monitoring mechanisms, I studied the pattern of preparatory reporting and data collection. Thereafter, I scheduled one or more meetings on fixed dates of the month, so that the rest of the days could be more effectively utilised for field visits and tours — not just by me but also by sub-district level officials.

After joining Paschim Medinipur I discovered that the pattern of weekly meetings at the block, sub-division and district levels — a legacy of the Literacy & Immunization Campaign started in 1989 — was still in vogue.[1] This continued despite the fact that the Literacy programme had virtually ceased to be a 'campaign', which by definition is time-bound and temporary, and had been converted into a routinised programme. Old habits die hard, and old administrative practices die harder. Therefore, I had to spend some time and energy to convince the Zilla Parishad leadership that since the literacy 'campaign' had now become a routine programme, following the present system of meetings yielded little benefit and was a huge drain on resources — of manpower, travel expenses, stationery, and above all, time. Perhaps, my argument that the weekly meeting regime cost each nodal officer at the block, sub-divisional and district levels, and several others, at least eight working days every month was more convincing. Therefore, I put into place a revamped system of supervision and monitoring of development activities, from the block level upwards to the district level.

Here I must make a disclaimer: the system of monthly meetings that I proposed was not an innovation. It was accepted practice when I joined as an SDO of Contai fresh from the National Academy of Administration. It used to be an important monthly event and we had to be prepared to take all manner of uncomfortable questions about the different schemes under implementation. Usually, the DM would follow up the grilling in the meeting with personal inspection visits to the weakest blocks or work sites. Thus, it was an abandoned practice that I sought to re-establish.

In Paschim Medinipur, thus, a monthly monitoring meeting was scheduled to be held by the 3rd of every month at block level, to be attended by all Pradhans, Executive Assistants and Secretaries of Gram Panchayats. From the visits made by officers to different blocks, and from the monthly meetings at the district level, it was observed that the monthly meeting at the block level was not held with due seriousness. Through circulars and verbal directives, I emphasised that it was vital that in this meeting, the Executive Assistant/Secretary/Job Assistant of the Gram Panchayat submit the monthly progress made by the different Gram Panchayats to the Panchayat Samiti and the BDO in writing. A review of fund position of the Gram Panchayats was also to be made each month along with that of the Panchayat Samiti. I had noted gaps in communication on a number of subjects, especially those pertaining to implementation of different schemes. Therefore, the guidelines of various schemes were also to be discussed in this meeting, particularly for the benefit of those Gram Panchayats where a particular scheme was not doing well.

The reports received from Gram Panchayats and the performance of the Panchayat Samitis and blocks were then compiled and sent to the district headquarters by the 8th of each month. A district level review meeting was scheduled for the 15th of each month, or if that was a holiday, on the next working day. This review meeting, chaired by the Sabhadhipati and the Collector, was attended by all Sabhapatis and BDOs, district level officers of relevant departments/sections, and the Karmadhyakshyas of Zilla Parishad.[2] All the developmental programmes were reviewed through the worst case method on the basis of the compiled district report.

On the 7th of each month or on the next working day, I fixed two meetings: the revenue mobilisation meeting at 2.30 p.m., and the industry development meeting at 4.00 p.m. The former enabled me to take stock of the revenue collection activities in the district, while the latter was meant to serve as a forum for coordination, facilitation and problem solving. At 2.30 p.m., on the 25th of each month, I fixed the meeting of the Executive Committee of the District Health and Family Welfare Society. The date for this meeting was fixed late in the month because after tracing the collection, compilation and transmission of health-related data, I found that the Health Management Information System (HMIS) report from the subsidiary health centre upwards does not reach the district headquarters until the 20th of the month. And without the data from the field, a review would be meaningless![3]

Nevertheless, I was not content to introduce a more streamlined schedule of monitoring meetings. I knew that over the years, as the number of development programmes implemented in the districts swelled, a tendency had developed at the block and the sub-divisional levels to supervise the implementation of these programmes from the office chair. This tendency had been shored up by the increase in the number of meetings of numerous committees, particularly at the block level. However, effective supervision and monitoring cannot be a sedentary exercise. Therefore, I found it necessary to encourage SDOs and BDOs to visit various work sites, such as health centres, primary schools and AWCs, so that they may not only supervise and monitor implementation of development programmes in the field but also take corrective measures with alacrity.

One of the chief difficulties in monitoring the execution of the range of development programmes and other activities was the absence of a pro-forma-based monthly reporting system that reflects the performance of key officials such as SDOs and BDOs. To meet this requirement, and to make BDOs and SDOs more field-oriented, with the help of my colleagues I developed two formats for monthly performance reports — one for SDOs and another for BDOs; the pro-forma for BDOs was first introduced in Cooch Behar district in 2002. The BDOs were asked to submit their monthly report in the pro-forma to the SDOs by the first day of each month, and the SDOs were to forward them to me on the following day. The SDOs and BDOs were instructed to immediately act on any problem that they encountered in their visits, and to draw the attention of the concerned block or sub-division level officers with intimation to me.

This pro-forma-based monthly performance reporting system was introduced in Paschim Medinipur from the month of July, 2004, and it was made clear to the officers that these monthly reports would form an important basis for their annual assessment. Although, to begin with, I was personally monitoring these reports, I also asked the enthusiastic district informatics officer to develop a computer programme to compile the inputs provided by the officers, to facilitate sustained scrutiny and assessment of the problems thrown up by the officers and of their performance.

I must add that from the very beginning of my tenure in Paschim Medinipur, the Chief Secretary on a regular basis monitored the progress of developmental activities that he had briefed me about on 5 March 2004 on. Paschim Medinipur was clearly in his sights. In the first couple of months I would receive a phone call from him on a weekly basis; soon this came to be a fortnightly event. I was also expected to send a report every 15 days to the government. This was apart from the video conferences of all DMs that were held by the Chief Secretary on a monthly basis, and which were presided over by the Chief Minister at least once every three months. Especially, once the government had identified the 4612 poor villages in the state, both the Chief Minister and the Chief Secretary personally monitored the visits by DOs to the villages and the implementation of poverty eradication schemes and improvement of public service facilities on the ground.

◎

Notes

1. In 1988, in the then Midnapore district, the authorities decided to include an awareness campaign for expansion of immunization for infants and pregnant mothers, and the Total Literacy Campaign was launched. Although the thrust was upon literacy, the campaign was called the Literacy & Immunization Campaign.
2. Karmadhyaksha is the Chairperson of one of the several Standing Committees of a Zilla Parishad constituted for implementing development programmmes under different subjects, such as public works, forestry, women and child development.
3. HMIS entails the monthly collection of data at the district and sub-district level of the health facilities and primary healthcare, such as infant and maternal immunization, incidence of diseases, and the responses of the health department. The data is analysed at the district and state levels for corrective action and intervention.

8

Pension for the 'Queen of Roses'!

◎

Several social security schemes have long been in place to provide relief
— albeit in small measures — to the poorest in our society. These include
regular pension schemes for the old, widows and the differently-abled,
and also scholarship and maintenance schemes for poor Scheduled Caste
and Scheduled Tribe students. Although the amount disbursed may be
small, it makes a difference to individuals who receive them. Therefore,
the emphasis in these schemes must be on regular, timely disbursement.
An examination of the cash analysis of blocks and checks during my
visits revealed that there was an unnecessary and painful delay in the
distribution of these funds. The vacancies, created by deaths of erstwhile
beneficiaries, and filled by those waiting in the queue, also needs to be
monitored, at least, on a monthly basis. Another set of social security
schemes for BPL families comprise National Maternity Benefit Scheme
and National Family Benefit Scheme, for pregnant women and wid-
ows. Here the delay is mainly in the processing of cases — which often
defeats the very objective of these schemes, that is, to provide one-time
timely relief!

Upon checking the attendance register of the block office I found
that even at 11.25 a.m. nine employees were absent. The BDO was
away to his former block in Purulia district in connection with a
court case. The Joint BDO was present but the attendance register
was not checked by him either at 10.15 a.m. or at 10.45 a.m., as
per rules.

After the attendance register I turned my attention towards the
cashbook. This is a register that speaks volumes about, among

other things, the amount of work done in the block, in financial terms, and the time taken to complete each item of work. In this respect it mirrors the level of efficiency of the block administrative machinery. My main interest at present was the status of social security and welfare schemes, since in this regard I had received complaints against the block office. An examination of the block cash analysis showed that over ₹500,000 received by the block for several social welfare schemes was lying un-disbursed. The break up of the amount stood as: ₹30,275 for Disability Pension; ₹1,169 for Widow Pension; financial assistance to destitute children to the tune of ₹26,694; ₹111,649 for National Old Age Pension Scheme (NOAPS); ₹25,000 for National Family Benefit Scheme (NFBS); and, maintenance charge to Scheduled Caste/Scheduled Tribe students, ₹57,120, was received on 3 March 2004 and ₹3,44,000 on 1 June 2004. It is a mystery to me as to why these have not been disbursed; apparently, it is a mystery to the block officials also!

The Block Welfare Officers (BWO) showed me the Widow Pension disbursement register. The number of pages contained in the register had not been certified as per rules on the first page and the pages were also not numbered. Widow pension from April–July 2004 had been passed for payment on 23 July 2004 and apparently the money orders had also been sent. There are a total of 15 slots for widow pension in this block (total population: 131,983; female population: 64,685) of which 14 were filled up. One case had been sent for finalisation at the district level. There are nine recipients of Disability Pension. It appeared that some of them had not received it since August and December 2003. Old Age Pension cases had been processed by the BWO and put up on 23 July 2004, and they had been signed by the Executive Officer on 2 August 2004; money orders were yet to be dispatched. Considering that money had been lying with the block for a very long time, this delay was unnecessary. In this block there are 46 recipients for Old Age Pension issued by the Social Welfare Department. The actual quota is 45, however, there has been a mistake at the district level in the apportionment of quota. This needs to be corrected and may be done expeditiously since one of the recipients is no longer in a position to receive the pension. He is dead.

I wanted to make a spot verification of performance pertaining to disbursement of pensions. Hence, I picked out three names in a single village. Then, accompanied by the Joint BDO and the BWO, proceeded towards Kumarhati village to check the position regarding the recipients of three widow pensions.

While I had been mulling over the registers in the block office it had been raining heavily. As we drove into Kumarhati the downpour had slowed to a playful drizzle. The burst of post-monsoon foliage along the way, the trees and bushes, all wore a freshly washed green. Water had collected in the ditches on the roadside and runnels sped along the pathways etched out by passing feet across playing fields. After parking the vehicle as we walked through the water-logged lane I was met by a sight replete with irony. On the edge of the road stood a line of water vessels—steel pails, plastic buckets, aluminium *gharas* with elongated necks, and large plastic containers that once held vegetable oil, all queued up to a short unobliging PHE water spout. Potable water is supplied at specified periods through the PHE water supply system, and local residents had staked their claim in anticipation. Meanwhile precious rainwater flowed nonchalantly away into the ditches. A line from *The Rime of the Ancient Mariner* came floating in my head.

On the way to meet the pensioners we came across Kokila Sheet and Subhasi Das, two members of an SHG. I requested them to tell me how their group was working and what they were doing. They told me that initially they had taken a loan to buy some ducks. However, the birds they had obtained soon died due to an infection. My query about vaccination was replied with the expected shaking of head. If only they had inoculated the ducks soon after procuring them, the hardy creatures would have been laying eggs by now. Yet, along with the ill-fated ducks they had also bought goats, which were doing fine.

We reached our first address where I met Tanushree Bannerjee, a widow pensioner about 35 years of age. She lives with her brother and mother. She has two children, a son and a daughter, who attend the local school. They live in a small section of an ill-maintained, double–storied house that belongs to Bannerjee's brother. Through the low doorway, protected by a none-too-clean rag of a curtain I peered into the dark recesses of the poorly appointed room. An unmade bed, a stool and a bicycle along one wall were the only fixtures. Bannerjee was grateful for the pension but, although unwilling to complain about the officials, she admitted that her pension often came very late. Her brother was more vocal.

Plate 8.1 Golaprani Das

Golaprani Das and Santirani Som, two other widow pensioners, live in a house with thick mud-packed walls and a straw roof, a little away from where Tanushree Bannerjee lives. As we walked towards the house, on one side of its forecourt I saw an old woman bathing near an unprotected ring well. Convinced that this must be one of the two pensioners, I watched as she slowly drew out water in a small pail from the well and poured it haltingly upon herself. This was Golaprani Das. Santirani Som was sitting on a *khat* in the wide mud-plastered verandah of the house. Both women were of advanced age, probably above 70 years. Silver hair framing their face, concurrent strings of wrinkles highlighting the weariness of their pale eyes, and wrapped only in white sarees with meagre black borders, the two old ladies were a picture of indigent Indian widowhood. I could not help thinking that both of them must have been attractive young women once. Indeed, fair Golaprani Das with her chiseled features must have been beautiful; hence, I conjectured, her parents named her Golaprani — 'Queen of Roses'. Santirani Som is largely immobile. She spends most of her time sitting or reclining on the cot in the verandah. The two ladies live in this house with relatives who take care of their basic needs, but who do not care enough to draw water from the well for them! Both obviously need the widow pension. And both state that they do not receive the money orders on a monthly basis! They last received a sum of ₹2000 about 45 days ago. In front of them I tried to make it clear to the Joint BDO and the BWO that disbursement of the due amount to widow pensioners, disability pensioners and old age pensioners, issued on a monthly basis and on time, is absolutely vital. As I was about to leave, I noticed that at the end of Santirani Som's saree's *pallu*, that curled around her neck, were tied two keys — they did not signify wealth, but self-respect and determination.

There was hope.

◎

9

Three Faces of Development

◎

A workshop on public health, nutrition and livelihood, organised by State Institute of Panchayat and Rural Development (SIPRD) and the district administration, began in the Dharampur Gram Panchayat office shortly after I arrived. The objective of the workshop was to exchange views with opinion leaders and people at the grassroots/target population about various aspects of, and the inter-relationship among, public health, nutrition and livelihoods. About 100 persons were present. Assembled under a bellicose orange and green tarpaulin with a purple fringe, the gathering included panchayat representatives, health workers, Anganwadi workers, teachers, and some local people.

Strangely, the main target group, that is people from truly tribal villages, was not present in large numbers. When I raised this concern with the Sabhapati and the BDO, a group of ladies from a tribal village was soon brought over. After the initial speeches and remarks that outlined the purpose of the workshop, elaborated upon by successive speakers, the group was divided into three sub-groups. Each sub-group dwelt upon a particular topic: availability and accessibility of public health and suggestions for its improvement; the nutritional cycle in the area and the gaps within it, as identified by the sub-group members; and finally, the existing sources of livelihood and what additional avenues of livelihood could be taken up. I divided my time with three sub-groups.

Although discussions on some of the issues, especially availability of medical facilities, were intense, I felt that a more thorough preparation would have helped us all. For this kind of exercise to be truly productive, it is essential to prepare a little in advance. For instance, it would have been particularly useful if three trained moderators had been prepared locally or had even been brought

Plate 9.1 Villagers participating in a workshop
on Public Health, Nutrition and Livelihood

from SIPRD. As it was, local officers had been deputed for this job
after just a quick briefing. This was not sufficient because at times
the discussion in different groups would either get much too abstract
or would run off in various directions. Overall, to me the result of
the discussion was not unsatisfactory.

Since I wanted to pay a visit to the PHC nearby, I left the workshop
mid-way. I reached the collection of single storey buildings to find
that the PHC had closed down for the day. I wandered around the
premises and took in a couple of cows pulling at tufts of grass in the
campus, while bolder Bengal Black goats loitered on the verandah
of the Out Patients Department. The PHC wears an abandoned
look; the regulation Public Works Departments (PWD) yellow (the
sickly shade of whitewash used by the Department on government
buildings almost all across India) has turned ashen on the cracked
walls, paint peels off the locked doors, and the missing top two
glass panes on many of the shut windows impart an expression of
hapless blindness. As a group of local residents collected I began
talking to them.

No government doctor has been posted here in the last few years,
they tell me. A doctor on contract attends patients at the PHC off
and on, but even he had left for the day. There is also a sub-centre

here, which too functions in fits and starts. No other staff member lives here; the residential quarters are also in a very bad shape. This area, which has a large adivasi population, sorely requires the services of a doctor who can serve the population in this and the neighbouring Gram Panchayats. After all it is meant to serve the suffrage of the Gram Panchayats of Dharampur, Baita, part of Lalgarh and of Dherua Gram Panchayat in the Sadar block. Apparently, neither doctors nor nursing staff are willing to be posted, let alone stay, at the Dharampur PHC, which is not more than about 30 km from the district headquarters. This is a story I have been told and retold by residents of many remote and not so remote Gram Panchayats of the district. We need to discuss and try to resolve this issue in the next District Health and Family Welfare Samiti meeting. Apparently, there is also a shortage of anti-venom serum and other medicines in this PHC as well as in the SHC. These deficiencies need to be taken up with the CMOH on an urgent basis.

In most parts of Dharampur, and its neighbouring Gram Panchayats, paddy transplantation is almost complete. The land is, again, undulating and the roads are made of compressed *kachha morrum*. The familiar houses are constructed of mud and straw. Some tiled roofs are also visible. However, both straw and baked tiles are being fast replaced by GI sheets. It is common for households in this area to keep poultry birds and goats. Even some diminutive herds of scruffy sheep may be seen from time to time on the scrub between paddy and forest, and ducks wherever they find water. Lumbering, black water buffaloes also dot the landscape.

Late in the afternoon, most workers in the field have called it a day after transplanting paddy all morning. Children are returning home from school on bicycles or on foot. One of the few bright spots that afternoon was the sight of a group of young school girls in red and white tunics, with rucksacks slumped on their backs, cycling back from school — a reassuring, but rare picture in these parts. In the village forecourts old and young men are sitting on grass mats playing cards. While some youngsters are either going to or returning from the village pond with a *gamcha*, a small bottle of mustard oil and a soap case — the daily bath. Through doorways I can see people sitting down for lunch on the hard mud floors, white rice glistening in the dark within. Otherwise, streets are deserted. After feeding their families and then having finished their own meal women sit in groups of two or three, combing and plaiting each others' long, well-oiled hair, or taking a brief siesta on *charpoys* in the mud-packed verandahs.

However, not everyone is taking rest. Fields that are yet to be sown are rectangles of activities. In uneven rows, wrapped in *saris* bright against the wet brown of the watered fields, women are bent over double, transplanting paddy. In some fields only two or three are at work.

I met Swapan Mahar of Shakhakoila village, Gram Panchayat No. 6 of Binpur-I Panchayat Samiti, on the banks of the Kangsabati, where it comes threateningly close to the PMGSY road under construction opposite his village. I had stopped on the broken but steep verge to examine the work being done on the road, and then stood gazing at the river. The ample Kangsabati, partially sated by the latest rains but ready for more, stretched in a generous curve between the grassy ridge on this side and the forest on the other. Masses of grey-black cumulonimbus sailed overhead, their reflection following them to the river banks. I *had* to stop and savour the scene for a few moments. As I stood taking in the scenery I noticed a middle-aged man, with but a *gamcha* wrapped around his middle, stop and get off his bicycle for a brief respite. I walked up to him.

His bare body glistening with sweat, Swapan Mahar was on his way back from the jungle after collecting a large load of dead palm leaves, which were tucked across the rear carrier of his bicycle. He told me that he would make these into brooms and sell in the nearby *haat* at about ₹2–2.50 per piece. Every week he made about 100–150 of these brooms. Swapan Mahar is a landless labourer who lives by the sweat of his brow, which he spills in the forest, fields in and around his village or, in the *boro* season, as far away as Keshpur and Narajole.

In the late Baisakh the wealthy farmers from Narajole, Keshpur block and other areas of the district come over to these parts in search of labour. They hire Swapan and his friends and pay their bus fare to Narajole. They work there for 10–12 days harvesting the fields; during this period they get ₹40 per day, and food. For sustenance they get a bit of *muri* in the morning before going to work. At about 11 a.m. they break for the first cooked meal of the day — mostly rice, some *dal* and whatever vegetables are available. In the evening they again get rice and anything else to go with it. However, the hirers of their labour do not pay for their ticket back;

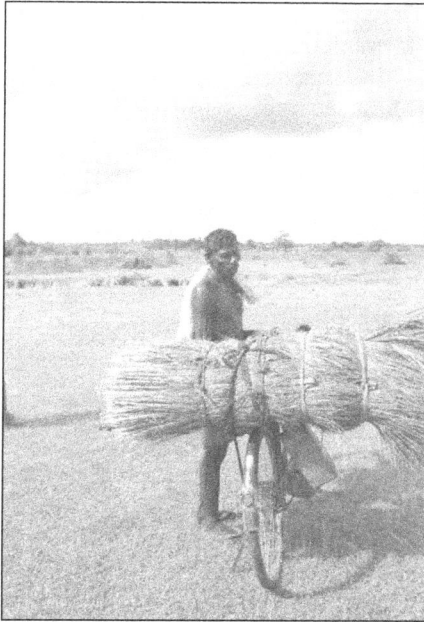

Plate 9.2 Swapan Mahar takes a breather

they have to pay this out of their wages. The last two years have been quite bad and virtually no paddy had been planted in Swapan Mahar's village. This year there has been enough rain for plantation to take place.

Swapan Mahar belongs to the Dom caste. At present his family consists of his wife, one daughter and a son.Swapan married his eldest daughter to a fish-seller two years ago. His daughter has been blessed with a son and is about to have a second child. The wedding came as a kick in the teeth for his son. The son who had completed his *madhyamik* did not want to stop studying. Among other things, Swapan gave utensils and ₹5000 in cash to his daughter's in-laws in dowry. He also gave his son-in-law a watch as a*shirwadi*. Soon after the wedding Swapan's son warned his father that if he wanted him to continue his studies then he would have to take private tuition. Swapan could not afford a tutor for his son, and, therefore, that was the end of it. His son, however, decided to drive a tractor, a mini-tractor common in these parts. Yet it has not assured him regular employment because several farmers own mini-tractors and are used to operating it themselves. The second daughter, the youngest, still goes to school. Swapan Mahar is now saving for her wedding.

◎

10

The Waterlogged Rice-bowl

◎

Shortly after daybreak when I left Midnapore, masses of grey-black clouds swept across the sky playing hide and seek with the sun, reminding us of the imminence of rain. By the time I reached the SDO's office, at about 8.15 a.m., the town was slowly waking up to its daily routine and the market was buzzing with morning *bazaar* shoppers.

I reviewed the flood situation and the relief effort with the SDO, the second officer, the Sub-divisional Relief Officer (SDRO) and the BDO, Ghatal. Evidently the flood waters had receded considerably in most parts of the inundated areas. However, parts of Ghatal Municipality and also of Ghatal block, especially the south-western areas, were still flooded. The main source of flooding water is the Ghetia Khal, which enters the Shilabati river at Rajagram near the Ghatal Municipality. The rainfall in the upper catchment of Shilabati also increases the water levels in the Shilabati river and, therefore, causes the inundation in the low-lying parts of this sub-division, which is a depression, shaped like a bowl. According to information received at the SDO's Control Room the release of water from the Cossye (another name for Kangsabati in its upper reaches) was stopped at 9 a.m. yesterday. Therefore, most checkpoints showed that water was flowing below the danger level except at Kalmijore where it was 4 cm above the danger level. At all other six monitoring points at Banka, Godighat, Bandar, Ranichak, and Gopiganj the water was flowing below the danger levels.

The SDO informed me that special medical teams had been visiting the four flood-affected areas, three blocks and one municipality — Chandrakona-I, Ghatal, Daspur-I, and also the Ghatal Municipality. Yesterday in Kharar *mouza*, Ramjibanpur Gram Panchayat of Chandrakona-I Block, 73 people were treated for diarrhoea. Yet this is not an area affected by inundation; people here use pond water for drinking as well as for other purposes — the main cause of the outbreak. Thirty ponds were disinfected yesterday and a medical team from Ghatal attended to the patients.

Upon enquiring about our state of mobility, I learnt that four speedboats had been stationed in Ghatal, which had been checked 20 day's back by a team of experts from the Civil Defence Department in Kolkata. Since the motors were not in working order, the head of the team had undertaken to arrange for repairs. Yet, till date none of the motors had been repaired. The Civil Defence Volunteers were manning the boats, but for all practical purposes the boats were useless because the motors were unreliable and the Civil Defence personnel did not wish to take any chances. Reportedly, the five boats, one large boat and four smaller speedboats, were also unstable. Thus, in the hour of crisis it was 'discovered' that none of the boats were in working order! This is symptomatic of administrative *dhappabaji*. What can be the objective of deploying unusable boats, except to go through the motions to deflect criticism for inaction before the floods, and to offer lack of repairs as excuse for inactivity after the deluge?

At this point I thought we should go see some of the affected areas.

Causeway no. 2, at the northern edge of the Ghatal Municipality, was still under 2 to 3 ft of water. Rows of trucks helplessly lined the road on either side of the causeway. From time to time buses full of people and goods stopped and disgorged passengers and their possessions on both sides. The passengers then climbed onto country boats that had sprung into service, to be ferried less than 50 m across to the other side to the empty buses waiting for their return journey. Primed by experience, local enterprise had been ready to plug the gap in an essential service so that life may go on.

At the causeway we boarded a country boat with an out-board motor and went across the inundated area towards Ajaynagar *mouza*. From the chug-chugging boat the entire area under a grey and silver strewn sky was a muddy sea dotted with green islands. Since the central portion of Ghatal sub-division is a basin through which the Silabati, and its numerous tributeries flow eastwards to meet the Rupnarayan, the *mouzas* — made up of several hamlets, are located on embankments that rise above the surrounding fields; ridges large and small planted with trees are built up with the houses. Elevating the homestead land has been the strategy of people who chose to settle in this rich bowl of fertile land that every monsoon inevitably floods, a stratagem that succeds in letting them live through the annual deluge and thrive by it. Hence, every monsoon turns the thickly populated ridges into islands, but after a few days or weeks the flood waters recede, leaving behind the rich silt that makes the sub-division one of the most prosperous areas in the state in terms of agricultural productivity.

As we made our way towards Ajaynagar, we saw country boats fitted with out-board motors ferrying passengers between the 'island' villages and Ghatal town. Among the commuters were several children carrying satchels of books on their way to school — life went on. We passed two boats rowed by two men each, one of them had two others squatting on the cargo. The BDO informed me that the rural road network in the area was poor and, due to the intensive cultivation of land, excruciatingly tortuous. Hence, people often waited to take advantage of the annual flood waters to transport building materials by boat, which could carry the supplies directly and quickly across the waters; it also works out to be significantly cheaper. Once the waters subsided construction work could be undertaken. I marveled not merely at the people's ability to adapt to the adverse circumstances but also at their talent for making the most of adversity.

As we approached the first 'island', through the branches of tall, green, spreading mango and peepal trees, we could see the yellow glimmer of straw or the occasional flashes of roofs built of GI sheets. Some cattle stood patiently chewing their cud under the trees, while half naked children watched us with interest from the top of rudely paved steps leading up the ridge. We climbed off the boat and went into the cluster of houses. Most people went about their daily chores unperturbed by the waters below their house. I found it remarkable that hardly anyone complained or demanded anything from the administration except for the occasional tarpaulin, as in the case of Kalipada Paria's damaged house in Pariapara.

It is evident that the people here are prepared for the floods, even for drinking water, which becomes one of the foremost needs at such times. In anticipation, in Ghatal, hand pumps are often located on the ridges; the few in the fields stand one legged but tall, on exposed metal tubes, prepared for the contingency of an inundation. Although I was not able to ascertain the exact number

Plate 10.1 Where roads do not reach, a boat carries building materials

of hand pumps in Ajaynagar, I saw four or five located in different parts of the village upon which over 3000 people depended for their potable water. No major incidence of diarrhoea has been reported, but the dangers of poor sanitation lurk around the corner — most houses have no latrines. Under the total sanitation campaign, people expect the government to give funds for the latrines. Those who fall in the BPL category have been provided latrines, but the others also expect to receive funds for setting up the same. This is yet another instance of the people's inexplicable dependence on government for things that directly affect their own well-being.

On a ridge in Ajaynagar two bare-bodied men were working to finish a wooden boat. Constructed of sal wood, it will finally cost about ₹8000. Although too late to help face the onslaught of this monsoon, it will come in useful in the years to come and not only during floods. During the winter and summer months it may be used as a fishing boat or as a mobile irrigation pumping station on one of the canals or rivers.

Our boat returned to cross the road and the inundated causeway to take us to the peripheral areas of the Ghatal Municipality, which were also flooded.

On this leg of the tour our first stop was Raghunathcharak, which falls in ward no.1 of the municipality. As in the case of the villages we visited, the houses in the municipality are also built on raised embankments. In Raghunathcharak, 10 hand pumps supply water for drinking and cooking purposes to the people in the neighbourhood. With some dismay, however, I noticed that the stagnant flood water was being used for washing clothes and even utensils. Thankfully, no case of diarrhoea, the principal worry in flooded areas, had been reported in this village either. While in Raghunathcharak, we visited a primary school where, although it was only 9.35 a.m., eight or nine children were present; one among them, a girl, was cleaning the two-roomed building. As it turned out, these children had been sent to school early by their parents who left home to earn their daily wage; school also doubles as a crèche.

Located close to the primary school is AWC no. 162, a flimsy structure made of bamboo covered with tin sheets; the walls are barely walls because they consist of series of bamboos stuck in the ground. The Anganwadi worker and helper are from nearby wards. There are three teachers in the primary school. One of them stays nearby and two of them come from far off villages. None of the areas, in this ward no.1 or in ward no. 2 that we visited next, have any latrines. Normally, defecation is out in the open fields, and during the floods in the water.

Ward no. 2, Kora, is also thickly populated. Although built on an embankment, some of the houses here are *pacca* constructions several storeys tall. Right now, people travel between wards in black canoes, dug-outs of palm tree trunks, which are broad at the base end and narrow at the other. A few small boats are used as well. Women and children also use these same means of transport to various places. As we approached the raised ward, I saw a bare-bodied father setting off to punt his 10-year-old to school in a dug-out; near the waters edge about a dozen of these canoes lay 'parked' under the overhanging branches of trees leaning over the waters. We disembarked near the 'parking lot' to have a closer look at the ward.

A line for cable television is running right along the embankments in this ward where hand pumps are still the only source of water! In a number of places relief tarpaulins were being used for drying and packing paddy. Apparently, making of joss sticks is a cottage industry in this area. Women sit in the small front yards of their homes covering thin bamboo spines with a dark adhesive mixture. I picked up a few fresh joss sticks laid out to dry in the sun and sniffed

Plate 10.2 Parked canoes and a boat

at them expecting the usually cloying aroma. Unable to smell any perfume as I wrinkled my nose, one of the residents explained that the fragrance was added once the joss sticks were dry. The women's task is limited to coating the joss sticks with the material provided by middlemen. They receive between 5 to 6 rupees per thousand of prepared joss sticks, which are then supplied by the middlemen to traders. At this stage the scent is applied to the joss sticks and then they are marketed. This business chain provides a small income to these families in rural Ghatal. However, not too many SHGs in this area appear to be engaged in this activity.

From the inundated wards we again headed for a few villages in Ajaynagar-II Gram Panchayat. Swarupnagar and Hatipara presented a picture similar to the one we had seen earlier in Ajaynagar. Few houses, very few indeed, have latrines. Again, people are waiting for the government to provide them subsidy for sanitation. Drinking water though was not a problem because there are a number of hand pumps, and they are functioning well. In Swarupnagar there is one habitation know as Silapukur that has no hand pump. Potable water, therefore hand pumps, is a primary requirement in this area. Disinfection of the existing hand pumps should be taken up immediately. Every ridge that houses a habitation should have at least one hand pump.

As our boat turned back, I wondered what could be done to improve the sanitation in these villages. The annual excess of water, and the havoc wreaked by it on potable water sources, posed a danger to health. But a more constant threat was lack of proper sanitation and open-air defecation. Ishwarchandra Vidyasagar, a scholar and social reformer and one of the greatest sons of Bengal, was born not many kilometres from Ghatal town. The people of the sub-division take great pride in owning Vidyasagar and in the traditions of education that have made Ghatal one of the most literate areas of rural Bengal. Yet when will the people recognise the need for sanitary latrines? When would they stop waiting for the government to grant a few hundred rupees to construct one?

◎

Food Entitlement:
An Awareness Campaign
◎

If Amlasole achieved one thing it was to turn the full glare of public scrutiny on people's entitlements to food under the PDS in the state. Apart from the Annapurna and Antyodaya schemes described earlier for ensuring food security of the poorest of the poor, the regular rationing system and other food linked schemes, such as the Midday Meal Scheme for primary school children, the Sampoorna Grameen Rojgar Yojana, where payment for work done was to be made partially in grain, the ICDS, and others also came under the scanner. The Supreme Court had, by its orders dated 28 November 2001 and 5 May 2002, made it incumbent upon the state to ensure food security through the wide variety of schemes that were under implementation but whose benefits seemed to evade those most in need.

In the middle of 2004, upon taking stock of the condition of the PDS in the district, I was shaken by the situation. In most Gram Panchayats of Paschim Medinipur the distinctive cards for Annapurna and Antyodaya had not been distributed. Many of the AWCs in remote parts suffered from shortage of stocks and erratic supply. Midday Meal was also yet to be introduced in a large number of schools, especially in the Junglemahals. And there was a perennial shortfall in supply of food grains by the Food Corporation of India (FCI). To make matters worse, the Food and Supplies offices in the district were inadequately staffed, and records and registers were in a conveniently terrible shape. Not surprisingly, ration shops were making the most of the situation. The shops would open only on one or two days a week, full quota of rations was seldom received by the poor in the distant areas, and in many places even the ration cards of the villagers were kept in the dealers' 'safe custody!'

I started by trying to strengthen the regulatory system in place. The DCF&S was instructed to draw up a schedule of inspection of the ration shops and to submit a monthly report regarding the number of shops inspected, the off-take from the shops, and regularity of their functioning. He was also to ensure that the ration shops functioned properly and were open for five and a half days as they were meant to. The ration dealers were warned against retaining ration cards and asked to issue the correct amount of rice or wheat to all ration card holders, especially the Annapurna and Antyodaya card holders. All ration dealers were also instructed to issue cash memos. Copies of orders passed by the Supreme Court in the Writ Petition No. 196/2001 were to be prominently displayed in all ration shops, if not done so already.

Deadlines for distribution of Annapurna and Antodaya cards were set, extended, and further extended to 15 August 2004 onwards. The DCF&S and all SDOs and BDOs were directed to take up this task on a priority basis. With the assistance of panchayat bodies, a drive was also undertaken to see that the Mid day Meal Scheme began in all the primary schools. I started calling the FCI on a regular basis while, with the help of the panchayats, arranging for the movement of food grain stocks to the Gram Panchayats, where SGRY was being implemented.

Yet a feeling grew that perhaps this was not enough. There were three reasons for this. First, more often than not, the target population did not know what benefit they could get and from where. Second, members of panchayats and lower levels of administration had no clear idea about the directives/guidelines of the schemes. And third, the effects of orders issued from the state and district administration from time to time in the last few years were not visible in most cases; even the directives of the Supreme Court had not filtered down. People were not acquainted with the schemes and, hence, could not receive what they were entitled to, let alone demand them. I felt that this was a gap that cried out to be bridged.

The poor are oftentimes voiceless because they are unaware. The plethora of government programmes for the poor often do not reach the intended beneficiaries because information about these is not accessible to them. The lettered, the 'educated', and, therefore, the empowered, wolf down the cherry, the icing *and* a large portion of the cake, leaving behind merely crumbs for the unaware. Since government creates schemes to benefit the vulnerable, it is also its responsibility to inform them of their entitlements. This is the unrecognised side of the right to information. With this conviction I decided that people should be made aware of their entitlements through a publicity campaign.

Again, initially, my proposal met with barely suppressed smiles of incredulity; perhaps it is true that fools rush in where angels fear to tread. Used to such dismissal, I sat down and chalked out the project. We then developed posters, handbills, and audio cassettes that spoke of the entitlements in different schemes — in Bengali and Alchiki (the script of the Santhali language). As was done for the election campaign, the posters and handbills were distributed and put up in public places in all the Gram Panchayats and municipalities, including ration shops. The audio cassette was also broadcast by van-rickshaw across the district. Finally, I also published a booklet in Bengali that gave details of the various schemes, informed of the timings of the ration shops, and included the orders of the Supreme Court and the complete list of all ration shops in the district by Gram Panchayat, and their location. I circulated this among all the offices, especially of the panchayat bodies and other public representatives. The posters and handbills may have played a role, but the van-rickshaw mounted, microphone aided publicising of the details of food related entitlements certainly had some effect. Reports began reaching Midnapore of altercations between ration dealers and local people who were insisting that they be given their full quota of ration, the shop be kept open on five and a half days as per rule, and so on. Several instances of villagers *gherao*-ing ration shops to enforce their demands were also brought to my notice.

By the end of my tenure in Paschim Medinipur I had achieved most of my regulatory objectives. More than 99 per cent of the Antyodaya Anna Yojana beneficiaries, including Lodha-Sabars, had not only been identified but had also been issued the card. The same was true for Annapurna. Midday Meals were being served in almost all the schools. Supply of foodgrains for SGRY had stabilised. Yet, what truly warmed my heart, whenever I heard of it, was the news of protest demonstrations and *jhamelas* that villagers created at many ration shops through the length and breadth of the district for their entitlements!

◎

PART II: SETTING COURSE

My frequent forays into deep and dangerous waters in the first few months helped me to not only chart the seas, but also enabled me to take steps to set the course of action. With the assistance of my team members I was able to develop tools that made this possible. Due to the the General Elections most developmental activities had been put on hold. Re-starting these and initiating new initiatives after the Amlasole explosion were priorities. The Baseline Survey and the VVI helped in pin-pointing the areas where development interventions were needed the most; these and the interactions with people also clarified priotities. By making the system more transparent and attempting to empower the citizen-customer, I hoped to create demands that could not be ignored after I moved out.

11
Raising Hope on Hard Laterite
◎

Although agriculture is the mainstay of the rural areas, lack of adequate irrigation infrastructure renders it dependent upon the monsoon's bounty. Behind this truism lie some uncomfortable details. Large tracts of lateritic regions, such as Sankrail Block, although drained by several rivers and streams, are short of irrigation water. The undulating geography creates streams that unless tended do not water the land but annually nibble away at the precious topsoil. Various projects being implemented in the district were aimed at building water and soil conservation systems. Alongside, it was necessary to re-direct the efforts of the people towards alternative occupations to supplement their income from basic agriculture. Based on available resources, within the perimeter of constraints, horticulture and animal husbandry offered opportunities for diversification of livelihoods.

The better part of the morning was taken up by a meeting in Jhargram on agricultural development in Paschim Medinipur district, chaired by the Minister of Agriculture of West Bengal, along with the Principal Secretary, the Director of Agriculture, the Sabhadhipati, ADOs and others. The discussion centred on development of agriculture in the tribal belts of the district.

Two kinds of schemes were in focus. The first was a scheme for promoting kitchen gardens among Lodha-Sabar and other tribal families. The two objectives of the scheme were to introduce horticulture/vegetable cultivation among these groups so that they may utilise their homestead land to generate some marketable surplus and to supplement their diet. The selection of appropriate vegetables for this kind of kitchen garden is crucial. After the discussion it was decided that *ole, kachu,* and other crops such as pumpkins and chillies should be taken up in these parts. Seeds and seedlings for these crops would be supplied to the beneficiaries after imparting a two-day long training programme to them. This would be preceded by a training of the instructors in each block. The training of the beneficiaries would be held at the village level. Essentially, this is the programme that we have chalked out for the RSVY agriculture component.

The second kind of programme was the diversification of crops in this area so that the farmers may get maximum returns on their investment and do not remain dependent on rain-fed crops. As pointed out by the Principal Secretary, Agriculture, it is necessary to make full use of the minor irrigation structures that are being built by various departments. Therefore, it is necessary to prepare lists of the new minor irrigation schemes undertaken in each block and Gram Panchayat of the district so that efforts of the Agriculture Department towards location of crops may be optimally targeted. Since the training, or extension, component can never be under-played, I emphasised that training of trainers should be taken up just before beginning the programme for the beneficiaries. It was also decided that attempts should be made for the convergence of schemes and funds of various departments so that maximum util-isation of available resources may be possible. These departments include Minor Irrigation, BCW, Rural Development, Agriculture, and Forestry and Horticulture. After the meeting, accompanied by the SDO, Jhargram, we left for Bakhra in Sankrail block.

First we visited the Comprehensive Area Development Corporation (CADC) project that extends over an area of 68 acres.[1] This project is meant for the Lodha-Sabar people. Eight persons employed by CADC, Debra, and eight Lodhas are working in that area. Progeny orchards of mango and guava have been developed here — the two-year-old guava orchard has come up well. They have also planted 90 quintals of turmeric in 10 acres. Some of the land is under marigold cultivation and there is also a small plot of gladioli. Three ponds have been excavated; whereas two of them are still incomplete and dry, one has about 2.5 ft of water. Short-term pisciculture has been started in this pond.

Produce from the vegetable plots is taken to the market in Midnapore; the flowers are taken to Kolaghat or Deulia *bazaar*. Though a fence of wire and cement concrete posts surrounds the entire 68 acre, the nearby villagers are regular predators and make away with guavas and other produce. During the last season the workers here sold 5 quintals of guavas. I suggested that the guava orchard, and later the mango orchard, could be auctioned every season. I could not, however, estimate what benefit had accrued to the Lodha population for whom this plot has been developed.

The BDO and the Sabhapati of Sankrail also joined us at the CADC project site. We went with them to see an 'Agro-Industrial Park', which in unadorned language meant a 26-acre plot covered with newly planted, about two years old, cashew plants. Apparently, the Panchayat Samiti is planning to lease out this developed land. Instead, I have suggested to the Sabhapati and the BDO to develop the land further, and in another year or two, when the cashew trees begin to bear fruits they may be auctioned seasonally. Thus, some revenue may be generated for the Panchayat Samiti.

From there we went to Bakhra village plot numbers 3 and 4. These plots, owned by 22 families of Lodha-Sabars who live nearby, comprise 22 acres which have been developed with the help of CADC. The BDO had visited the place last year and so had the SDO when they had seen the plot taken up for extensive vegetable cultivation. Although we expected to see the same during this visit, we found only about an acre and a half of the area was under vegetable cultivation. Instead, guava had been planted all over the land, but without any inter-cropping. Lodha women and men were working in the vegetable field. I have instructed the BDO to hold a meeting of the Lodha owners on site along with the representatives of the Agriculture and the Animal Resource Development (ARD) departments to see how better the area may be utilised. I also suggested to those present to excavate the naturally depressed area in the centre of the plot for rainwater harvesting and short-term fish rearing. Essentially, at this stage the project needs some hand-holding by the BDO and the Sabhapati. Without regular support of the Panchayat this entire venture may be lost. There is a potential here for turning around people's lives, the lives of the Lodha-Sabar families who even though they own the land now, but have little skill.

We had been travelling through vast stretches of land — bare, idle land that it hurts to see. This uneven region, composed of laterite soil and rock, receives poor rainfall. However, little effort appears to have been made to turn this land to good use. The Forest Department has developed a few plantations of cashew and eucalypti. I also came across some Arjun tree plantations. Yet all around us lies tremendous untapped potential for plantation of these and other varieties of trees.

Tarun Das, the head teacher of Bakhra Primary School, our next stop, was absent; that left only one teacher in a school for 106 children. At that moment only class-III and IV students were present. Only nine out of 19 students were present in class-IV, and 17 out of 35, about 50 per cent, in class-III. 15 out of 33 children were present in class-I, while 14 out of 20 attended in class-II. About eight to nine children in each class appeared to be regular absentees. The head teacher had gone off at about 1 p.m. to submit the monthly returns at the office of the sub-inspector of schools. Since only one teacher is present today, children of class-I and class-II had been dispersed earlier. Although 60 schools are covered in this block under the cooked Midday Meal Scheme, it is not running in this school. Proposals for 91 more primary schools have been sent to the SDO, which I asked him to follow up immediately. An additional classroom is being constructed on one side of the primary school under the SSA project; work is progressing briskly.

Next, we visited Bhalkisole village in Khudmorai Gram Panchayat where nine new houses built under the PMGY and nine upgraded houses are located. The houses are built of mud and have asbestos roofs. The scaffolding, supporting the roof from inside, is made of wood, and rather poor wood at that. The size of the room also appears to be rather small.

This is a fully Lodha populated village. Child marriage seems to be quite common in this tribe. I noticed a number of very young and anaemic mothers. The child-mothers were unaware of any immunization other than 'pulse polio'. It may be useful to set up an outreach camp for immunization in this village on a regular basis under the existing programme.

There is a three-room primary school in Bhalkisole and also an AWC. Drinking water is not a problem here since there are a number Mark-II hand pumps around the village. Eucalyptus plantations are also coming up in this area. The young saplings, about 2.5 ft tall, are fenced in by a row of nettles. However, large tracts of land are still lying bare, pristinely fallow. Apart from grazing cattle, the land has not been put to much use.

As I was leaving I noticed two very old women slowly making their way towards our vehicle. Grey untidy hair and a once white sari now carrying a million stains hinted at their story. I went forward to meet them. Their demands were simple enough: a house and Old Age Pension. But is the system ready to accede to such simple demands?

◎

Note

1. Comprehensive Area Development Corporation (CADC) is an agency under the P&RD Department, Government of West Bengal, that undertakes area development interventions based on agro-climatic requirements through 21 projects in 16 districts of West Bengal. Its activities include development of inputs for agriculture, pisciculture and animal husbandry, water harvesting, and skill development of people in the rural areas.

12
Peeping in Nooks and Crannies
◎

During my tours I had noticed that a common cause of delay in implementation of schemes was the time taken in the preparation and finalisation of estimates. This was a bit of a mystery because the same schemes were taken from one year to the next. Yet every time a scheme was to be implemented the wheel would be re-invented all over again: the drawing board would be taken out afresh, drawings and estimates laboriously prepared, approvals taken at various levels, notices issued for tender, and so on. Infrastructure schemes, such as for buildings and roads, were particularly prone to such procedural delays. To untie the knot, I decided that standardisation was the only answer. This would not only reduce delay but would also ensure a certain degree of uniformity and quality of the schemes across the district, apart from instilling some discipline in the processing of the estimates. Nonetheless, I also realised that a major ingredient for the success of this 'rational' solution would be consensus. Therefore I decided to hold a workshop.

On 28 July 2004 a workshop on rural development schemes was organised in Midnapore, attended by the key panchayat functionaries of all three tiers. The Secretary of the P&RD Department was also present. During the discussions, inevitably, panchayat representatives raised the issue of stalling the process of implementation due to delay in getting technical clearance of different schemes at the Panchayat Samiti or the Zilla Parishad levels. The reasons for delay were examined and heatedly debated before it was unanimously resolved that for a number of common schemes taken up by the Gram Panchayats and Panchayat Samitis the plans and estimates should be standardised. Eight such schemes were: AWC, SSK building, road, dug well, storage godown for SHGs/Gram Panchayats, primary school building, production-cum-storage facility for SHG, and kitchen shed for Midday Meal Programme.

It was agreed that the model estimates of these schemes would be prepared by the District Engineer, Zilla Parishad, and circulated among the Panchayat Samitis and Gram Panchayats. If these bodies followed the model plans and estimates, sanction for the scheme would be issued

by the competent authority within a week. On 15 September 2004
I circulated the compendium of 'Model Plan & Estimates for a Selection
of Schemes' to the panchayat bodies as promised.

Upon reaching Lalgarh early, I descended upon Mrinal Kanti Halder, the BDO, at 7.20 a.m. After a hot cup of tea in his quarters, we left for the village Tarkilata to inspect the water harvesting structures being constructed there by the Water Investigation Department under RSVY. Apparently, some confusion still persists about the eligibility of the rates for earth excavation work being offered by the Minor Irrigation Department, especially because the rates have been fixed on the basis of work performed.

We reached Tarkilata at about 7.55 a.m. A 50 m long by 30 m wide water harvesting tank was being excavated here. Although interrupted by the early morning showers, work had already started. About five to six labourers were working and more were on their way. At the deepest point, in the centre, the tank was about 2.20 m deep. It is finally meant to be 4 m deep. I wondered if the command area of the pond was not too limited, proscribing its utility as an irrigation source. Perhaps, we need to review the size of the tanks being constructed under RSVY; emphasis, instead, should be placed on *sech bundhs*.

Plate 12.1 A tank being excavated in Tarkilata

The land on which the pond is being excavated belongs to Uday Mahato, who himself is also engaged in the process. Others working with him are local adivasis and Lodha-Sabars. Uday Mahato explained that, apart from using the tank for irrigation purposes, he intended to engage in pisciculture. Actually, the site of the *pukur* is not as bad as I had initially thought. On the northern side of the *pukur* lies a forest. Through the forest snakes a drainage stream which runs right into the pond; that is why the people here have selected this spot. Apparently, the water from the canal is also brought here. On an average 70–100 people have been employed in excavating this water harvesting tank. After the first few feet of top soil the diggers had hit laterite and even lateritic rocks, which were being broken and excavated.

A well, constructed a few years back, is providing good drinking water to this village; it has a cemented platform and a high parapet — the kind of parapet we need to construct around all dug wells. The platform and the parapet have been completed during this year. In Lodhapara there is a well that is still lying incomplete. One of the properly constructed wells is located in the Mahatopara.

The second tank that we visited is located adjacent to Lodhapara. Lalu Sabar, the panchayat member from this area came over. According to him about 80–120 people are working here. I asked Dinu Sabar, and a few others who were present, about the number of people engaged in this task daily. They said that 20–25 persons, i.e., about 10–12 Lodha families have found work here on a regular basis. A total of 35 Sabar families live in this village; the others are employed in the other tanks. There is another well in Sabarpara that is lying incomplete. Concentric concrete rings have been crudely fitted into the well, but there is nothing else to protect it from the contamination of flowing rainwater. Little wonder, therefore, that the water in the well, at a depth of about 6 ft from the surface, is filthy. The difference in the quality of the earlier well in the better off and politically alive Mahatopara is obvious.

Tall, concrete electricity posts came up in the village about a year back, but cable lines have not come yet and neither has electricity. In a few houses transistors are playing. Yet, wonder of wonders, panels for solar lighting perch incongruously atop a number of decrepit houses. The nearest primary school is at Purnapani, about 2 km from this village; the high school is at Lalgarh. A Madhyamik Shiksha Kendra (MSK) had been sanctioned for Tarkilata, but mysteriously it has been relocated to Kukurmouri. We visited a health sub-centre in the village itself. Conversations with the villagers indicated that it opens regularly on Mondays, Wednesdays and Fridays. I checked the stock of medicines; they had been issued regularly and the supply was satisfactory.

Two electricity posts stand right in the middle of the village, between the Adivasipara and Mahatopara on one side and the Lodhapara on the other. Another water harvesting tank is also located near the Mahatopara. It stands on the land of Tilak Chand Mahato, whose son, Tapan Mahato, is purportedly an ex-People's War Group member. The tank is about 30 m wide and 50 m long. It is, however, located in an area bordering cultivable land. On three sides of the tank lies land owned by the family of Tilak Mahato and a few neighbours. The water storage capacity and irrigation potential of this *pukur* is high because even this late in the year water is seeping through and accumulating on the north-eastern side of the pond.

One thing is clear: Lodha-Sabars and other adivasis of this and the neighbouring villages are getting employment during this lean period. According to Lalu Sabar, a panchayat member, and other villagers, the water tanks near the Mahatopara, the first one that we saw, and the one in Lodhapara, are going to retain water only for six months in a year. In October–November they would use the water collected to irrigate the *kharif* crop in the nearby fields, and it could also be used for short duration pisciculture. The third water harvesting tank created in Tilak Mahato's land is likely to retain water for the entire year.

Ever since it was installed about two years back by the PHE Department, the Mark-II hand pump in the centre of the village has not been working. I asked the BDO to either have it repaired or removed. As we stood near the well-worn pathway discussing the hand pump, some villagers with *kodals* spades over their shoulders walked by. I stopped them for a chat. Bablu, Sudhanshu, Sadhu, Choto, and Shakti Sabar, were five Lodhas on their way to work. All were from Tarkilata and Khas Jungle. Although they were reasonably satisfied with the current availability of employment in the earth-work schemes around here, according to them not a single Indira Awaas house had been built in their village for any Lodha. Perhaps, this difficulty can be resolved by better utilising the Lodha Development Scheme.[1]

Sadhu complained that there is no *morrum* road to their village. However, there is a *pacca* well, with parapet, that supplies clean water and they are happy with it. But the tube well, about four years old, has not been working for the last one and a half to two years. It strengthens my belief that we should have more dug wells, properly protected dug wells, rather than going in for tube wells, which are difficult to build and maintain and expensive to renovate.

At about 9 a.m. we left Tarkilata for Routara village, 20 minutes away. At the border of Routara and Purnapani we saw a newly constructed primary school. The Purnapani Primary School is a single-storeyed structure that measures about 100 ft in length and 15 ft in width. This long brick building is divided into four rooms with three windows and two doors each. Originally, ₹2.5 lakh had been sanctioned for this, and in the expectation of more funds from the Zilla Parishad, the villagers insisted upon extending the building. The additional funds never came. Hence, now it stands incomplete and unused. No doors and windows have been installed as yet; the walls are unplastered and the dung strewn floor un-cemented. Before it becomes a permanent monument to unrestrained ambition and profligate promises that have become a feature of panchayat-led development administration, we need to complete the building immediately. To begin with, at least two of the rooms should be finished within the next few weeks, so that it may be used by children for the purpose it is meant for, instead of serving as a resting place for cattle and goats. This neglect of timely construction is particularly galling because about 300 m away stands the original one-room primary school building, an old and sturdy structure but crammed with over 150 children! The local Anganwadi, inexorably without a building, is attached to the primary school and also uses the old premises. I have suggested that once the new building becomes functional the old primary school building should be repaired and made the permanent venue for the AWC.

As we stood outside the incomplete building discussing what needs to be done, we saw a herd of cattle being taken into the jungle to graze. Around their necks the slightly built cows wore small and large wooden bells — a type I have never seen before. The bell is a purse-like wooden container, with the centre painstakingly hollowed out and filled with wooden balls, that roll and produce a resonating murmur as the cattle move. Unlike the sharp tinkle of metal bells, the cloudy ring of the wooden bell has the unsophisticated sweetness of jaggery. Come even-fall the unbroken rolling of the bells, each distinctive as a signature, makes it easy for the owners of the cattle to locate them in the forest. Of course, metal bells are too expensive.

Khas Jungle, the neighbouring village, is inhabited mostly by adivasis, particularly Lodhas. This is one of the poorest villages I had visited with some of the worst houses I have ever seen. Some of them would not qualify as houses at all! Aghast, I came upon Ramani Sabar's lean-to. Exposed on three sides, with utensils lying on the ground and her clothes hanging on a rope strung between two posts that support the torn black tarpaulin tied to the poorly made wall of bamboo staves and mud whose shade is her house, the 60–65-year-old Ramani huddles inside with a few of her family members. Often at night she takes shelter in the primary school. Incredibly, Ramani's is not the only house in this condition; in Lodhapara several such rooms recline on thin bamboo elbows sheltering entire families.

In certain ways this was a defining visit because it made me resolve what I had been contemplating for some time — taking up a separate housing programme for the Lodhas. Due to their small numbers and scattered habitations their suffrage has not the same value as that of other tribes and communities. Hence, while distributing IAY houses the panchayats find it convenient to overlook them. Unless a separate housing scheme is designed and implemented exclusively for the comprehensively indigent Lodha-Sabars, this vital need will not be met. Such poor and politically feeble groups need special consideration from the state. I determined to make it happen.

A sum of ₹10,000 was given by the Panchayat Samiti to Himu Sabar under the IAY. Now his dwelling is an 8 ft wide by 10 ft long structure; a four-*chala* GI sheet roof held up by six slender concrete posts. Himu Sabar lay wrapped up in a *chaddar*. He got up at the sound of our voices. He was suffering from swollen feet. Caused by the sting of an insect, he informed that it was a common affliction in these parts. The Sabars, as most other poor, do not wear any slippers; they have no slippers to wear.

There are 39 Lodha families in this *para*. The need for a good road is expressed by everyone, especially because health care is available only in Lalgarh, 10 km away and fitfully connected by public transport. The last time any work was done on the road was

Plate 12.2 A Lodha house in Jungle khas

Plate 12.3 Himu Sabar's Indira Awaas Yojana House

about 25 years ago. I think repairs can be taken up under the SGRY, even from the Zilla Parishad share.

Later we visited the water harvesting tank being excavated in Routara on the land of Mahendra Dasgupta in Lodhapara. Mahendra Dasgupta is the postmaster. The Lodhas here have received *patta* for land but not many till their own land. Instead, I am told, they 'lease' out their plots for a few rupees or for a few bottles of local liquor. Further, the land allotted to them or bought for them from the Lodha Development Fund is often not the most fertile available and is usually located on high ground. Thus, the Lodhas are a people caught between the forest and waste land.

Work on this water harvesting tank stopped when a depth of about 6 ft to 8 ft was reached. An underground spring flows into the tank and a good deal of water has accumulated in it, which is why the Minor Irrigation Department has suspended its work. The site selection here appears to be faulty. A second pond that I visited in Routara in Lodhapara, the land once again belongs to Sudhir Dasgupta, Mahendra Dasgupta's brother. About 60 people are working at this site. The pond is located at the end of a sloping forest area. So it is expected that surface water from the forest will drain into it. It seems that we are constructing *pukurs* on private land, on the land of the large land owners. I enquired about this and found that since adivasis had little land they were most unwilling to spare it for the creation of a water harvesting structure.

Bhanga *bundh* in Purnapani *mouza*, which was never completed, can be taken up for excavation. It can supply water for irrigation to a fairly large area due to its large size and excellent location. A large number of Lodha and other adivasis own land in the command area. The BDO should check this site and have it surveyed by an SAE.

The last water harvesting tank is on Malay Dasgupta's land. Here the workers had gathered and were complaining against the contractor. According to them the contractor takes the measurement and makes payment after three and sometimes even after four days. The average wage that they get is ₹25 per day or even less! I spoke with the overseer, who does not keep the measurement book at the site, and asked him to ensure that not only is the measurement done every alternate day but full payment was also made on measurement days. He was warned that no payment will be released for the work if faults like these persist. We also need to take this up with the Water Investigation Department.

On the way back we stopped at the SSK in Thakurpara-Durlavpur. It is functioning in an octagonal shed used by the community for *hari-kirtan*. I was told that there are two *sahayikas*, teachers locally appointed by the panchayat, working here. Only one *sahayika*, Sabitri Roy, was present today. According to her, 40 students are enrolled in this SSK. The number of children enrolled in Class-I is eight. Yet the primary school is only about 50 yards away! What is the point of conducting an SSK in a *hari-kirtan* shed when a primary school is located close by? Indeed, SSKs — an excellent alternative primary education initiative of the State government — are meant to be set up to serve habitations distant from existing primary schools. Since the SSK does not have even have a shed of its own, let alone a well-constructed building, it is no surprise that the cooked Midday Meal Scheme is also not running here.

It would appear that this SSK was set up not to serve children of the locality but to provide employment to someone; this is often the consequence when local politics gets the better of reason and need!

◎

Note

1. Lodha Development Scheme is a scheme under the Backward Classes Development department for improving the condition of life and livelihood of the Lodha tribe members in Bengal. It has several components, such as provision of homestead land, housing, drinking water, irrigation facilities and alternate means of livelihood aimed at providing them with skills and resources.

A Baseline Survey

◎

As mentioned earlier, the initial Baseline Survey of 48 villages in five blocks started on 13 June 2004. The results of the survey were submitted on 16 June. Based on the results a number of measures were forthwith taken up in selected villages; these were mainly schemes for rainwater harvesting, cashewnut plantation and *tassar* host plantation.

On 25 June I presented the findings of the survey in a meeting held in the Development and Planning Department at Kolkata, chaired by the Minister of Planning and Development. It highlighted the various problems faced by the people of the villages, particularly with respect to irrigation, livelihood, infrastructure, and access to public facilities. I also proposed a strategy for development of the area called the 'Program for Rapid Area Development'. At the end of the meeting the Secretary, P&RD Department, handed over to me a list of 520 villages, identified by the P&RD Department as the most backward in Paschim Medinipur. The list was prepared by identifying villages with the Scheduled Tribe population greater than 50 per cent, marginal workers[1] above 20 per cent, and with an earthen or *kuchcha* road to the village. (Later, when selecting the 4612 poorest villages in the state the P&RD Department reduced the criteria to two: one, the percentage of marginal workers and non-workers; and two, percentage of female literacy.)

To survey the 520 villages, teams consisting of officials at the block level were formed. To equip the team leaders and members to carry out the survey with a degree of professionalism within the short time available, a training workshop in Participatory Rural Appraisal (PRA) was organised on 27 June at the Administrative Research and Training Institute, Salbani, conducted by the trainers from the State Institute of Panchayats and Rural Development, Kalyani.[2] The survey of the 520 villages began the following day.

Soon it became evident that the list supplied to us did not cover all Lodha-Sabar villages, while some of these also did not qualify as very poor villages in terms of the parameters used for identifying them. Hence, some villages were dropped from the list, while names of other villages, forwarded by the BDO, Sabhapati and others at the local level, that deserved more attention, were included.

Finally, 747 villages were surveyed under the Baseline Survey, taken up in Paschim Medinipur district between 10 July–31 August 2004. The following outputs were produced by the survey teams at the end of the survey: a notional map of the village and its environment based on PRA; a village profile based on the data collected; list of the schemes for income generation for people who owned land, and schemes for people who did not own land; schemes for the improvement of physical infrastructure; and, schemes for improvement of social sector infrastructure.

The Baseline Survey data contained 52 fields of information: demographic parameters, such as total population, number of males and females, Scheduled Caste/Scheduled Tribe, number of households, number of Lodha households, population of Lodhas; land use parameters, such as area under irrigation, area under cultivation; physical infrastructure parameters, such as roads and irrigation facilities; social infrastructure parameters, such as primary schools, SHCs and ICDS centres; and, income source parameters such as agriculture services and business.

To summarise the analysis of the data, 19 villages did not have any drinking water facilities at all, out of which six were villages inhabited by the Lodhas. The total number of families covered by the survey was 7617. Only 60 of these 747 villages had SHCs whereas ICDS centres were located in 324 villages. 370 villages had primary school facilities while 274 had SSKs. 160 villages had neither a primary school nor an SSK whereas 92 of the 747 villages had the privilege of having both a primary school and an SSK. In all, 132 villages had neither a primary school, nor an SSK, or even an ICDS centre. The data indicated that 254 villages in the sample had no irrigation source at all.

On the basis of these queries six lists of villages were generated: without any drinking water source; without any irrigation facility; without any *sech bundh*; without any irrigation pond; without any irrigation dug wells; and those dependent only on dug wells.

Lists of these villages were sent to the concerned blocks and the BDOs were instructed to ensure that available funds from the RSVY, SGRY and other programmes were utilised immediately for creating the absent facilities in these villages. Indeed, the data was utilised extensively to locate resources available under the RSVY programme exclusively in the surveyed villages. An attempt was also made for convergence of the resources of other programmes for this purpose.

The Baseline Survey served two purposes: first, it was used for locating schemes to fulfil identified needs in the surveyed villages — the primary objective of the survey. Second, it provided important pointers for analysing the census data for developing the VVI that was to come later.

◎

Notes

1. A marginal worker is defined as one who is unemployed for less than 180 days in a year.
2. PRA is a set of methods employed for gauging the condition of a rural area for developmental purposes by enabling the local residents to participate in the assessment process. Called the Rapid Rural Appraisal in the 1980s, it was developed as a counterpoint to the top-down approach of development administration initiatives undertaken since the Second World War; by the 1990s it had gained currency in the developing countries of South Asia and Africa as PRA. It insisted not only upon local participation but also the utilisation of local knowledge, and planning for development based on priorities that emerged from the participatory process.

Another Explosion

◎

On the evening of 14 October 2004 I received a telephone call from the BDO, Lalgarh. He informed me that a landmine explosion had been triggered by the LWEs in Bankisole village near the Ramgarh police outpost, a few kilometres from the block headquarters. Several policemen were feared to have been killed in the blast. I tried to get some more details from the SP; however, he too had just received a similar outline of the incident. He only added that the personnel killed belonged to the EFR. I made a few more phone calls, one was to the Home Secretary in Kolkata whom I gave the few details I had. At about 7.30 p.m. I set off for Lalgarh.

By the time I reached the Ramgarh outpost it was almost past 9 p.m. The SP had already reached and he told me what had happened. A section of EFR *jawans* had left on a patrol at about 3.30 p.m. About 2 kms from the outpost, as they were crossing a bamboo footbridge over a narrow stream in a single file, the explosion had been set off killing six *jawans* in all. The LWEs had also fired with automatic weapons upon the scattered *jawans*, who returned the fire, but the militants retreated into the jungle. Five bodies had just been recovered, of which three were terribly mutilated. One *jawan* could not be traced. As the inert forms were brought into the camp I could only think of the mindlessness of the tragedy. The blood-soaked uniforms of the killed *jawans* and their crumpled body lay in a truck as their fellows, silent in shock, prepared to send them to the EFR headquarters in Salua, near Kharagpur.

Within half an hour the missing *jawan*'s body had also been discovered, lying about 40 ft away from the site of the explosion! Shortly a *jawan* came up to the SP: the missing *jawan*'s daughter was on the phone. She wanted to know whether her father had been found. What should he tell her?

After talking to the police officers and some of the *jawans*, I returned to Paschim Medinipur with the unheard wailing of widows and children ringing in my ears.

◎

13
A Field Channel
Runs through Eden

◎

Early in September the P&RD Department had forwarded a district-wise
list of backward villages to all the districts. In all it had identified 4612
villages that had been selected on the basis of two criteria: where more
than 60 per cent people were either marginal workers or non-workers,
and where 70 per cent females were illiterate. The source of data was
the 2001 Census. The DMs were asked to visit these villages, send reports
to the government, and immediately take up developmental activities
for the inhabitants of the identified villages. The Chief Minister and
the Chief Secretary themselves monitored the visits to these backward
villages and the DMs' reports were followed up.

Upon reaching the Jhargram block office I checked the attendance
register. Eighteen out of 47 employees were yet to reach office at
10.20 a.m. The register was not being checked regularly by either
the joint BDO, who had apparently been entrusted with the responsibility, or by the BDO — as head of office — either at 10.15 a.m.
or at 10.45 a.m.

I also checked some leave applications against absence noted as
earned leave in the attendance register. SAEs Phalguni Chakraborty
and Subrata Kumar Bal had both applied for earned leave and had
been allowed the same by the BDO. However, the applications
are not in the format prescribed and have not been filed properly.
I was sure that no entry had been made in the service books either.
I checked and found my surmise to be correct.

The tour register is divided into sections of different categories
of employees, instead of a chronological list as mandated. I have
instructed the BDO to open a new tour register and to maintain
it regularly and properly. All tours proposed to be taken by the

employees should be entered in advance in the register. No gap should be kept between the lines and a serial number should also be maintained.

Accompanied by the SDO and the BDO, I left for Auligerya village, under Nodabahara Gram Panchayat, situated about 5 km from Lodhasuli. Since tourists from Kolkata are fond of visiting these parts, a number of guest houses have sprung up in this area. The *morrum* road we were driving on passes through the middle of a thin strip of Sal forest. From time to time, through the sparse Sal lining both sides of the road, we caught glimpses of paddy fields. A portion of this land receives irrigation water from the canal system.

Bhutapara is a small *para* on the southern side of Auligerya. As we approached the nearest house, we could see a small group assembled in front of a hut. In a corner of the mud-washed courtyard a small *puja* site had been prepared. A couple, Nathu and Laxmi Sabar, had kept a *mansik*, a pledge of offerings or sacrifice, for their daughter who had been ill. Now that she was well again a *puja* was performed in their front yard last night and a goat sacrificed this morning. Bhutapara is busy with the ceremony and in preparing for the feast that is to follow.

A little further along we come across an IAY house built about nine to 10 years back standing rather uncertainly without repairs. It is built of mud with a *tali* or tile roof. There is a dug well on one side of the Lodhapara, which has a parapet but no platform. About 8–10 families draw water from this well. The water was at a depth of about 35 ft. Nearby, Batasi Sabar, a widow, lives in a small shed made of bamboo with mud plaster and covered by a very poor straw thatched roof. All alone in the world, Batasi Sabar depends on the widow pension that she receives from the Welfare Department.

Most of the houses were empty since the inhabitants were in the jungle collecting sal leaves, the main source of income for Lodhas during this time of the year. The walls of Gour Sabar's hut are made of sticks bound together and plastered on the inside with mud; its roof is made of date palm fronds. Sal leaves were spread out to dry in the front yard of this hut. I saw another well about 15 ft. from Gour Sabar's house, next to Batasi Sabar's hut. It is lined with rings, concrete rings, but without the benefit of either a parapet or a platform, it sorely needs to be disinfected.

We came across another IAY house constructed in 2002, in a relatively better condition. It is interesting to note that except for the new Indira Awaas houses most Lodha houses do not have any doors. They may have a crude frame made of sticks and leaves to cover the doorway but proper doors are uncommon. The houses that have doors are seldom locked, and locked Lodha houses are rare indeed; for these people — caught between the forest and the plains — have nothing to conceal and nothing worth stealing. One may almost gauge the 'prosperity' of the occupant of each house by merely checking if it has a door, and if it does then what is it made of, and whether there is also a provision for locking the door.

We also saw the house of Nabin Sabar, which is being constructed under the SGRY Individual Beneficiary Scheme for Scheduled Castes/Scheduled Tribes. Made of bricks till the lintel level, and then with packed mud above that, it has a GI sheet roof laid on the wooden bamboo frame. Besides joining the bricks, in most houses, mud is also used for covering the walls from the outside and from the inside. This might be an alternative model for construction of Lodha houses on a large scale under the project that we are preparing.

As far as the Lodhas can recall only five Indira Awaas houses have been constructed in this village of 114 Lodha families. In any given year not more than one new Indira Awaas house has been constructed by the Panchayat Samiti. At this rate it will take about 110 years to cover all the inhabitants of Auligerya — if we start even now!

The yard in front of most houses, beaten smooth over time, is truly an extension of the huts. Most dwellings have a small mud stove in the front yard. Some of them also have a *tulsi* plant in the front, or some flowering plants. Near the door, usually, lie a bucket and a rope, and a mortar and stone slab for grinding spices. The only festival among the Lodhas is the *Badhna*. Right now the ladies of the village are preparing for it.

Lalu Sabar's homestead is at the edge of Lodhapara. His hut is slightly built but larger and better kept than most. In his small yard Lalu Sabar has done a fine job of cultivating vegetables and also planting a number of fruit bearing trees. Fruit trees, such as jackfruit, mango, papaya, and also cashew, and some vegetables, such as brinjals and beans are growing in his kitchen garden. Lalu Sabar's front yard is lit up by roses and marigolds.

I found that the 2 km-long field channel re-excavated by the Soil Conservation Department under the RSVY is already being utilised and utilised well. It carries water from the Auligerya *sech bundh* to

Bairagidighi past Auligerya through a large swathe of cultivated area, which includes land owned by Lodhas. About 15 *bighas* of this land here, and many acres owned by the others, are being irrigated by the water brought by this field channel. As this is primarily a Scheduled Tribe and Lodha village, 'others' comprise mostly adivasis. The field channel is about 18 inches deep; it ends at Bairagidighi village which is the far end of the 2 km.

Kamal Sabar, our self-appointed guide, showed us the land that was given to Lodhas under *Patta*. According to them the area is about 100 acres or 300 *bighas*. In the vicinity of the village are situated two large water harvesting tanks, about 100 m by 30–40 m, which two old men insisted was made in the time of Pandit Jawaharlal Nehru, the first Prime Minister of India. They are silted and dry and now no longer in use. If they are deepened by another 5–10 ft the water could be utilised by the Lodhas for cultivation of vegetables and other crops in the adjacent area.

The Health Centre at Nodabahara is near the Gram Panchayat office. The 'road' from Auligerya to Baidyanathdihi is a narrow *morrum* track which loses itself in a grassy field as we approach Baidyanathdihi. This is exactly the kind of location that was meant to be taken up under the PMGSY road construction scheme but has somehow escaped selection. There is a raised track that could be broadened and turned towards the existing *morrum* road. A few culverts would also need to be built.

We were on our way to Baidyanathdihi to inspect the SSK being constructed there. The track has now turned into a single-file footpath over which our vehicles gingerly criss-cross. The SSK in Baidyanathdihi is at present functioning in a mud and GI sheet structure about 18 ft by 18 ft. The new SSK building being built right behind it is being constructed at a cost of one lakh rupees. It has two rooms of the same size, 12 ft by 12 ft with a window in between. I think they will only partially serve the purposes of the school. There are 87 children enrolled in this SSK, although only 35 were in class today. There is a tube well installed in the front of the SSK but sanitation facilities also need to be built.

Lastly we visited the Auligerya *sech bundh*, which is the main source of irrigation for the immediate neighbourhood, and also in the off-season — October–November — to areas as far away as Baidyanathdihi. However, there is a consistent spill over the *pacca* dam built in 1996–1997 under Jawahar Rozgar Yojana (JRY), which is flowing away along the stream.[1] We need to create another *sech bundh* a little downstream which could be used to store water and to supply it to the fields in the lower areas, which are at present short of water. I have asked the BDO to have the site examined by the SAEs, conduct a survey and to submit a proposal by 30 November 2004. Apart from this no SGRY work, especially earth-work, could be seen in the two villages that we visited today. This is a pity because August, September and October are one of the leanest phases of the year when Lodhas go without work because they are landless.

◎

Note

1. JRY was a programme comprising a cluster of schemes that included wage employment and asset creation, housing — the IAY — and provision of drinking water under the Million Wells Scheme. Initiated in 1989, its main thrusts were ensuring wage employment for the unemployed and the underemployed and on creation of rural infrastructure for the poor. Later it was replaced by the MGNREGS.

14

A House for Pramila Sabar

◎

Accompanied by the SDO, Jhargram, and the District Engineer, Zilla Parishad, I reached Lohamelia village in Patasimul Gram Panchayat, Jhargram block, at 8.40 a.m. The total population of Lohamelia village numbers about 650, out of which 300 belong to the Schedule Castes. There are 56 Lodha families residing in this village. The objective of today's visit, apart from an overall examination, is also to assess and identify the requirement of houses, in view of the Lodhas' needs, under the special housing project for Lodhas that we are preparing.

In Lodhapara the first house that we reached belonged to Karuna Sabar, who seems to be better off than other members of his tribe; Karuna's aged mother, Shakuntala Mallick, and her daughter-in-law were drying sal leaves tied in bundles in the hedge-enclosed plot, behind the house. The parapet of the well nearby is almost level with the ground and has no surrounding platform. It was half-filled with branches. Upon asking Shakuntala Mallick, she told me that about a month back a cow had fallen into it and ever since she and her neighbours had stopped using the well.

Nearby is the house of Pranami Sabar, who was also spreading out sal leaves to dry in her yard. I asked her if she had got the Antyodaya card and ration. She informed that her card was with the ration dealer. Twenty days back she had received 14 kg and 300 gm of rice at a cost of ₹42. A receipt had been issued to that effect.

By then a number of Lodhas had collected in front of Pranami Sabar's house. Their response to my question was the same: they had deposited their cards with Shudhangsu Mahato, the ration dealer in Mohanpur. The cards were to be stamped before they could get them back. However, there was one old man, Anant Sabar, who stated that he had his ration card with him, stamped and revised. I requested him to get it for me so that I may examine it.

Yudhisthir and Bela live with their one-year-old daughter Patoli in a tiny hut occupying less than 80 sq. ft. It is less than basic. Atul Sabar and Gurbari Sabar also stay nearby in a one-room hut. Their card is also deposited with the 'control', as they call the ration shop. I sent one of the accompanying block officials to fetch the dealer. Within 15 minutes the worried dealer arrived with the deposited cards; they had been stamped. He was also issuing cash memos. I asked the block officials to ensure the return of the cards to the beneficiaries immediately — the same day. This matter needs to be reviewed at the district level.

Passing through the Mahato *basti* we examined three wells. One of them, with a diameter of about 4 ft, had a number of rings missing. Water glimmered at a depth of about 30 ft. The second well, also quite deep, was in better shape. This one and the next one that we saw had high parapets and platforms. The third well also had a couple of rings missing and needed to be repaired. Without much ado these repairs should be taken up by either the Gram Panchayat or the Panchayat Samiti. Across the path from Mahatopara lives the slightly built Karna Sabar with his family. Karna and Sumitra Sabar have three children, Jahar, Soma and Julie Mallick; the youngest daughter was born on 21 February 2002. I checked little Julie's Health Card. She has not received all the doses of immunization. The last set of doses, against measles and for Vitamin-A, were administered to her on 7 January 2004. Karna's father's name is Rabin Mallick. Mallick is one of the titles used by the Lodha-Sabars.

The District Engineer and I decided to discuss the requirements of the house with Karna Mallick. He told us that 30 *pons* of straw were needed to thatch his house. One *pon* is two handfuls of straw and each *pon* costs about ₹20. Balak Sabar is a local expert who knows how to make roofs of straw. He is one of the few Lodhas in Lohamelia who has acquired the skills for constructing mud houses and thatched roofs. Normally, only the Mahatos and adivasis possess housebuilding skills. Balak Sabar takes two days to lay the roof and he charges ₹60 per day. All the houses do not have windows. I asked some people the reason for this; Karna's answer was: for fear of visiting elephants who often explore the inside of the hut by thrusting their trunks through the windows. But general insecurity seems like the main reason. Since ventilation and lighting are essential I suggested using *jaffreys*, pre-cast cement grills; they were open to the idea and willing to accept it. We also suggested that Karna may think about extending his hut forward and building a verandah which may serve as a kitchen during the monsoon. Apparently the hut cannot be extended forward without consulting their *gunin*, soothsayer; and Mahato, the local *gunin*, has forbade the extension of the hut!

Patla Soren's house was damaged by an elephant last month. The broken front wall, which reveals the plan of the house, is yet to be rebuilt. The house has two rooms; the outer L-shaped room has a paved floor. At the end of the small limb of the 'L' is located the kitchen, whereas the front room, the longer section, is used as a store. The inside room is for sleeping.

Anant Sabar is one of the better off Sabars; he owns three *bighas* of land. His house is a double-storeyed structure made of mud, where his three sons live. For himself he has built a small hut at the back. He stays there during the summer months; the rest of the year it is used as a kitchen. Anant Sabar showed me the AAY card which, unlike the others, he had got back from the 'control' a week ago.

Apart from a few Napits (the barber caste) such as Gopal Manna, Mahatos and Lodhas form the bulk of the population of the village. Manna's homestead has a well-built mud house and a kitchen garden. He is also the motivator for the TSC Programme in this village. A well outside Kalipada Sabar's house had been covered with branches of leaves because the parapet is very low, only about 18 inches high. Small children might fall into it and, therefore, the people prefer to cover it rather than using it. We looked at another well in the front yard of the house, which is ringed but also without any platform or parapet — just one and a half rings to the well. The water of this well is used for drinking and cooking.

To peek at past work, we also visited two Indira Awaas houses; the first one belongs to Kharus Sabar and his wife Tuli Sabar. This IAY house was built in the year 2000. At present it has no windows and but one corrugated iron door. The rest of the house is again divided into two small rooms. The other house that we saw was built under the IAY scheme in the year 1983. It has mud walls and is covered by *terracotta* tiles. The empty windows of this 21-year old house have stopped waiting for the window panes, meant to be supplied along with the house. The owner has filled up the space with bricks. Once the house had a verandah but the tiles covering the verandah are gone; the missing tiles reveal a story. Madhu Sabar, the owner, is known to be inordinately fond of his drink. Some time back, on a thirsty evening he made a deal with a friend: he sold off all the tiles over the verandah for a few gallons of rice beer! Out of 55 Lodha families here, three have received IAY houses thus far, including the two that we saw. One adivasi family is the recipient of the fourth IAY house in the village.

This addiction to liquor is almost all pervasive among the Lodhas. Evening visits to their habitations are pointless, for by the time darkness falls they are quite incapable of conversation. Most days they do not even wait for darkness. A lot of their earnings are spent on *hanria* or *mahua,* country spirits. This is one of the main causes for their lack of savings and consequent vulnerability. Along with other aspects of their life this also needs attention. The question is: how do we go about it?

Kalu Sabar is an enterprising man who has started a small shop. He sells biscuits, a few vegetables and bread. Kalu also keeps some ducks, which were at present in a bamboo cage under a tree because they pose a threat to the paddy in the fields nearby. He is an uncommon example of a Lodha entrepreneur. In his yard I noticed a child in a soiled blue frock and vermilion in the parting of her hair shyly watching us. This was Kalu Sabar's daughter, about 12 years of age, who had just been married off. Kalu could not remember the name of his son-in-law, and I was too taken aback by the sight of the child to ask her name. I did ask her if she went to school, to which the answer was the expected 'No'.

There are three ponds on the eastern side of the village. Two of these are private ponds belonging to two Mahato families. The third, which is twice the size of the private ponds, is on vested land and according to the villagers was constructed by an NGO in 1978 or 1979. However, the water does not last in these three ponds beyond December or early January. Yet there is scope for short-term pisciculture in these ponds. The large pond either belongs to the panchayat or is under its control, but this too has not been utilised for rearing fish.

The people here, especially Gopal Manna and some Lodhas, requested me to examine a site about 1.5 km from the village for the construction of a *sech bundh.* We walked across the paddy fields where patches of golden Aush awaited the sickle while Aman paddy had begun to ripen into shades of plump green. The site was right next to the forest and comprised a long segment of vested land. Though, it is located in Montipa village, the benefit of the water conserved here would be received by the fields in the leeward side of the *sech bundh*. If the *bundh* is constructed now it will be functional only next year but the work could be started right away since the area was lying fallow. I asked the BDO to get the area surveyed by an SAE immediately and submit a proposal under the RSVY.

In the middle of the village is a large vacant area with two structures; one is a Shiv *mandir*, which is still under construction, and on the other side is the now abandoned *pacca* primary school building. The school is about 18 ft long and 12 ft wide, with a wide verandah on three sides. It has four window frames and two door-ways, but neither window panes nor doors. At present it serves as the AWC. Chinta Mahato is the Anganwadi worker who comes from Montipa about a kilometre and a half away. If this building is repaired then it would prove useful for the centre. Alternatively a new Anganwadi building can also be constructed here. I asked the BDO to take steps for repairing the AWC. Lohamelia has 12 Mark-II hand pumps, but none of them is working. I have taken a photograph of one such defunct tube well. This hand pump was set up here in 1983. The hand pump standing next to this AWC is also not working. Nearby, there is an old well with a platform and a high parapet, which has also fallen in disuse because it has not been cleaned or disinfected in a long time. The Gram Panchayat has also constructed wells here. These are ring wells but without any platform.

While I was there, a number of Lodhas had collected in front of the AWC and I could sense that they had a grievance to share. In brief it was as follows: There is a village right across the forest about a kilometre from Lohamelia. Some vested land there had been developed and was being cultivated by the Lodhas of this village for about 15 years. However, that is an all-Mahato village and they have dispossessed the Lodhas — driven them away. The vested land is still lying vacant. Those who have taken over the land by force already possess land. I asked the SDO to enquire into the matter and inform me.

Afterwards, as I was getting into the vehicle a middle-aged woman came forward and demanded that I visit her homestead. Although it was late I felt I must not disappoint her, especially when she told me that when she had heard that I was in Lohamelia she did not go to the field to work. That is, she had forsaken her day's wages so that she may request me for a house. I find the continuing expectations of the poor from government both astonishing and a little frightening. I went over to Pramila Sabar's house.

Pramila Sabar and her diminutive husband, Hari Sabar, live in a thatched, polythene covered hut about 12 ft long by 15 ft wide. Although they inhabit a tumble-down hut they have planted marigolds in their yard, which are blooming a bright orange. In their kitchen garden grew potatoes, peas, *lau*, beans, and *arhar* plants, which towered over me. There was a jackfruit tree and other fruit bearing trees such as mango and *sajne,* drumsticks. These are all signs of industry and hope. Pramila's son works with about 15 others, making plates from sal leaves in the electrical machines that the local *mahajans* have installed. If such machines are provided to some of the younger Sabar they might be able to make better use of the sal leaves that they collect. If not under the IAY then under the special Lodha housing project being prepared, a house must be built for Pramila and Hari Sabar.

◎

15

Of Chickens and *Sech Bundhs*

◎

Under the RSVY we attempted to projectise the schemes undertaken. That is, schemes under different sectors such as agriculture or animal husbandry were not implemented as stand alone, one-time inputs. Instead, they were being planned as multi-faceted interventions with various inputs made over a period of time and with constant monitoring and supervision. For example, in the poultry project under RSVY we included a Training of Trainers programme; selection of beneficiaries from identified villages with the help of panchayats; a two-day training for them; provision of 10 28-day-old chickens, 10 kg of feed to the beneficiaries, weekly monitoring by Pranibandhus for the next five months, and vaccination treatments, etc., during this period. Earlier, normally, one or two one-day-old chickens were provided to the beneficiaries; and that was it.

In the morning, I attended two meetings in Jhargram. The first, chaired by the Secretary, ARD Department, was with the representatives of eight SHGs and the BLDOs of this sub-division. The eight SHGs located at block headquarters, near the BLDOs' office, had been selected for rearing one-day-old chickens. These would be supplied to them by the ARD Department, which after 28 days would buy them back for distribution to beneficiaries under various schemes, particularly the RSVY. We discussed the provisions of this scheme and gauged the ability and willingness of the SHGs.

Initially, all eight SHGs expressed their eagerness to take up the responsibility. However, later it was found that the group from Gopiballavpur-I, selected by the Sabhapati, had not passed its first grading[1] and had no access to the Revolving Fund.[2] We also discussed whether any of the groups had any experience in poultry farming and were told that six of the eight groups, or the members of these groups had experience in rearing poultry. Finally, nine groups were identified, two in Gopiballavpur-I and one each in the other blocks for operating the scheme. It was also decided that instead of laying down rigid parameters of 7 sq. ft per 200 chickens, elaborate arrangement of lighting, etc., the local knowledge and experience of the members of different SHGs would be utilised, and the schemes initiated even with a smaller number of chickens than originally envisaged. The Sabhadhipati, Paschim Medinipur Zilla Parishad, also addressed the meeting.

After the meeting there was a small function in which the first set of poultry units under RSVY were distributed. The 319 bene-ficiaries selected from the villages surveyed in the Baseline Survey, all belonging to the schedule tribes, had been asked to come over to the BLDO office, Jhargram. We had designed the programme so that on their second and last day of training the beneficiaries would receive the chickens. After the training, the Sabhadhipati and the Secretary, ARD department, handed over the first units to the bene-ficiaries. Each of them was given 10 kg of feed and 10 28-days-old chickens that may be expected to start laying eggs after four to five months. The feed is a one-time provision to tide the chickens over for the first three months. There was great expectation among the recipients but most of them were poorly prepared for taking charge of the chickens; some had brought small bags (*jholas*) and others small boxes to carry the chickens back home. Since larger cardboard boxes had to be arranged for, the distribution was delayed. At least we learned a lesson: next time larger boxes with holes for ventilation should be organised for carrying back the chickens.

Once the distribution had started, accompanied by the SDO, I left for Jamboni at about 3.00 p.m. to inspect some of the sites of water harvesting structures being excavated by the Water Investigation Department under the RSVY.

In the fields on both sides of the road green-gold paddy was ripen-ing; harvesting would probably begin by the middle of this month. Sowing for Aman paddy in most of the hilly and forested blocks of Jhargram sub-division starts early, and, therefore, harvesting also begins earlier here than in other blocks of this district. Most of the Aus paddy has already been harvested; some of it is still lying in the fields in sheaves, drying under the still warm November sun. After harvesting, in anticipation of the festival season, most adivasi houses have already been mud washed with white soil extracted from precious deposits in the jungle. In preparation of *Deepawali*, or *Kali Puja*, which is a major festival in these parts, women and children may be seen adorning the walls and doorways of their houses with flowers and leaves and other traditional designs painted in different shades of earth — black, red and yellow — and whatever colours they can lay their hands on.

At about 3.40 p.m. we reached Belia village in Dubra Gram Panchayat. A water harvesting tank is being excavated here on the *Patta* land of Hariram Deheri and Kanai Deheri. It measures 50 m by 30 m. Sixty persons have been working on this tank and a depth of about 3 m has been achieved until now. Due to the harvesting season the number of persons engaged has come down to around 30. Subal Sabar and Damu Sabar also have a share in this water harvesting tank since their *Patta* land is being excavated. Yet the utility of this tank is likely to be limited because of the small catchment area. Nevertheless, if they store water in these tanks, as they say they will, brought by the Kangsabati feeder canal, perhaps, its utility might increase.

We proceeded to the site of another water harvesting tank on the other side of this village. This one is located below a stretch of forest about a kilometre from the road. We walked over the *aals* to have a closer look. Bhuban Chandra Rana of Belia village, a job worker employed by the contractor at this site, was present here. It is an excellent location for a *sech bundh*; the entire surface water of the forest and of the paddy fields lying further up drains this way. Due to seepage of water from below, after a depth of 1.5 ft work had been stopped. The job worker tells me that they have been drying the tank and have also dug a channel to ease out excess water. Now that the water has been drained the excavation should continue. It is likely that workers may strike more water after digging a little bit so I have asked them to continue the excavation even if intermittently.

As we headed for Benadihi, we passed the 'Rajbari' in Chilkigarh village. The most imposing parts about this Rajbari are the gates. For beyond lies only the falling mansion of the former *Zamindar*.

We turned left near the PHC, Chilkigarh, and engulfed in red dust went up the road through a sal forest. Of the two, the first water harvesting tank being constructed here is on the land of the two Dutta brothers! These are similarly large in dimension and are adjacent to the Kangsabati feeder canal. Digging has been completed to a depth of about 4 ft. Work is going on but the number of people engaged here has also decreased, as it has at another site about 100 m away. People, including Lodha-Sabars, from Benadiha village are also getting work here. The excavation at both these sites started about 25 days ago. The second pond is being excavated on the land of Marwari Soren. While I was inspecting the tank and talking to the villagers, I received a call on my cell phone from an old school friend, now a doctor in New Zealand. Felt strange; he seemed several worlds removed.

On our way back, we stopped at the second tank that is under excavation. The contractor's man there was complaining that it had become very difficult to excavate because they had hit rocks; actually these are lateritic rocks and, therefore, more negotiable. To soften the plot they have to water the area before digging.

In a field nearby a football match was in progress. Over 300 spectators were cheering the teams. Under tall trees in one corner of the field there were stalls of ground-nut sellers, *paan*-sellers, vendors of sweets, *pakouri*, and the ubiquitous *hanria*. The atmosphere was festive, and, although in smaller numbers, groups of women were also present. Most of the people here were youngsters. If sports could be promoted in this area, and football and volleyball kits distributed to clubs, then perhaps the youth here would be better engaged rather than idling their days away or taking to paths of violence.

In Murakati village, Lalbundh Gram Panchayat, we inspected another harvesting tank being excavated here, adjacent to the forest and next to the road. On an average about 1.5 m of excavation had been completed. Much work remains to be done. Each day about 100–110 people had been working here, but since harvesting began here too the number of people had come down considerably to about 20–25 per day. The long, forest side of the tank has been cordoned off from the jungle by a wall of red earth excavated from the tank. I wondered why, since this would prevent the surface water run off to enter the pond. However, according to the people who had collected there, if water flows into the tank directly from the forest it will bring in quantities of sand. I went and had a closer look at the sandy area on the other side, and found their apprehensions to be true. The plan is to divert the water along the elevated bank to an entry point at the far end of the tank. I was glad to note these arrangements that indicated the involvement of villagers in implementing the scheme. This is a good project also because there are no large *pukurs* or *bundhs* in this area.

Evening had fallen by the time we went from Murakati to Jamunasole, a distance of about 4 km through the forest. I noticed a channel running beside the road. The BDO told me that this had been made with funds from the Watershed Development programme; it carries water from the reservoir at Jamunasole, Gidhni Gram Panchayat, to villages more than 2 km away. Along with water harvesting structures we also need field channels to carry excess water to storage tanks lower down or to facilitate irrigation in dry periods. We must advise the line departments and panchayats to take up such schemes, especially under RSVY.

Soru Sabar, son of Naresh Sabar, owns land right next to the water harvesting tank that is being dug at Jamunasole. His field is very low. Soru Sabar had just harvested his paddy and was in the process of taking home the last bundles. According to him, irrigating even the *kharif* crop is a problem here. Often in October–November not enough water is available to irrigate the paddy crop. This is the chief problem throughout Paschim Medinipur.

The tank at Jamunasole runs from west to east. They had struck water in the tank, which at its deepest point is about 12 ft. The western side was more shallow since the seeping water had led to suspension of work. Before starting work again they had to evacuate the water. The drainage canal from the reservoir up the road, Jambundh, also passes next to this tank. The new tank can receive excess water from Jambundh through this narrow channel, as does Alibundh 2.2 km away. Ramesh Roy, the contractor for this tank and also for one in Lodhapara at Tarki in Binpur-I Block, confirmed that the excavation of the tank in Tarki and of two tanks in Routara was complete. It is likely that because of the shortage of labour the excavation of the Jamunasole tank would be completed only by the end of December.

Local inhabitants told me that right now there is no dearth of work. Harvesting is in progress, the construction of a road in the forest has been taken up by the Forest Department, and now this irrigation scheme. What people want and need anywhere is regular work; I think this is the foundation of happiness in any society.

◎

Notes

1. First grading is the assessment of an SHG after the initial six months to determine, based upon its activities and its savings, whether it is ready as a group to receive and utilise the revolving fund for income generating activities.

2. Revolving fund is an amount loaned to an SHG that has passed the first grading, which the group may use as a corpus for issuing loans to members of the group for various economic, and even social, activities. Provided jointly by public sector banks and the government, the amount an SHG is eligible to receive as its revolving fund may range from ₹25,000–₹40,000.The fund is of a revolving nature, since members who take loans are responsible for returning it at the earliest so that other members may in their turn also avail of the facility.

A Crop Calendar

◎

To rephrase a hackneyed truth, agriculture is the mainstay of the vast majority of people in India; the agricultural cycle determines not only the levels of prosperity but also the life cycles of the people, their social engagements and political struggles. With a focus on expanding livelihoods, improving the agricultural resource base is one of the primary aims of development administration. To do this we must understand the periodicity, variety, extent — both temporal and spatial — and quality of agricultural production in an area, its relationship with other sectors of the local economy and its impact on them. Any method or tool that helps us to come to grips with these dimensions of agriculture would enhance the accuracy of plans and the effectiveness of their implementation. One such tool is the Crop Calendar.

Originally, I had developed the concept and then designed the calendar in 1995 during my tenure in Bankura district. As ADM (Development) I was trying to promote watershed-based development, and one of the key challenges we faced was introducing newer and improved varieties of crops. The data on agriculture was all there but, as it usually happens, it was not readily available. The Principal Agriculture Officer of the district, Dr Ajit Maity, and the Collectorate assisted me in collecting the figures, and with the help of the National Resource Development and Management System (NRDMS) officer I organised them to create the calendar. Although I tried to use the calendar during my tenure, but once I left Bankura, like the passing year the calendar was also abandoned. After almost a decade, in Paschim Medinipur, the cussed administrator within me prompted a fresh attempt to re-introduce it.

The Crop Calendar was an endeavour to map the agricultural activities carried out in various seasons throughout the year in each block of a district. For interventions in employment generation to succeed and be sustainable it was not only necessary to plan in detail, but also for the area selected to be homogenous in terms of topography, vegetation, ground and surface water availability, average rainfall and other such independent variables. In this respect, a district is too large an area to plan for, and a village, or even a gram panchayat, too small. Most development blocks, however, can be viable planning units. Therefore, I selected the block as the unit for developing Crop Calendars in the district of Paschim Medinipur.

The objective of preparing the Crop Calendar was to provide administrators and decision-makers a tool for planning a wide variety of development activities; it is meant to be an instrument of both analysis and planning. As a map of agricultural activities, read with the data accompanying the calendar, it informs the reader about the period, the activities, the crop variety, and the availability of employment in different parts of a block; with this information an analysis of the strengths, weaknesses and opportunities of interventions may be made. And on the basis of this the gaps may be addressed through an extensive plan.

The Crop Calendar of each block is in the form of a chart that illustrates the sowing and harvesting periods for all the major and most minor crops cultivated in a block. The graphic representation enables the user to swiftly assess the cropping pattern and crop cycle in the block, during different seasons throughout the year. Both the Gregorian and the Hindu calendars were used and the crops were grouped together according to the Bengali cropping seasons to aid understanding and utility at the local level. To complement the Crop Calendar we also enclosed a map of the block and a data bank consisting of certain basic data sets of the block.

The map showed us the Gram Panchayat boundaries and the location of Gram Panchayat headquarters, the block headquarters and the *haats* and markets in a block. The data bank afforded basic data pertaining to geography, demography including figures for different types of employment, land use patterns, soil quality, irrigation, agricultural infrastructure, *haats* and markets, crop diversity, their acreage, their productivity and yield. The aim of the data bank and the map is to make the Crop Calendar more meaningful and the planning exercise accurate. Both the map and the data bank may be improved further. There could be additional maps showing the soil quality, the land use pattern, the ground water availability, the surface water availability, and the road network. The data sets could be further refined to provide Gram Panchayat based figures and information on subjects such as employment, land use pattern and irrigation facilities. I tried to make the best use of the NRDMS facility in Paschim Medinipur. However, the additional maps we needed in turn required better computing facilities.

Interventions in agricultural sector usually prove to be interventions in the entire economy of a particular region; the contrary is also true. A large number of departments could utilise the Crop Calendar for planning development schemes and their implementation. Two such departments would be: P&RD and Department of Agriculture. Apart from these, the Calendar would be useful to several other field departments, such as Departments of Minor Irrigation, Animal Resources Development, Cottage & Small Scale Industries, and Agriculture Marketing.

In sum, the Crop Calendar is a tool for planning and analysis based on quantitative data and confirmed information. However, its utility depends upon the willingness of the planners and decision-makers at the district and sub-district levels to use it, and to utilise its data for planning and implementing the vast range of developmental programmes that the government has taken up.

Hoping for the best, and first having convinced the Sabhadhipati of the Zilla Parishad, I made a presentation on the Crop Calendar before the members of the Zilla Parishad, the Sabhapatis of Panchayat Samitis, BDOs, and officers of related departments. I also handed each of them a copy of the calendar relevant to their block or jurisdiction and requested them to use it for planning purposes.

I do not believe that I was able to institutionalise it.

Crop Calendar
Block: Nayagram

Block: Nayagram

SEASON	Sl. No.	NAME OF THE CROP	January / Pous / 1	February / Magh / 2	March / Falgun / 3	April / Chaitra / 4	May / Baishakh / 5	June / Jaistha / 6	July / Ashar / 7	August / Shraban / 8	September / Bhadra / 9	October / Ashin / 10	November / Kartik / 11	November / Aghrahan / 12	December / Pous / 1
			RABI SEASON			SUMMER SEASON			BHADUI SEASON			WINTER SEASON			
RABI SEASON	1	Potato		▓	▓								■	■	
	2	Wheat			▓	▓							■	■	
	3	Sunflower			▓								■	■	
	4	Mustard & Pea	▓	▓									■	■	
	5	Til, Khesari, Moong & Musoor (types of pulses)										■	■		
	6	Gram				▓							■	■	
	7	Sugarcane	▓	▓	■										
	8	Arhar		▓	▓			■	■						
	9	Vegetables											■	■	

(Continued)

(Continued)

		Sowing / Harvesting calendar
SUMMER SEASON	1	*Boro Paddy, Sunflower*
	2	Groundnut, Maize & *Til*
	3	Vegetables
BHADUI SEASON	1	Aus Paddy
	2	Groundnut & Maize
	3	*Babui* Grass
	4	Vegetables
WINTER SEASON	1	*Aman Paddy*
	2	Green Gram & *Tori*
	3	*Kulthi*
	4	**Vegetables**

Vegetables: Brinjal, Ladyfinger, Pumpkin, Gourd, Cucumber, Beans, Carrot, Beatroot, Cabbage, Cauliflower, *Palon*, Radish, *Jhinga*, Chilli

Note: ■ ■ ■ Sowing Period
▮ Harvesting Period

Basic Data: Nayagram

	Baligeria
Block Headquarter	
Distance from District Quarter	120 km.
Geographical Area	50170 ha.
Gram Panchayats	12
Mouza	336
Inhabited *Mouza*	291
Gram Sansad	93
No. of Households	20513
Total Population (2001)	123937
Male	62629
Female	61308
Scheduled Caste Population	22757
Scheduled Tribe Population	49387
Literate	**57426**
Male	36714
Female	20712
Total Rural Families	32645
BPL Families (Survey-2002)	15506 (47.5 per cent)
Small Farmer Household	4892
Marginal Farmer Household	8625
Total workers (2001)	66453
Total Main Worker	40995
Cultivators	15431
Agricultural Labourers	15728
Household industries	1556
Other Workers	8280
Marginal Workers	25458
Non Workers	72695

Land reforms (area in hectare)	
Total Land Vested	3680
Vested Land Distributed	3276
No. of Vested Land Beneficiaries	22274
Patta Holders	21754
Bargadar	2074
Land use (in hectare)	
Net area under Cultivation	23760
Area under Pasture, Orchard, etc.	200
Cultivable Waste Land	805
Forest Land	15113
Area under Multiple Cropping	1420 hectare
Irrigated area	6280 hectare
Sources of Irrigation (in numbers)	
RLI	12
MDTW	11
STW	225
Dug well	1000
Pond/Tank	260
Road Length (in km)	259 km
Bank Branch	09
SKUS	29
LAMPS	02
Mouzas with Electricity	73 (25.09 per cent)
Haat/Market (in numbers)	24
Private	13
Market Committee	6
Government	5

Area, Production & Productivity
Block: Nayagram

Name of Crop	Area (in hectare)	Production (in metric tonne)	Productivity (kg/hectare)
Paddy			
Aus	1440	2350	1633
Amon	15480	25880	1672
Boro	1630	2630	1617
Wheat	1230	2280	1857
Maskalai	70	40	511
Oil Seed			
Mustard	1110	500	451
Til	220	130	600
Potato	460	9390	20317

Village *Haats* and Markets: Nayagram

Name of Village *Haat*	Date Established	Name of *Mouza*	J.L. No.	Area (in acre)	Days	Nature of *Haat*	Average no. (per *haat* day)
Nekrasole *Haat*	1960	Nekrasole	170	0.60	Saturday	Private	800
Ugarsand *Haat*	1910	Rajpahari	9	1.20	Wednesday	Private	1500
Chandabila *Haat*	1955	Chandabila	27	1.50	Monday	Market Committee	500
Negui *Haat*	1977	Sana Negui	49	1.99	Tuesday	Government	6000
Totasai *Haat*	1962	Totasai	8	2.00	Sunday	Market Committee	1000
Khakrei *Haat*	1930	Khakri	60	1.50	Monday	Private	700
Bachurkhoyard *Haat*	1950	Bachur Khoyard	34	1.00	Thursday	Market Committee	600
Kalma Pukuria *Haat*	1975	Kalma Pukuria	75	0.75	Thursday	Private	1800
Chhoto Jharia *Haat*	1972	Chhoto Jharia	60	1.50	Saturday	Market Committee	2000
Marchi *Haat*	1965	Marchi	60	0.50	Saturday	Market Committee	500
Bara Negui *Haat*	1955	Bara Negui	52	0.50	Sunday	Market Committee	700
Kharika *Haat*	1970	Kharika Mathani	148	2.97	Wednesday	Private	2000

Name	Year	Place	No.	Value	Day	Ownership	Amount
Nayagram *Haat*	1920	Nayagram	144	1.00	Monday	Government	600
Khudmarai *Haat*	1950	Khudmarai	232	2.00	Saturday	Government	700
Kumarpur *Haat*	1920	Birkanda	223	2.00	Thursday	Private	800
Basupat *Haat*	1971	Basupat	254	1.00	Sunday	Private	800
Bauskuthi *Haat*	1974	Bauskuthi	159	1.00	Sunday	Private	700
Sahashra Linga *Haat*	1880	Sahashra Linga	191	0.78	Tuesday	Private	600
Baligeria *Haat*	1870	Patharband	199	1.16	Friday	Private	5000
Ramkrishnapur *Haat*	1972	Ramkrishnapur	176	0.52	Monday & Thursday	Government	600
Nagripada *Haat*	1972	Nagripada	178	0.52	Wednesday & Sunday	Nagripada H.R. School	500
Dhumsai *Haat*	1958	Dhumsai	323	2.00	Tuesday & Saturday	Government	1000
Paika Jhauri *Haat*	1979	Paika Jhauri	330	0.75	Monday & Thursday	Private	1000
Keshor Rekha *Haat*	1979	Keshor Rekha	182	1.00	Thursday	Keshor Rekha Jr. High School	800

16

Harsh Reminders

◎

The LWEs appeared to have spread to blocks other than those initially identified. From time to time I received information about their movements in blocks such as Salbani, Jambani, Jhargram and Gorbeta-I. In the evening of 17 November they shot dead a police officer of the district intelligence branch at a haat near Lalgarh. The SP and I visited the site later that evening. I was a little disconcerted to find that the haat where the officer had been killed was adjacent to the Forest Range office — in the block headquarters. The bloodstains on the gravelly ground showed in the moonlight.

Even during my inspections of on going schemes, especially dhal bundhs, water harvesting tanks and roads in the forested areas, I was aware that among the groups of people I met and talked to were elements belonging to the extremists. On some occasions the BDO or another local official discreetly pointed them out to me. I had also learnt that in many cases where such schemes had been initiated two or three persons had enquired about the work and the system of wages paid out to the people engaged at such sites. Although aware of the potential danger of visiting remote extremists-affected areas, and despite receiving two threatening letters supposedly written by the extremists, I never felt threatened by them. Indeed, the LWEs had never interfered with developmental activ-ities implemented by the government or by the panchayats. Therefore, despite the warnings and the anxiety of the SP, I never toured with an armed police escort. Of course, I never revealed my destination until I reached it. Surprise was my only precaution.

On 23 November the Chief Secretary had held a video conference of all DMs. Apart from reviewing various programme he made an important announcement: the State government had decided to initiate an Old Age Pension Scheme exclusively for the scheduled tribes. All scheduled tribe persons above 60 years of age, belonging to the BPL category in ITDP blocks, and not receiving any other pension, were eligible. The DMs were directed to identify such candidates for immediate selection under this scheme. The aim was total coverage of the eligible candidates; no ceiling on the numbers was fixed.

On the cemented parapet of a well on the outskirts of the village Choto Pelia, slogans in Santhali, written purportedly by the PWG against the elections, greeted us. A little further down, on the wall of the AWC facing the road, in red dye it was inscribed: 'Polici Raj Khatam Karo — 'Janayudha' or End Police Rule — People's War.

The AWC was being run in a ruined one-room building without a roof. Enclosed by the four walls a dozen children sat on the floor with the sun shining overhead! Rupali Hansda, the helper in the AWC, was present but the Anganwadi worker was not. She told me that no food had been supplied to the centre for the last one month. Hence, today also no food was being cooked. The attendance register is not available with the helper. Earlier, in November, the ICDS Supervisor had visited the centre, but no report in this matter seems to have reached the CDPO or come up to the district level. Some medicines were also supplied but they are kept with the Anganwadi worker. The food is cooked in a nearby club. According to the helper, the children enrolled in the AWC have been immunized. Immunization of 0–6 months old children, however, has not yet taken place. The day-long Pulse Polio campaign was last held on the 21st of this month, that is, three days back; this AWC was also a Pulse Polio Centre and all the children took the drops. When we left the AWC at 9.20 a.m. Lakshmi Hembram, the Anganwadi worker was yet to reach her post.

On our way to Kumar *bundh*, a *sech bundh* that the BDO has proposed for re-excavation, we pass through Choto Pelia, a tribal village. The scattered huts, although not signifying prosperity, were of reasonable quality. Goats tied to the walls and busy chickens pecking away at the ground indicated that the villagers are keen on livestock.

The BDO told me that the *pacca* road to Choto Pelia, and Kumar *bundh*, was built about five months back on *ryoti* land donated by the adivasi owners. It is not as if the people here do not want development or do not wish to contribute to their own development, the main problem appears to be in our efforts to channelise development funds in these areas.

From Kumar *bundh* village we turned on to a broad mud road, known as the 'British road'. Apparently it was built during the British times, and buses used to ply on this road from Midnapore to Sijua. From the condition of the road I could gather that not much repair or widening or strengthening of this road had been done since the Britishers left. Now buses have also stopped using this route.

Kumar *bundh*, which is at the edge of the forest, is classified locally as a *dhalbundh*. A *dhalbundh* is a rainwater harvesting tank which arrests the flow of rainwater on a slope (*dhal*) and stores it for irrigation purposes. This *bundh* has silted over and weeds more than 4 ft tall have conquered it. But this *sech bundh* has both a large forested catchment area and a large command area, which is owned by the adivasis. Along with the *bundh* an irrigation channel needs to be constructed. Earlier two crops were grown in the nearby fields because water was available. Now, because the *bundh* is silted over, only one crop is grown here apart from some wheat and vegetables. At present, the water is barely knee-deep. Even the local people do not remember when it was excavated. Some of them stated quite facilely that it was built in the time of British rule. During my visit to these forested interiors of the district some of the harshest words that I have to hear in the context of any public facility — a well, a *bundh*, or a road — are: '*Eta Britisher aamoler*': 'This is of the British period'. I dread hearing them, for they ring like an indictment!

Jamadar Tudu, a squat and greying elder, was harvesting his paddy in the field nearby. In reply to my query he told me that the *bundh* was not excavated during his time, in fact, it was created during his father's time. Due to siltation the upper reaches of the *bundh* have been reclaimed by the people here and is under cultivation. Baneswar Murmu has occupied a portion of it. As I can see, 80 per cent of the paddy in this area has been harvested; according to Jamadar Tudu after this they will not have any work for several months. I have asked the BDO to start re-excavation of this *bundh* immediately under National Food for Work Programme (NFFWP).[1] He told me that already the labour list is being prepared and the work can be started within a few days.

We then went to Madhupur *khal*, which is basically a perennial stream adjacent to Arulia and Kumar *bundh*. If a check dam is constructed here it would serve two purposes: one, it would create an automatic reservoir of water, and two, it would also serve as a bridge for the people to cross over the *khal* during the monsoons. This would be a large project but would be well worth implementing. I have asked the BDO to prepare a preliminary plan. In view of the size of this project the technical expertise of the Zilla Parishad engineers could be utilised. The District Engineer should visit the place immediately and prepare a plan and estimate.

The road, meandering through tangles of lantana and a cashew plantation, eventually traversed sal forests before bringing us to Uparbundh.

Khudiram Murmu, a grizzly 60-year-old, was busy with a sickle in his paddy field. This *bundh* is on *ryoti* land and is owned by five or six scheduled tribe families. Situated on a slope, right below the forest from where the water drains into it, Uparbundh also has a good catchment area. But like Kumar *bundh* this reservoir is also silted and shallow. According to Khudiram Murmu, it was constructed during his grandfather's time; he said that re-excavation was taken up last year on one side of the *bundh* but it has not been significantly deepened. Shareholders in the *bundh* also rear fish in it, and earlier in the year some fingerlings had been released in its waters. After chatting with us Khudiram Murmu went back to his field. Not content, I followed him into the field all by myself.

I started talking to him about the paddy yield this year and other such things. Khudiram Murmu told me that the late rains this year had come as a boon, and only because of that he had been able to cultivate the area adjacent to the *bundh*, which otherwise would lie fallow. He told me that one person can harvest about five *kathas* of land in a day, starting early at about 6 a.m. (although watches are unknown to people like Khudiram Murmu) and working till late afternoon. Harvesting can be back-breaking because he has to bend low and cut handfuls of paddy with a sickle, gather them, and lay them out to dry. Until the last sheaves lie on the ground the process is inescapably repeated.

We next went to Kumar *bundh* village, a 100 per cent tribal populated village, where we first stopped at the house of Gurbari Hansda. She lives in a mud dwelling with a tin roof overhead. Gurbari was applying a layer of red mud on the walls of her house. Her eight-year-old daughter was also assisting her — part work and part play. The newly harvested paddy lay in a neat block about 7 ft high in her courtyard. Next to her house Gurbari and her husband have planted some *arhar*, pulse. Although they own land, but it is *danga* (upland) and not irrigated; therefore, it cannot be fully utilised.

Chintamoni Murmu is about 70 years old and lives nearby. She is a fit candidate for receiving Old Age Pension under the new scheme of the BCW Department. Butni Murmu, her daughter-in-law, has two children who have started attending the primary school where cooked Midday Meal is being served. However, younger children, who have not yet been enrolled, are also going to the primary school but they have been denied food. I tried to explain to them that younger children should be enrolled in the AWC and nutritional support for them will be ensured at the ICDS centre.

About four months back a tube well was constructed in Kumar *bundh* village and it is now being used as a source for drinking water and for other purposes by the villagers in this area. However, they complained of the presence of inordinate amounts of iron in the water. Other schemes are being taken up in this village under RSVY. Although three wells, with parapets and platforms, are providing good water, the tube well has become the main source of drinking water.

Bhusan Kisku has a grandson about six months old whom he has named Chetan Kisku. Son of Mangli Kisku, Chetan was born on 19 June 2004. I examined his health card with some satisfaction since he had received all the immunization shots except for measles and Vitamin-A. Supply of the measles vaccine, dependent on the three central laboratories, has been erratic in the entire state.

We found Premchand Hembram sitting on a low *charpoy* outside his hut. He was modest about his age but I am sure he must be nearing 70. He does not work any more because, as he says simply, he cannot. From his appearance too he looks a tired, old man. He is another candidate for Old Age Pension.

Narayan Murmu and Som Murmu, a middle-aged couple, were threshing paddy with a manual threshing machine. They have harvested their paddy recently; despite the single rain they received, the crop has been satisfactory but the yield is not as good as it could be. Moni Murmu is the old mother of Narayan Murmu. She was carrying a sack of harvested paddy to be dried — another candidate for the Old Age Pension Scheme.

Chandra Soren, a man of about 45, just then walked into Narayan Murmu's courtyard. He was carrying a quail in a cage in his left hand and a lump of earth in the other. I asked him where he was headed. He said he was going to feed white ants to the quail and proceeded to do so. The lump of earth was actually broken off from some unfortunate ant hill. As he tapped the lump and crumbled it on top of the cage, white ants rained down and the quail greedily pecked away. Chandra Soren catches other quails with the help of this caged female whose calls attracts others; they come up to the cage to be ensnared in a bamboo trap. But Chandra does not sell the quails he catches. On a good day he may catch six or seven birds, adding some meat to the family's meals. Chandra Soren had a long black feather sticking out from behind his ear. Wondering if it had some tribal significance, I asked him what it was for. His answer: for cleaning his ears!

Some houses in this village use solar lighting and some even have electricity. There are also some shallow tube wells in this area and a few manual thresher machines. Both are shared by the other villagers, without payment of rent. This sharing of their resources seems to be common among adivasis where the sense of community has survived the winds of commercialisation. In front of some houses the paddy was already being boiled before being turned to par-boiled rice. Large black earthen hanrias were steaming on wooden stoves. This seems to be one of the better tribal villages in this area; the main problem here is insufficient irrigation.

Later, at 11 a.m., we arrived at the Kumar *bundh* Primary School and found that it was open. Atanu Saha has been posted here as the assistant teacher. He was present and so were most of the children. Kaliram Soren, the head teacher, who lives in the village had not yet come but was expected shortly. There are 91 children in this primary school, which has one large *pacca* room and an old mud and tin room. I could not see any sign of expenditure done on the school building from the maintenance grant, which is provided on a regular basis and that has been provided here also. The assistant head teacher informed me that everything was controlled by the head teacher. I suggested that they could at least purchase a few balls for the children to play with. There is also a tube well at the primary school, which provides drinking water to the people of this locality. It was set up about a year ago.

On the way to Ramgarh we went to Bansberh, which I had visited earlier on 14 April 2004. The three new dug wells in the three adjoining villages that we had promised have been constructed; I could see them being used. The BDO, Bansberh, pointed out one of these new wells to me. Two women were carrying away pots of water from the well while a man took a bath on the encircling platform. I asked him *'Tale, kuon ta hoeche?'* — 'So, the well has been built?' In response to this stupid question he poured a bucket of water over his head and cried *'Eito, chan korchi!'* — 'Here I am, taking a bath!' This moment will stay with me.

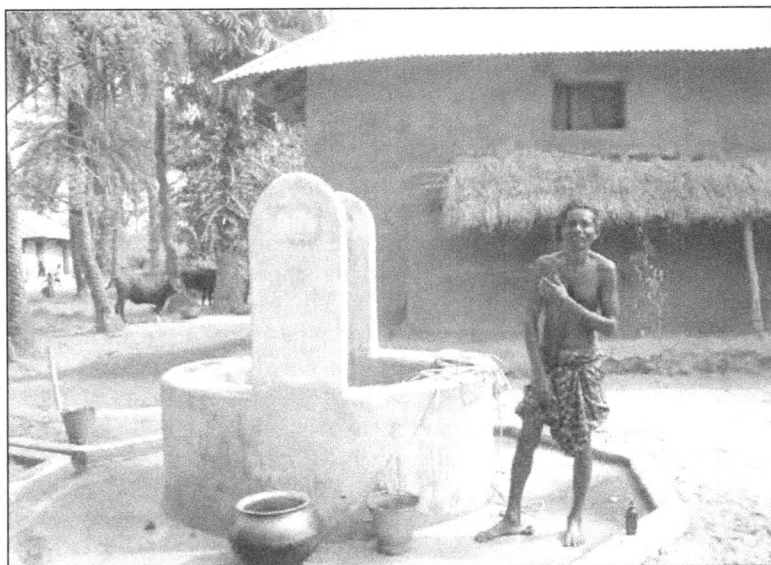

Plate 16.1 *Eito chan korchi!*

We walked through the village to the Upar Bansberh *bundh*, which is proposed to be re-excavated. Since I could see streams meandering down the wide watershed, I discussed the possibilities of more *sech bundhs* with a few villagers. They confirmed that there are a number of springs in this area and a few earthen *dhalbundhs* could be built to hold the water. About a kilometre from Bansberh village, a *dhalbundh* is situated at the edge of a forest, which serves as its catchment area; it also receives water from another large *bundh* higher up from where excess water flows down to the lower reservoir through a channel on the western side. Through siltation the Upar Bansberh *bundh* has also become shallow and needs to be re-excavated. All the land in its extensive command area is owned by the adivasis. At the *bundh* itself we discussed the issue with the people from the village. I asked them when they could start work.

Since a few more days of harvesting remain they agreed to begin re-excavating the *dhalbundh* the following week.

After visiting Upar Bansberh *bundh* we walked about 1.5 km through the forest up to the Neyar Bansberh *bundh*, also a source of water to the lower *bundh*. This also needs to be re-excavated. The villagers there agreed to start this process after the Upar Bansberh *sech bundh* re-excavation is completed.

Under the NFFWP it is imperative that construction of water harvesting structures is taken up simultaneously in a large number of villages or perhaps even a cluster of villages. It would not be prudent to construct a number of water harvesting tanks in a single village at one go because shortage of labour in these thinly populated areas will delay the progress of work.

We also visited the primary school at Bansberh that I had found to be in a derelict state on 14 April 2004. Now it has been repaired and a new school building will also come up here. The money for the primary school has also been sanctioned and the BDO told me the work would start soon. Cooked Midday Meal prepared by an SHG is being served here. Once the new primary school building is constructed, the mud building, in which the primary school is being held now, should be handed over to the AWC, which has no building of its own. There are 57 children enrolled in the school and 45–50 of them attend school regularly.

When we were returning, bullock carts full of hay and harvested paddy were being taken back to the villages. The bullock carts did not have wooden wheels but large metal ones. This is perhaps a sign of progress in the bullock cart economy.

◎

Note

1. Introduced in November 2004 in 150 backward districts of the country, the NFFWP was a precursor of the Mahatma Gandhi National Employment Guarantee Act. Its main objective was to ensure employment and food security for the rural poor through the creation of economic, social and community assets. Under the programme, wages were paid to the workers in both cash and grain. The programme was fully funded by the Central Government.

17

In the Name of Greed

◎

After lunch we left for Lalgarh and crossed the river Kangsabati by a boat. The fair weather bridge was washed away by the last monsoon and the new one is yet to come up. We headed for IET Greens.[1] This company, that has entered the Agro-Industry business in a big way, has set up a very large farm, about 300 acres in area, near Dahijuri. However, when we began checking on the *Pattas* given to the Lodhas and whether they were in possession of the land, we found that IET Greens had occupied and then taken over the *Patta* land given to 25 beneficiaries, 19 of whom were Lodhas. *Pattas* were given to them between 1990 and 1993. I instructed the SDO to ensure that the land is returned to the Lodhas and that action is taken against IET Greens.

This morning a First Information Report (FIR) was filed against the company and the *Patta* holders were brought over to the site. Police arrangement too was made, and the Sub-divisional Land and Land Reforms Officer (SDL&LRO) and BL&LRO, with a complement of *amins*, had been demarcating the plot since early morning. Now they were waiting for us.

At about 3 p.m., on reaching IET Greens we found that demarcation of most plots had been completed and the possession of land had once again been given to most of the *Patta* holders. The land has been very well developed into large plots of pineapple, teak, papaya, mango, etc. A large pond about half an acre in area, excavated on land that belongs to the Lodhas, now belongs to three *Patta* holders. I spoke with the *Patta* holders, among them were two women. They told me that initially they had been given ₹1000 by IET Greens and had been told that they would be given work on the land. Most of them neither received any further amount of money nor any work. Today they got the possession of their land once again, but I could sense in them the fear of being turned out by the owners of IET Greens. Therefore, I got them together and spoke with them: this was their land, they must cultivate it and they had nothing to fear. If at any point of time, anyone tries to intimidate them or dispossess them once again they should immediately report the matter to the nearest official or directly to me. The assurance seemed to assuage their fears a little but this place would have to be monitored very closely.

I have asked the SDO to draw a comprehensive plan for the development of this area. The Lodha families in the other parts of the block, who are below poverty line (and how many are not?), can be allotted a house each on that plot of land. Irrigation facilities may also be created in the form of tanks or irrigation wells for their use. All this can be done through a variety of ongoing rural development programmes. I have asked them to dig a trench right along the boundary between their lands and the land owned by IET Greens. A separate entrance to their area also needs to be made through the wire fence that surrounds it. IET Greens is also in illegal occupation of at least 14 acres of vested land. This land should also be distributed to landless Lodhas and they can be settled in this area along with other communities. The SDO must hold a meeting with all the relevant officials in this regard and submit a plan by next week.

From Dahijuri we proceeded to Dalkati, which we reached at about 4.25 p.m. I wanted to see how the chickens distributed to Lodhas and other tribals on 4 November 2004 were doing. Yellow stickers proclaiming that the household has been provided with chickens under RSVY programme are stuck brightly on most of the houses. The first house I visited was that of Chotu Digar. She is about 55 and lives in a small broken hut. All her 10 chickens were doing well. She said that the feed provided had finished and now she is unable to feed them. I tried to gently explain to her that providing more chicken feed is not possible. In the neighbouring house one of Phatick Mullick's ten chickens died on the way on the day of distribution itself. The others were doing well.

Further on I checked the health card of Molly Mullick's son, Ujjawal Mullick, born on 19 May 2004. He has not received any of the shots except the first one (BCG). Of course, Pulse Polio has been administered. There is a great deal of excitement in the village over the chickens; it is also evident in the way they are taking care of the birds.

Construction of dug wells has been started by the villagers already. They apparently cut 1.5–2 ft of ground in this season when it is still soft and before the sun hardens the earth. Every week they will dig a little deeper until by March–April they reach an adequate depth. Every house here has a dug well. In one house a chicken fell into the well and from another house one was stolen.

Sukumar Mullick, a resident of Dalkati, is one of the receipients of a Medium Term loan. He resides in this village and organises the people here. All of the 152 families of Lodhas who reside in this village should be given poultry units. This has already been decided and should be implemented as early as possible. This must be one of the largest concentrations of Lodhas in a village.

Plate 17.1 Chickens safe under a mosquito net

A *Pranibandhu* had visited this village in the morning and vaccinated all the chickens. Bhutnath Datta requested me to see his chickens also as I was on the way out. We went to his home and in his small courtyard found his 10 chickens enjoying a pampered life under a baby's mosquito net!

Antyodaya Cards have been received by all the Lodha families. They have got 17.5 kg of rice but no wheat, which has been received in other blocks but not in this one. The family ration cards, according to them, have not yet been distributed to them. Putting up posters and announcing on microphones about the food security programme has not been done in this area either. I instructed the SDO to review both the programmes and report to me within three days. There is no alternative other than keeping at it.

Almost after a month of the raid I received a letter from the government. IET Greens Limited had complained to a senior minister that my action had been illegal and disruptive; I was asked for a clarificatory report. Although I took some time to respond to the direction, I presented a comprehensive report highlighting the facts. The company had been in illegal occupation of a large area of vested and Patta land in three mouzas. The encroachment of Patta land belonging to the members of the tribal community, including the Lodhas, had deprived them from cultivating and making use of the land allotted to them. Under my direction an FIR was lodged against IET Greens Limited at the local police station, and under the relevant provisions of the WBLR Act[2] the land was restored to the Patta holders belonging to the Lodha-Sabar community on 24 November 2004.

With some temerity I also pointed out that it had been the oft stated position of our Government that the landless poor should be given Pattas of ceiling surplus land for cultivation. However, Lodhas and other adivasis in north-western Paschim Medinipur had often received the patta in name alone. Furthermore, I emphasised, if the poorest of the poor of this area were to be assisted to stand on their own feet, the administration could not ignore the dispossession of their land by unscrupulous businessmen and so-called industrialists.

Probably my clarification was accepted because I heard no more from the government in this regard. Ironically, IET Greens Limited also filed a writ petition in the High Court, Kolkata. Although I expected to be made a respondent in this case, surprisingly IET Greens Limited chose not to drag me to the High Court.

◎

Notes

1. Name of the company has been changed.
2. Enacted in 1955, the West Bengal Land Reforms (WBLR) Act aimed to reform the laws pertaining to land in the wake of the abolition of estates in the State. It sought to initiate new forms of land use and their regulation, the vesting and distribution of ceiling surplus land, and for reframing land relations between the owners of land and sharecroppers.

A Village Vulnerability Index
◉

On 28 July 2004 I called to congratulate Mr B.N. Yugandher, who was the Director of the National Academy of Administration, Mussoorie, when I was under training, as he had recently been appointed Member of the Planning Commission of India. Bubbling as ever with enthusiasm Mr Yugandher chatted with me about Midnapore. He informed me how the last of the three British DMs of Midnapore to be assassinated had met his end at the hands of the revolutioneries while attending a football match; he, proceeded to ask me what I was doing in the field, and the main problem that I faced. I mentioned to him that one of the principal problems was prioritisation of sites for developmental activities, for, in a given district, poverty-stricken areas co-exist with well-off ones. After discussing the issue, he first suggested, then urged me to develop a tool for identifying vulnerable areas; it would help to prioritise among villages for decision-making at the Gram Panchayat level. I promised him to do whatever I could.

A month later, perhaps after a conversation with Mr Yugandher, Dr Suryakanta Mishra, the then Panchayat and Rural Development Minister of West Bengal, also called and asked me if I would try and devise a Village Vulnerability Index (VVI). The Panchayat Minister did not leave it at that. Every few weeks he kept calling to find out how the VVI was progressing. Although up to my gills in work, after conducting and compiling the results of the Baseline Survey, I began working on the VVI.

But what makes a village vulnerable? My first task, therefore, was to clarify the context and definition of the vulnerability of a village. Undoubtedly development administration was the context of the VVI. The stated priority of the Government of India (GoI) in this regard was: poverty alleviation to raise the overall standard of life of people. Consequently, rural development programmes have two main objectives: to improve the income generation potential of the rural population, and to enhance their quality of life through provision of a variety of public services. From these twin objectives flows our definition of village vulnerability: *it is a measure of (a) the extent of a village's susceptibility to hunger; and (b) the extent of the ability of a village to access public facilities for improving the quality of life.* In keeping with the definition, the objective of constructing a VVI was to identify the most vulnerable villages, in terms of susceptiblility to hunger and poorest access to public amenities.

In India, the need for developing a VVI has grown ever since its independence in 1947. Since 1960 not less than 12 committees, under the aegis of the Planning Commission of India, have attempted to identify the most backward regions and districts in the country. Almost all of them have focused upon the district as the unit of analysis. A few have tried to identify backward regions within states — which are also ultimately agglomeration of districts. These studies have utilised data from a variety of sources, primarily the national sample surveys. Yet census data has never been used as the basic data set for analysis of poverty or backwardness of an area.

Over the decades there has also been a steady attempt to decentralise and to channelise scarce developmental resources to population groups most in need of them. In 2001–2002 the GoI identified 150 most backward districts in the country on the basis of three criteria: Scheduled Tribe population, agricultural productivity and agricultural income. In 2002 a special development programme, the RSVY, was formulated to target additional untied funds at the rate of ₹15 crore per district for the most backward districts in the country.

The problem, however, lies at the sub-district level; for most of the identified backward districts are not uniformly backward — with centres of prosperity and pockets, large and small, of acute poverty. It was vital, therefore, that disaggregation in the quest for the most backward does not stop at the district level but reaches down to the lowest administrative unit — the village. Yet there was no system of identifying the most backward villages in these backward districts.

The urgency for developing a system for identifying the most backward villages for targeting development investment grew out not only from the historical evolution of development strategy and programmes in India, but also from the very nature of development programmes. Developmental programmes may be either re-distributive or distributive. Most re-distributive programmes, by their very nature, target the potential beneficiaries of these programmes. This occurs due to two reasons: one, because benefits of most re-distributive programmes can be disaggregated; and two, because the beneficiaries of re-distributive programmes are easily identifiable. A classic example is the distribution of ceiling surplus land.

Distributive policies, however, for the most part entail the distribution of goods and services that may not always be disaggregated, such as a new road. Since a majority of the goods provided under the distributive developmental programmes can not be disaggregated, we are faced with a problem of prioritisation among competing groups for these goods and services. Although over the years governments at the central and state levels in India have attempted to target the most needy population groups, these attempts have been inadequate because they do not take into account the intra-village disparities in needs at the sub-district level.

A VVI would enable the government to identify the villages that are in greatest need of distributive developmental programmes whose goods/benefits may or may not be disaggregated. Therein lay the utility and need for a VVI.

In the absence of any other comprehensive village level database, selection of indicators for the VVI was restricted to parameters available in the Census 2001 data sets for Pashim Medinipur district. The challenge was to identify those parameters that would most efficiently indicate the two dimensions of vulnerability identified.

On the basis of the Census 2001 I developed a data base. Initially, two sets of independent and dependent variables were distinguished. With the invaluable assistance of Motiur Rahman, the District Informatics Officer, I then generated frequency tables and plotted the results on charts to examine if the selected parameters were correlated, and, if so, to determine the nature and strength of the correlation. The emerging trends were examined, analysed and crosschecked before selecting the final set of indicators for the construction of the VVI. The selected parameters were assigned an internal range of scores, and also a weight based on certain criteria. The 7581 populated villages in Paschim Medinipur district were then assessed on the basis of the VVI and a score was awarded to each on a scale of one to 100; the greater the score the more vulnerable the village.

The Proof of the Pudding

The findings of the VVI were presented before the P&RD and Industries ministers, the Chief Secretary and several senior Secretaries to the Government of West Bengal on 8 December 2004 in Kolkata. After their endorsement I made a concerted attempt to persuade the three-tier local government bodies in Paschim Medinipur regarding the utility of the VVI.

Initially, a list of the most vulnerable villages in each developmental block, and a map based on the list, was provided to the heads of each Panchayat Samiti and the BDO, among others. They were first asked to visit the identified villages and verify the efficacy of the VVI. Once they were satisfied, 1424 of the most vulnerable villages were selected for targeting development investment, under the RSVY, the NFFWP, and other routine programmes.

By the end of the financial year 2004–2005, implementation of a variety of employment generation and asset development schemes — ranging from excavation of water harvesting structures to sericulture — had been taken up in each of the 1424 villages. On 31 March 2005, in anticipation of my departure from the district, and to put the facts transparently in the public domain, I held a press conference at the Collectorate. In the course of the well-attended press briefing I also released a compendium of schemes, with all relevant details, taken up for implementation in the 1424 most vulnerable villages in Paschim Medinipur.

I had hoped that this step would ensure that even after I had gone the schemes would be under public scrutiny. To the best of my knowledge, not a single reporter from either the print or the electronic media visited any of the schemes in the next few years.

By February 2005, with the help of Motiur Rahman, I had also applied the VVI to all 37,963 villages in the 18 districts of West Bengal and analysed the results for each district. But that is another story.

◎

PART III: FULL STEAM AHEAD

Undoubtedly ever since I joined the district, I had pursued the implementation of existing development schemes. Yet the focus was on the standardised schemes not emphasised by priorities. The experience of the previous months, churning of data and information, and interaction with people at all levels, made our task clear: to target development investments at specific groups inhabiting vulnerable villages, in the key areas of food security, physical infrastructure for basic public services, water harvesting for water security, livelihoods, and housing for the Lodhas. Of course there were points of convergence. For instance, excavation of a water harvesting *sech bundh* was a three-pronged effort aimed at food security, livelihood creation and ensuring of long-term water security in parched areas.

Since my time in the district was short, engaging the cooperation of various other departments, the three-tier Panchayat bodies, and people in the large number of identified vulnerable villages, our team moved full steam ahead. The following months were a period of frenetic touring, persistent persuasion, hands-on supervision, and issuing of directions — and at times of threats, to push for execution of schemes and initiatives in an area forgotten by the 'mainstream'.

18
No Roads Lead to Tamakbari
◎

On the night of 4 December a large group of armed LWEs descended upon the village of Kankrajhore in Binpur-II block. They picked out leaders of the CPM, beat them up, leaving three unconscious, and threatened the labourers working on the construction of a pacca road between the village and Odolchua with dire consequences if they stayed on. Then they poured diesel on a truck and an excavator used for the road project by the contractor and set them on fire. After making it plain that they did not want a macadamized road in these parts, they proceeded to the picturesque Kankrajhore Forest rest house situated at the base of a wooded hill facing the valley. Breaking open the doors, they systematically detonated explosives in it. When I set eyes upon it a few days later, it was beyond repair.

According to our VVI, Tamakbari village, with a score of 89.75, is ranked the 12th most vulnerable village in the district. According to Census 2001 it has a population of 88 persons of which 90 per cent belong to the Scheduled Tribes. At about noon, I first went to the Block Office with the SDO to pick up the SAE because the BDO was on leave and the SDO was not aware of the location of the village. Then we headed towards Tamakbari in Manidaha Gram Panchayat.

About 2 km past the Gram Panchayat headquarters, we turned right onto an earthen track. Along it, about 1.5 km from the state highway lies Rupsa village followed by Barhamchatti, which we passed on our way to Tamakbari. The 'road' to Tamakbari, along a stream, peters off at Barhamchatti. About half a kilometre further along, pushed by the village houses on to the border of a thin stream — locally called *khal* — the track narrows to a foot path. Tamakbari is on the other side of this *khal*, visible over empty fields a further kilometre away.

Over the shallow but flowing stream there is no culvert! To reach Tamakbari one has to jump across the water or wade through it. I hate to think of how, in the middle of a rainy night, a pregnant woman in need of emergency medical attention would make her way across the pathless paddy fields and this nonchalant stream. Why could the Panchayat not construct a culvert costing a few thousand rupees and a path with the SGRY funds?

Jumping across the canal we walked along the still wet *aals* of the recently harvested fields to reach the village. The undulating land slopes down from the forest about 1.5 km to the north. Along the way, I noticed stretches that had not been cultivated at all. As we approached the village we found it to be a cluster of huts occupying a gentle hump surrounded by trees; a 30-year-old eucalyptus towers above the habitation. Under the tree we met Sital Hansda, a resident of Tamakbari, who claims he is 65 years old. He informed us that 15 families live here, all Santals.

Pratima Majhi and Rikta Mondal are the two *sahayikas*, both from other villages, who are running the local SSK under a mango tree on the southern side of the village. A low mud house with a broken straw-and-bamboo roof is the southern most house in this *mouza*. The low open doorway revealed on the near floor a bent aluminium plate with the remnants of a just concluded meal. Taking advantage of the absence of occupants of the house, chickens hurriedly pecked away at the last grains of rice clinging to the plate.

Adar and Malati Murmu are the residents of this house. About three years back, their house, one half of which is still in ruins, was almost destroyed by a *kal-baishakhi*, thunder storm; they have not been able to rebuild it. I asked them how many chickens they kept. At this aspersion of wealth they laughed, and told me that all their chickens did not lay eggs, not many of the eggs hatched and of the hatched chickens not many survived because they were too poor to have them vaccinated. Adar Murmu has received a *Patta* for 0.82 acres of land from the government in another village, but he has built his house here, on his father-in-law's land — which, he reminded me, is not his land. The Murmus share the one tube well and a Mark-II hand pump set up about five years ago among these huts.

Turning to the SSK we found that the register showed a total of 49 children enrolled: 21 in class-I, 13 in class-II and 15 in class-III. Prasenjit and Ajoy Kisku, two brothers about 10 and 11 years old, were hanging around there. They go to Tamakbari Primary School in Sarengasol village, which can be seen about one and a half kilometres away to the east; the school meant for Tamakbari, that still carries its name, is located in another village! Apparently, there are several such schools which were meant to be located in one village but have actually been located in another — primarily because the village of choice is more populous, and has fewer tribals. I was told that another SSK is running in Rupsa *mouza*. Though a plot of land has been identified for the SSK in Tamakbari, and its owner is ready to donate it, but until now the Panchayat has not sanctioned funds for the construction of the building.

The villagers showed me the land, owned by Raghunath Hembram, which they had selected for the SSK. It lies mid-way between the first and the second *paras* of Tamakbari. In all, there are three *paras* — or habitations — in Tamakbari. The furthest, bordering the forest, is Nutanbasti; the one in the centre is Majhpara; and the one nearest to the strenuously approached road is Sitalpara.

As we were walking through Majhpara, in the fore-court of a house two children sat eating rice with cauliflower curry; no *dal*. Beside a hut, under an overhanging roof, illegal distillation was going on. I noticed two dug wells in Majhpara with rings, but without either parapet or platform. I saw many dogs here — there are many dogs in all three *paras*. Beyond Majhpara on the *aal* in the middle of the paddy fields, two teenage boys sat with a transistor radio with the wire antenna strung upon an erect bamboo stick. They were listening to (what else?) racy Hindi songs. We were walking through fields that had been ploughed after the paddy harvest. The farmers will sow wheat and mustard here, the main *rabi* crops to be harvested the following spring.

According to Sital Hansda, a resident of Majhpara, they were celebrating *Choto Makar* today. I asked him what did they do on *Choto Makar*. His reply was: everyone is happy, and they have liquor, chicken and pork. Festival days are days on which the poor try to forget that they are poor. But it is not easy, for as we had just seen, even on such occasions most of them have little more to eat than rice, a vegetable and salt.

We reached the *zamindari bundh* on the northernmost slope of the village. A very old *bundh* now swollen with silt, it still provides water for irrigation to the fields bordering the tank. A small brick and concrete check dam on the eastern side of the *bundh* holds the water over flowing through the outflow channel. It was built eight years ago in 1996 by the Gram Panchayat or the Panchayat Samiti. Occupying about 5 acres, the reservoir of the *sech bundh* itself is extensive. However, it needs to be re-excavated and deepened. Laying down field channels on both sides of the reservoir would also help the villagers make better use of the water. Situated right at the edge of the forest, the *bundh* receives the water from the catchment area higher up the slope, from the expanding green of the forest beyond.

Nutanbasti, the third habitation within this *mouza*, is located at the edge of the forest. Nutanbasti, which is almost half a kilometre away from the Mark-II hand pump, apparently lacks a reliable source of drinking water. It lies on the north-eastern extreme of the scattered *mouzas* that make up Tamakbari. An unprotected dug well is the lone source of water here.

The area around the *bundh* once belonged to a local *zamindar* — the Chatterjee family who stays in Midnapore. After land reforms were undertaken in the late 1970s and early 1980s it is now owned by the tribal population; they cultivate a second crop in a part of the land by using the water from this *sech bundh*. A new *sech bundh* can also be made near Nutanbasti, higher up the slope. It would be possible to link the new *bundh* with the old one.

I noticed that some mustard had been planted in Nutanbasti, while seedling were being prepared in small beds of paddy. Two streams flow through the undulating *ryoti* land. The villagers have directed the flow of water to their own fields by digging narrow channels; they hold the water for some time within the high *aals* of their fields. The second *khal* flows past Tamakbari on its eastern flank, carrying water from the Tamakbari *bundh*. A check dam can be built right near Majhpara, opposite Raghunath Hembram's house, so that some of the precious water that now flows away may be held for a few months to irrigate crops. We could ask the Forest Department to survey the area and submit a proposal for water conservation in this area.

Like the road, the TSC has also not yet reached Tamakbari. The Gram Panchayat members told me that they have taken it up in the village, but it is obvious that TSC has not been promoted here. I told the residents that unless the programme is implemented immediately and they build sanitary latrines for all the houses within December, we will not be able to make any *sech bundhs* that we had discussed with them in detail.

Women and children of Tamakbari are immunized at the SHC near the Gram Panchayat office. There is no AWC here; the nearest one being at Sarengasol which also has the primary school. I checked the health card of Sohagi Hembram's son, Sanjay Hembram, who was born on 25 October 2003. His mother is pregnant again and has received six of the eight shots she is supposed to. Chandni Hembram, daughter of Biren Hembram, is about 13–14 years old. She is afflicted by polio and is physically challenged. She needs some prosthetic aids because it is difficult for her to walk and even to go to school. A SHG has been formed here in Tamakbari but is inactive.

On our return trek, when we reached Sitalbasti we found the SSK reassembled; this time instead of the six there were 20 students, still short of the 49 students supposed to be present. However, there is no shortage of books in the SSK.

The local people told me that a number of villagers had left to work in the Sabong, Pingla area, which they described as *namal* — low-lying area. This annual migration is a common practice during the lean, post-*kharif* months in most of Paschim Medinipur. Adivasis leave their un-irrigated lateritic lands to earn a living in the low-lying fertile belt of the Gangetic Plain that is a part of this divided district. To the west, adjacent to Tamakbari, is Tiakata village, the next most vulnerable village in Medinipur Sadar block. It is ranked 56 in the overall vulnerability list. Some of its inhabitants have also gone to the *namal* in search of work.

We also inspected a potential site for a small check dam a little south of Ghentu Murmu's house. This is also a likely spot for holding a large body of water. We need such small dams down all the different streams in watersheds around the district.

I do not know whether Tamakbari deserves to be ranked as the twelfth-most vulnerable village in the district. Yet it is a vulnerable village because although only about 20 km away from the district headquarters it is a village with potential unutilised, a village neglected, a village which can do much better than it is doing at present. This long *mouza* populated by Santals lies between two *khals*, an archipelago of tribal habitations left to their fate. Its principal problems are communication and lack of irrigation facilities — or rather the lack of structured irrigation facilities — drinking water sources, education and healthcare. Our first step should be to build a culvert over the *khal* followed by a path or road to connect the village to the rest of the district.

◎

19

Some Tourist Spots

◎

Accompanied by the DFO, Midnapore (east division), I reached Chandra Forest Range Office at 11.00 a.m. The forest officers had selected this site for developing it into a tourist spot and today we were to inspect it. The Chandra site is just off the state highway from Midnapore to Lalgarh, on the edge of a *sal* forest. Venerable old *sal* trees encircle the spot, which, since it is only about 22 km from Midnapore, can attract townspeople and tourists alike. The idea was to create a water body in the nature of a *bundh* at the lower end of the slope. Yet I was disappointed to find that the forest officers had selected a spot high up on the slope for the water harvesting tank. After discussions, in which doubts about the viability of the spot were thrashed out, all of us agreed that this would not be the best spot for the tank. Walking down almost to the edge of the slope fringed by thick-girthed sal trees, we selected a spot for the water body. Further 25 m down the incline meets the road. I suggested to the DFO that he may consider developing the *dhalbundhs*, the water harvesting structures being created under RSVY at the edge of forest at several places, as tourist spots. FPCs or SHGs active in the area could also be involved. We had sanctioned one scheme at Tamakbari, which I had visited the day before, and that could be a likely location.

Next we went to Dadhrasole village where near a large cluster of adivasi huts, an orchard plantation has been developed in an area of four hectares, under the RSVY. There are 280 guava plants, a like number of lemon plants, 150 mango, 280 *chiku* and 150 pomegranate trees planted here. The FPC in the village is responsible for its maintenance and they are using the drip irrigation method — with a local twist. A covered earthen pot with a hole on one side, through which water drips gently via a piece of cloth to the root of the plant, is buried in the ground up to its neck. Once a week, the vessel is replenished.

From Chandra we proceeded to inspect the site of the Eco-Tourism Centre to be funded under RSVY. This spot is located near Gurguripal village, about a kilometre from the main road. A series of reservoirs were created by the construction of earthen dams across the watershed under the Kangsabati Watershed Catchment Area Development Project several years ago. The project has ended but there are no funds available for the development of the area and the reservoirs created under it. FPCs located in the villages along the watershed could contribute to the enhancement of tourist attraction and benefit from it.

The main reservoir is quite an ideal location for development of an Eco-Tourism Centre. A large kidney-shaped water body, green and placid, lies at the centre; a spill-way at the lower end carries the overflow to the next water harvesting structure lower down the incline and so on. Our aim is to create basic infrastructure such as footpaths, toilets, drinking water facilities, some picnic canopies, an Eco-Interpretation Centre, and a deer park. Some child-friendly features such as slides, see-saws, etc., would also add to its charms. Such amenities would ensure that people come here and enjoy themselves without straining the forest. A plan drawn up by the DFO, Rupnarayan Division, had been submitted, to which I recommended a modification. Instead of locating the deep tube well which they propose to set up at the entry point, which is about 300 m from the edge of the reservoir, I have suggested that it should be located on the other, the higher, side of the lake so that expenses on the pipeline may be reduced and the water tower may also be used as an observation post for bird watchers. Since the sal forest all around is dense and has regenerated luxuriantly, a number of jungle trails could also be developed.

Overall, from the points of both infrastructure development and sustained employment, this is a site where investment would be worthwhile.

◎

20

The Bleakest Village

◎

Today a meeting was scheduled at 2.00 p.m. at the SDO's office regarding the activities of LAMPS. Since the *kendu patta* collecting season is around the corner, the items on the agenda would focus on the activities of LAMPS and the role they may play in supporting the local population. However, I first intended to visit two of the most vulnerable villages in the district — Junglekhas and Dainamari — both in Jhargram block itself.

A few kilometres before Jhargram town, near Sabitri Mandir, from the state highway we turned right onto a *morrum* road being repaired under the SGRY programme. Going by the manner of the repairs, the results are likely to be sub-optimal. We stopped to have a closer look. The workers were either merely spreading the *morrum* over the pot holes, or first shovelling stone chips into the gaps and untidily covering them with the red lateritic gravel. If the sides of the road are not strengthened with boulders and earth, this patchwork of *morrum* is unlikely to last through the next monsoon.

For a while the road winds through the sal forest and emerges into open land on the right with the sal trees accompanying us on the left. A number of small villages are scattered in this forested area.

Junglekhas includes, in sum, six families living in six houses dotting a length of road. Beyond the houses extends the hard, un-irrigated, and currently uncultivated land fringing a scruffy forest. Kalachand Mandi and his wife, the occupants of one of the houses, have just been blessed with a son. I checked the infant's health card. The child, named Laxman after the hero of the epic Ramayana, has received only one BCG shot until now. For immunization, people of Junglekhas must travel to Nalbana where the health centre is located, or to Chanpasole where an outreach centre is held in a primary school. Although the outreach camps are meant to be held every week or every fortnight, according to Kalachand Mandi, this outreach centre is held once in a month or two months!

Kalachand had recently received 10 four-week-old chickens under the animal husbandry scheme of RSVY; while half have perished, the other five are thriving. Bharat Murmu, an older neighbour had also

Plate 20.1 A typical village well in Junglemahals

been given 10 chickens of which nine have died — four or five of them died the day they were received. Evidently, the poultry birds given here have not been vaccinated! This should be taken up with the BLDO immediately; the surviving birds must be vaccinated and the dead ones replaced.

Four of the huts are built around a small mud-plastered court-yard. A modest heap of recently harvested paddy lay in one corner of the courtyard, and sal leaves were carelessly spread about to dry. Junglekhas village is surrounded by forest and people here are principally dependent on either the forest or the distillation and brewing of illicit liquor, which finds a ready market at the nearby Banstala Railway Station.

Across the road from Junglekhas is Jambeda, a much larger village. There is an AWC here, but women from nearby houses told me that the Anganwadi worker and the helper come here for only an hour or so. According to them, there are about 50 children enrolled in the centre but the stock of food has already been exhausted. CDPO, Jhargram, should be asked to look into this matter; this is a clear case of neglect. With no building or even a shed to house it, the Anganwadi is held under a tree; both the helper and the Anganwadi worker commute from other villages.

Even a cursory glance across the beaten path indicates that the people of Jambeda are probably better off than Jungelkhas. A couple of *pacca* houses can be seen through the trees; a motorcycle stands in one fore-court, while in another courtyard a new Hero Honda two-wheeler without a number plate is displayed — to evoke admiration or, perhaps, jealousy.

In Junglekhas, on this side of the earthen track, there is a well with a broken platform and a fractured parapet. It supplies most of the drinking water to people in the habitation, including, Raghab Mandi, an old man whose name has been enlisted as a prospective old age pensioner. I try to prod his memory. When he was a child there were three families in Junglekhas; now the number is grown to six. Raghab Mandi's house was destroyed by elephants about two years back. He still has not been able to completely rebuild it. The villagers here are Santals and own no land because they are living at the edge of the forest — actually, within its perimeter. The little land they do possess is at a distance in Chanpasole and is *danga* in character. Behind the house that Raghab Mandi has now built,

I found lovingly tended rose bushes and marigold plants in full bloom. I asked him whether he sold the flowers, and he answered no, the children had planted them on their own because flowers are beautiful. But his house is made of mud with a straw and bamboo roof.

Haren Soren is the owner of the fourth house. He had received 10 chickens out of which two got lost. In contrast to Jambeda the piles of recently harvested paddy are much smaller in Junglekhas. Yellow stickers marking out the recipients of RSVY chickens are pasted on the doors of these houses.

A widow, Ramani Soren, lives in the sixth house in Junglekhas. She also received 10 chickens out of which one has 'disappeared'. The chickens have grown rapidly into hens and she is happy to look after them. Ramani Soren's house is well constructed and well maintained. In the backyard there is a kitchen garden in which some radishes and creepers such as beans have been planted. Soren has also planted some cashewnut trees, which are about two years old. But there is no source of water for either the kitchen garden or the stunted cashewnut tress.

Jambeda has an SSK, where most of the children receive primary education, but no primary school. The primary school is located about 2.5 km away at Chanpasole, where the ration shop is also located. An old lady, Manu Mahato, with a grandchild on her hips tells me that the infant has received only one immunization shot. Six families and 28 people comprise the total population of Junglekhas. Perforce, they are dependent on forest or on illicit distillation of liquor for their livelihood. The main problem here seems to be of water for drinking and for irrigation: the lone well with a broken platform and parapet is the only source. The outreach services are not functioning properly. The BLDO has not yet sent anyone to vaccinate the chickens — another indicator of the malady of neglect. Although in terms of remoteness Junglekhas is not poor; it is only about 10 km from the main road, the railway station is about 2 km away, and the relatively better off Jambeda right opposite. That is why the condition of the people of Junglekhas village is not worse than what we find them in.

We proceeded towards Dainamari, one of the most vulnerable villages in the district, and, as it turned out later, in the state.

On the way to Dainamari we crossed a stream by driving through its shallow bed. During the monsoon months the engorged stream cuts off Dainamari from the main road and Jhargram. We stopped and examined the place. I think it may be a sound location for a check dam that could be built of locally available boulders; this would provide a reservoir for irrigation and also serve as a bridge, at least for people on foot. We then passed through the village of Naniakunti where a Gram Panchayat member's house displayed the posters on Food Security Schemes that we had disseminated.

One of the heartening features of the villages here is that most of them have football grounds. Football is very popular in these areas and should be encouraged.

In Dainamari, at about noon an SSK class was being held under the open sky next to a tall Mahua tree. Raghunath Mahato is the SSK *sahayak* here, a physically challenged person who seems to be serious about his work. He informed us that the children on their own are not interested in attending classes; their parents also are indifferent to their education. Therefore, on some days Mahato has to go from house to house to call them to school. The SSK is located at a central point between Dainamari, Kalsibhanga and Nutandihi.

Dainamari is a fully Lodha populated village.

Bhairabnath Bhakta and Jaleswari Bhakta have just been blessed with a granddaughter who is only 17 days old. They call her Jyotsna and her proud grandmother carries her in her arms. They live in a small hut, made of mud and straw, and draw drinking water from a dug well. A heap of paddy straw crowds a corner of their small courtyard; the sum total of their harvest, it is an embarrassed pointer to the size of the area they cultivate. As we walked out of her courtyard I realised that all the children had left the SSK and followed us into the village. Jaleswari Bhakta scolded the boys, who had come there to gawk at the vehicles 'as if they have never seen one before'. Perhaps out of context (and maybe not) she tells us that elephants often visit Dainamari. Despite her poverty and the bleakness of her circumstances, providentially, Jaleswari Bhakta's self-respect is intact.

In front of the doorway of a neighbouring hut an old woman, Bimala Mallick, is laying out portions of sal *dhuna* or resin on tiny, beautifully folded sal leaf bowls which she will sell for one rupee each. She goes to a nearby village to sell her ware. Bimala Mallick told me that as she cannot work very hard she only collects the *dhuna* from the forest. Her late husband, Mohan Mallick, had owned no land; since his death several years ago, she does her best to make a living from the forest.

Chickens had been provided under RSVY to all the families in this village on priority but most of them have died because they had not been vaccinated. Nevertheless, some goats, which were also distributed, can be seen. Dug wells are the only source of drinking water here but none of them are properly built. Most are but rudely dug cavities in the rocky ground. Some dug wells have rings but no parapet or platform. These should be disinfected immediately; under the new scheme they also need to be firmed up and protected.

The villagers told me that some years ago the Forest Department had built a water harvesting structure at the edge of the forest below which lies land owned by the Lodhas. We went to have a look at the long tank formed by a check dam beyond the huts. At this time of the year it has shrunk to a tiny pool in the deepest part. Hence, in this season the inhabitants of Dainamari use the *pukur* only for bathing. If this tank is expanded by extending the check dam, the increased capacity may enable it to provide some water for irrigation, at least during the dry late *kharif* season. Or maybe not? Actually a series of surface water harvesting structures need to be constructed at points down the slope to hold the rainwater.

There is a lot of open land around the habitation but hardly a fraction of it is under cultivation. Here also the main difficulty is irrigation; another problem is ownership of land, which is mostly *khas* or vested. *Pattas* could be given to the Lodhas, for whom work is limited to manual labour, because most people have very little land and only the forest to depend upon. Yet the inhabitants have tried to develop a kitchen garden around each house.

Dainamari village is an example of what has happened to the Lodhas. They have been brought out of the jungle and have settled on the worst possible land available. Few natural resources, either water or land, are available to them; perforce, they depend on the forest and their labour to eke out their livelihood. The wells in Dainamari, at least two of them, could be made *pacca* and a platform and parapet could also provided.

◎

21

Urban is Rural

◎

In Ghatal sub-division there are five 'rural municipalities' — an oxymoron if ever there was one!

The purpose of the tour to Ghatal Municipality, with some public representatives, was to visit a few important sites where development schemes are to be taken up. The town itself appears to be a part of a rural landscape. Our first stop was to be ward no. 7 located on the bank of the Jugni River that flows into the Damodor. As we drove through Ghatal town, a very old municipality, I noticed that most of the houses were double-storeyed; many of them built on pillars or on raised platforms because of the annual ritual of floods. Normally, even within the town, flood waters rise up to 8 or 10 ft. Out of 17 wards only three, situated on relatively higher ground, escape submergence. A host of muddy water bodies in and around the town provide water for bathing, washing and cooking utensils for the people living nearby. As a result, the number of outbreaks of diarrhoea and dysentery in Ghatal sub-division is the highest in the district.

As we left town (only later did I realise that we had actually been within a town all the while) we found that in the fields on both sides of the raised *morrum* road, a crop of mustard was almost ready for harvesting. Fields were being prepared for the *boro* paddy crop in the short spring that comes treading on the heels of an all too brief winter. For *boro* paddy cultivation, construction of *boro bundhs*, temporary dams for irrigating the second paddy crop after winter, is taken up on different rivers and water channels throughout the sub-division. Thirty *boro bundhs* are built every year on rivers, streams and canals. Consequently, in this sub-division most of the SGRY fund is spent on *boro bundhs*.

We stopped to take a look at Hingopur Tiapara Primary School. Nandalal Majhi, the head teacher, was supervising all the classes.

Another teacher, Kumar Maity, was on leave and the third, Prashun Chandra Mondal, was yet to arrive. There are 109 students enrolled in Classes I to IV in this school, which has 50 children in the 'infant category'. This was something new that I came across, but appears to be quite a common feature in many primary schools in Ghatal — primary schools also serve as crèches for the local labourers' children. Although there is an Anganwadi nearby, people take their children there in the morning for the meal, and then bring them over to this school. The primary school perches right on the banks of the Jugni River, on the arc of a meander. Each year, nibbling at the banks, the Jugni creeps closer, thus, threatening to eventually devour the school building. This is the primary concern of the people here and I was called to find a solution for it — I do not think anyone has yet found a quick, low cost solution to a meandering river.

Hingopur is in ward no. 7 of Ghatal Municipality; it wears the appearance more of a dishevelled village than a municipal ward. Most of the houses here are built of packed mud and asbestos or GI sheets. They are all built on platforms of packed earth or of sacks filled with sand or clay. Hand pumps are the main source of drinking water. We walked some distance on the river bank to the place where, in the last monsoon, the river had sliced away a portion of the bank and taken a few houses with it.

The problem of embankment erosion has to be referred to the Irrigation Department, which may be asked to draw a scheme for protecting it. I am not sure how feasible such a scheme would be or where the funds may come from.

I was fascinated by the sight of a number of boats floating on the river, with mechanised diesel pumps fitted on board. A local innovation, these are mobile lift irrigation schemes. In this area, criss-crossed by several serpentine streams and canals, the rowboats fitted with pumping machines are widely used. There are about 150–200 boats in a stretch of about 3 km along this river. During the monsoons these boats, about 20 ft long, are vital for communication; and during *rabi* and *boro* months, for instance now, they are used as mobile lift irrigation units. The machines are rented out at ₹50 per hour inclusive of diesel. Quite a number of people are engaged in running them. I think this irrigation scheme can be made a part of the Special Component Plan (SCP) or Tribal Sub-Plan (TSP) scheme.[1] They could provide employment to many youth. Large number of manual paddy threshing machines are also being used in this area. They are rented out at ₹100 a day. Sometimes the rent also depends upon the amount of paddy to be threshed. Tarpaulins, supplied during the earlier floods, are now being used to dry threshed paddy.

All roads here are raised; they are about 7 or 8 ft above the ground level. Driving along the bank of the river to the site of a *boro bundh*, built on the Jhumi River, we reached the almost completed *bundh*. Situated in Mansukha-I Gram Panchayat, it is about 60 m long and will cost ₹310,000 to build. Three *boro bundhs* will divide the Jhumi River into a series of reservoirs for the coming season. There is one at Balrampur about 2.5 km downstream from this point. During May, before the monsoon commences, the *boro bundhs* have to be slashed through the centre so that flood waters do not wreak havoc on the banks; once the waters rise, the raised sides of the *bundh* get washed away in any case. Right next to the *bundh* under a *bargad* tree is a lift irrigation machine that draws water from this section of the river and supplies it to about 50–60 acres of land on the other side of the river bank.

A *boro bundh* is constructed almost entirely of sand and sandy-earth taken from the side of the river. The face of the *bundh* is firmed up with thick rolls of straw tied together and then nailed into the *bundh* with bamboo staves. These rolls of straw form the front of the *boro bundh* and rise from the bottom in step-like layers, each successive layer protecting the earth packed behind it. The Mansukha *bundh* will be 17 ft high and 90 ft wide. To stabilise the dam, thick rolls of woven straw are laid at different depths of the bundh. along the length of the compacted earth; 50–60 people have been employed in its construction.

Fields on the banks of the river are rich with potato plants and other seasonal vegetables including mustard, which is flowering. According to the panchayat functionaries, hundreds of acres would be irrigated by the three *boro bundhs* on the Jhumi River. About 15–18 ft above the water, bridges made entirely of bamboo connect the two banks at intervals along the river.

Our team also visited the site of a market complex being established under the 10th Finance Commission scheme.[2] It has three large sheds in the centre with small shops on three and a half sides and a toilet unit. Strangely, however, there is no provision for even a rudimentary drainage system.

Sultanpur village in Sultanpur Gram Panchayat was our next destination, where we were to inspect the site of a canal excavation scheme that had been submitted under the NFFWP. On the way we drove through a number of villages. The difference between the Junglemahal and these villages becomes evident if one takes note of the large number of *pacca* buildings that have come up in this area; in Jhargram *pacca* structures are a rarity, while here they are the norm. Other than the *pacca* buildings there are houses made of packed mud on bamboo frame. A *morrum* road to Sultanpur, that perhaps had a black top once, joins the state highway at Palpukur in Kharar rural municipality. These rural municipalities have neither drains nor paved roads nor public lighting. For all practical purposes they suffer the same disadvantages as villages.

Both sides of the state highway are thickly planted with acacia and eucalyptus. A number of deep and shallow tube wells dot this alluvial plain — bare after the paddy harvest. Yet the fields are already being prepared for the *boro* crop. The old deep tube wells are still being run by the Agri-Mechanical Division, but the newer ones, which have come up in the last three to four years, are being handed over to beneficiary committees who have the responsibility of maintaining them. Only such an arrangement is sustainable.

According to the local people, the *khal* at Sultanpur is about 3 km in length and almost encircles the *mouza*. However, it is choked with silt. The local people are of the view that it should be re-excavated so that it can store the flood water for use during the *boro* season. I think it would be well worth taking up under the NFFWP. They have submitted a plan and an estimate of about ₹9 lakh. This can be sanctioned in the next allotment. About 150–200 small and marginal farmers who own land on both sides of the *khal* would stand to gain — most of them belong to the Scheduled Castes.

As we turned to go back, I found about 10–12 children collected around the parked vehicles. I asked them whether the school was open, they said yes; that they were not present in class was obvious. This has become a problem. Children may be enrolled in a school but they are not attending it regularly and the parents do not seem to mind it.

This part of the district has a large number of livestock — cattle as well as goats. Cattle dung in various forms is being used as fuel. It is patted into *gunthe,* dung cakes, or just shaped into lumps that are dried and used in the earthen cooking stoves. That Ghatal is a large producer of milk and milk products, was underscored by the number of people seen carrying milk in large aluminium cans, either on both sides of a bicycle or on their shoulders, to the collection points. Over the years, dairying has grown steadily in Ghatal sub-division.

The Krishi Karmadhyakshya told me that there are certain low-lying areas in Ghatal sub-division that remain fallow not only during the *kharif* season when they are under water, but also during the *boro* season, because there is no source of irrigation in these areas. A plan needs to be prepared for utilising these areas also.

At the block office, I reviewed the estimate of the scheme that we had just visited — the deepening of Sultanpur–Garkhai *khal*. According to the estimate 4 km of the canal bed is proposed to be excavated till a depth of 35 cm, a little more than one foot! This is an absurd proposal which appears to have escaped close scrutiny by the BDO, the Sabhapati and the Purto Sthayee Samiti — the Standing Committee on Public Works of the Panchayat Samiti. Such a scheme can only lead to wastage of funds. The proposed depth of the excavation is much too small for it to make a difference even in the short-term. I requested them to recast the scheme by reducing the length of the area to be excavated while increasing the depth so that it may actually be used for storage of water. After discussion it was decided to excavate the canal only in two sections of 500 m each. Each section should be about 4–6 ft deep so that the water may be retained in the resultant tank and used during the *boro* season. Since there are a number of such canals which dry out after the monsoon, we may think of drawing a plan for creating similar water retention structures in these canals. Such 'water retention structures' would be the appropriate form of water harvesting in areas with heavy rainfall and water logging, but with canals that drain the water out of the area soon after the monsoon.

Bheri Balaram Kundu, as it reads in the land records, is the name of a village comprising all three houses situated on the *bundh* of a *bheri*, a large tank. This was a *zamindari bundh* and people have settled down here in the last 8–10 years. This minuscule habitation has been identified as one of the two most vulnerable villages in Ghatal block.

Kalipada Samanta is one of the house holders; he and his family live in this tiny village less than 500 m from the state highway. Kalipada works as a daily wage labourer. Swapan Dolui and Ram Samanta are the other two heads of families in the habitation. The latter is the son-in-law of Kalipada Samanta, and he has just constructed a house of bamboo and packed mud with concrete pillars and an asbestos roof. Swapan Dolui works in a *bhusir dokan*, a cattle-feed shop, in Ghatal. Barely 20 ft wide, the *bundh* is formed of a high heap of mud. Kalipada Samanta's house is on top of the *bundh*,which widens to about 30–35 ft before narrowing again in the place where Swapan Dolui's house stands. Kalipada Samanta has planted chillies, tomatoes and radishes in his homestead. He built his house about eight years ago; in 1996.

Swapan Dolui built his house about three and a half years ago. Like other houses of the poor in this area, it is made of bamboo plastered with mud. During the monsoon, when the flood waters inexorably rise, families move on to the higher ground next to the road and near the bridge — sometimes for 15 days, sometimes for a month or even longer. The source of drinking water for the families here is a hand pump near the Kali temple about 300 m away, and the children go to primary school just on the other side of the road. The village is right on the outskirts of Ghatal town. Water of a narrow canal next to the embankment is used for cooking and other purposes!

I took a photograph of Kalipada Samanta. After taking the picture, as we were leaving, I heard his wife, who may have been jealous, tease him, '*Byas. Buroke dhare niya jabe!*' (That's it. Now they are going to arrest the old man!) — a reflection of the popular image they have of their government?

◎

Notes

1. The SCP for Scheduled Castes and TSP for Scheduled Tribes are two strategies formulated by the Government of India and implemented by the State Governments for delivering special development schemes to members of the Scheduled Castes and Scheduled Tribes. The aim is also to ensure that benefits from the general sector of the Annual and the Five Year Plans reach Scheduled Castes and Tribes at least proportionately.

2. 10th Finance Commission refers to the 10th set of recommendations of the West Bengal State Finance Commission, set up under the Article 243 Sec I of the Indian Constitution. The State Finance Commission is mandated to make recommendations on a periodic basis of devolution of funds to Panchayat bodies in the State for developmental purposes and for their improved financial functioning.

22
Revisiting Fundamentals
◎

Paschim Medinipur was one of the districts selected for implementation of the NFFWP from the year 2004–2005 onwards. To this end we received an allotment of ₹2 crore and of 2481 metric tonnes of rice. Having discussed the programme with the Sabhadhipati and Karmadhyakshya of Paschim Medinipur Zilla Parishad, the BDOs and Sabhapatis sanctioned 91 schemes in 14 blocks under this programme. Work in most of the schemes had either begun or was about to begin. One scheme — the re-excavation of Kumarbundh sech bundh, Binpur-I block — was nearing completion. Nevertheless, certain problems confronted the implementation of the programme.

The most immediate problem that may prove to be the Achilles heel of this programme was a shortage in supply of food grains. Paschim Medinipur district had not received a single kilogramme of rice under the NFFWP from the FCI. Therefore, we had to make the allotment for these schemes solely on the basis of the funds received, that is, only cash but no grains could be paid as wages. Since one of the aims of NFFWP is to ensure food security among the poorest farmers and landless labourers in the lean seasons of the year, the unavailability of rice for the programme threatened to defeat its purpose.

Another major problem likely to arise was due to the partial release of funds made until now. December, January and February are the months when most agricultural workers do not have employment in the un-irrigated areas of this district. This is the period when this programme could offer maximum benefit to the target group. However, unless the rest of the funds were released immediately the working season would pass in vain. Waiting for the the Panchayat bodies and concerned government agencies to utilise 50 per cent of the funds and then releasing the remaining funds could cause fatal delay and prove counterproductive. The chief reason for this was that excavation or re-excavation of water harvesting structures, which was our main thrust under NFFWP, was not a scheme that could be completed quickly; those starting in December 2005 or January 2006 were likely to extend well into February. Submission of

*Utilisation Certificates, a mandatory stipulation for further release of
funds, in late February may, therefore, be too late. However, if we could
receive most of the funds now we may be in a position to start and finish
a large number of schemes spread across the district before the end of
March 2005. This, I informed the Government.*

After attending the platinum jubilee function of Lalgarh Ramkrishna
School and making the obligatory speech, I left for Routara village
to review the ongoing RSVY programme. Four water harvesting
tanks under construction there are at various stages of completion.
I wanted to see if the progress was as per schedule. In these parts
there is hardly any *kharif* cultivation and the lean period for the
landless labourers has commenced; provision of employment during
this period is the main objective of the RSVY and the NFFWPs.

The first water harvesting tank that we visited in Routara is on
the outskirts of the village. Excavation of the tank was over and it
was satisfying to see water collecting into it — dark and muddy,
but water nonetheless. According to Bakul Hembram, who owns
land nearby, the brown pool created by the seepage is already
about three to 4 ft deep in the new community reservoir, which
is about 60 m long and 20 m wide. The sides of the tanks have

Plate 22.1 Routara village tank

been paved with boulders and patched with dried-up grass, which prompted by the rains will re-appear as a green buffer against erosion. At the far end a channel leading out of the tank has also been dug for the release, and also for storage of excess water. On the side, where we stood on the yet unmarked red banks under a palm tree, a pipe with a large diameter has been fitted connecting the tank to the fields — at present lying barren and bare. With the help of a shallow tube, pump water will be pumped out to irrigate these fields. Villagers here plan to use such pumps to draw out the water from these water harvesting structures. In the plots adjacent to the tank, farmers have already begun to prepare the ground for *boro* crop, paddy variety number 136. As per the guidelines, the Minor Irrigation Department has also set up a brick and concrete signpost announcing that the scheme was undertaken under RSVY. I am glad I had turned down, insisting that we could all do with less ceremony, a cautious proposal to inaugurate such water harvesting structures. Besides, how does one inaugurate a water tank?

The second tank is located about 150 m from the first one; since the water levels had come down, there was very little water in it. This tank is located on the slope just below the forest on the land that stretches gently downwards to the thirsty fields. There is a gully on one side that carries water from the forest down to these parts; rainwater, otherwise dispersed and wasted across the incline, will now flow into the tank through the passage leading into its western side.

Jogeswar Hembram and Pradhan Hembram were working on the land on which the tank has been excavated. The land belongs to Bakul Hembram's father; they also plan to take up seasonal fishery in it. The sides of the water harvesting structure also have been well constructed and its consolidation with boulders is underway to protect the channel and the banks. Bakul Hembram told me that the yield this year had been good and now they were preparing for the *boro* crop. Small plots were being prepared to raise paddy seedlings. I asked them why they did not grow *moong*, a pulse; his reply — seeds are not easily available. There is a scope for extension work as well as for the introduction of pulses and oil seeds in these parts. The RSVY board has been defaced at this completed tank, apparently by children. The Minor Irrigation engineers will have to be asked to make the lettering on the plates with cement. Otherwise, even when the tank is full of water some visiting central government team may question its existence!

After circumambulating the second tank we walked through the sal forest towards the third tank located at the other end of the village. Nearby, strung up high on a tree was a painted tin billboard that drew attention to 'Samadhan Coaching Centre, English Medium-er sakal bishayer Class-I to X CBSE, ICSC (F) coaching-er babyastha ache. Echhara-o bangla medium-er sakal bishay etc', (Also other than this all subjects in Bengali-medium).

Late one afternoon in 1990, when I was an assistant magistrate undergoing district training in North 24 Parganas, while wandering around in a village in Amdanga block, I had stopped by the hut of a part-time van-rickshaw puller, a landless labourer. As we chatted, and I sipped the freshly plucked green coconut his wife had pressed upon me in a gesture of hospitality ubiquitous in rural Bengal, I had noticed in the corner of the courtyard a child sitting on a frayed mat apparently being taught by a youth. I learnt that my host, the part-time van-rickshaw puller, had engaged a tutor, a high-school student, for his eight-year old son who attended the local primary school, for a sum of ₹15 a month! On catching sight of this advertisement in forested Routara I felt the same astonishment that had jarred me 16 years ago. For improving their lot the poor recognise the value of education as much as the well-off, but their options are much fewer. Our school system is unequal to their expectations. Therefore, private tuitions have become common even in the remoter parts of Jhargram and other tribal areas.

In her forecourt we came across Panmani Hembram, certainly over 65 years old, sewing together sal leaves into plates. These sal plates will fetch ₹50 for 10 bundles, a 100 plates comprising a bundle. In this season, when trees shed their leaves, there is a shortage of sal leaves so the price has gone up; normally it hovers around ₹30–₹35 per bundle. The older women can manage to stitch together only about 300 plates in a day, the younger ones up to 500.

There is a well with a broken parapet and broken platform near Panmani Hembram's house. The well was constructed in 1975 and has not been repaired since. This should be taken up for repairs under the special housing scheme that we are preparing. It provides water to most of the families in this area.

In their courtyards husbands and wives were threshing paddy on the pedal-worked paddy threshing machines. Newly-threshed paddy was drying on the mud-plastered ground. A housewife holding a little baby gently paced up and down, turning over the golden grain with her bare feet to let the sun do its job well.

The third tank on our list is on plot number 147, which belongs to one Sudip Dasgupta. The entry point of water from the jungle is on the southern side of the tank, which is about 50 m long and 25 m wide. This tank too was almost complete; just the dressing of one of the sides remained. To ensure retention of water, polythene sheets have been laid at the bottom of the tank; some people complained that the polythene liner was too thin. An outlet has been created by inserting a concrete pipe in the north-eastern corner of the tank. The pipe is right at the top edge of the tank and I wanted to know why this had been done. I was told that if it was lower the water would flow out early in the rainy season. According to them the depth of the tank is about 12 ft and they expected it to be full to the brim after the rains. We visited the end where the outlet has been located; the depth here is 15 ft while at the other side, on the higher end of the slope, the tank is 12 ft deep. Some fields in the command area are green with potato crop, but a large area is still unoccupied. Most of the land here belongs to the tribals. Narrow, shallow channels need to be cut across the command area to carry the water to fields further away; prefabricated field channels could be used here extensively.

Before leaving Routara, I dropped by at the primary school to see if there had been any change since my last visit on 4 October 2004. Cooked Midday Meal is being served since the last two months at the Purnapani Primary School, which is right next to the Routara village. The supply of raw materials in primary schools has now been stabilised.

The road that takes us from Routara to Tarkilata is in a jarring condition; the topmost layer of gravel has disappeared in most sections and large pot holes mark its course. We reached Tarkilata at 1.50 p.m. In this village also, a number of water harvesting structures have been taken up for excavation under RSVY. The tank in Lodhapara of Tarkilata village is also nearing completion. About 25 persons are engaged here; most of them have just left after their day's work. The job worker for this scheme told me here that they would take seven more days to complete the work; certainly by *Makarsankranti*, 14 January, the work should be done. That would be another reason to celebrate.

There is a SHC in Tarkilata village manned by one male health assistant. It is housed in an earthen and GI sheet hut; not bad, considering the number of SHCs that do not have any building at all!

Electric poles have come up since my last visit and electric lines have also been strung. Villagers are waiting for the day when electricity will course through these wires. Hopefully, that will not take very long.

On the way back near the Jhitka SHC we stopped to visit Bhumijdahasole village. Chickens under RSVY were distributed here on 28 November 2004, and I wanted to see how they were doing and how they were being kept. The first person we came across was Snehalata Sabar, around 60 years of age, who was sitting on a *khat* next to her home. Across the *khat* and over its sides was draped a *mashari* (mosquito net) provided by the H&FW Department under the malaria prevention scheme. In this improvised coop under her *khat*, within the safety of the mosquito net, the chickens seem to be thriving. Instead of using the mosquito net herself Snehlata Sabar was using it to secure her chickens!

Under the RSVY agriculture scheme 20 persons in Bhumijdahasole have been given 10 kg of wheat seeds each. The BDO here has provided two Lodha families with shallow tube well pump sets and holes have also been bored in the ground. It is hoped that farming will provide them a worthwhile engagement. Nebu Sabar's house is, at best, a huddle of bamboo and palm fronds. None of the walls is complete. I noted a number of Lodha houses that can be replaced under the proposed housing scheme.

Thakurdas Sabar is weaving a basket from strips of what looks like cane but is not. Flourishing wild in the forest, it is the stem of a creeper called '*atang*'; basket weavers like Thakurdas Sabar collect it from the jungle from time to time around the year to weave their wares. Thakurdas makes about 10–12 baskets in a day and each sells for ₹12. The baskets come in two sizes; the one he is weaving now is of a smaller size with a diameter of about 3 ft, while the larger ones are 4 ft across and cost about ₹15 each.

Jhitka is just a kilometre away and, apart from the SHC there, it also has an ICDS centre and a Tribal Welfare Centre has also been constructed here. Two shallow tube wells that have been set up in Jhitka, used also as hand pumps, provide both drinking water and water for irrigation. Indeed, the results of the shallow pump set up about two months ago were already visible. The fields, that were bare after the paddy harvest, are now green in patches. Farmers have planted wheat and mustard and also some vegetables. The shallow tube well-cum-hand pump scheme can also be taken up in other places.

I spoke with a few children only to find that most of them did not attend the school at Jhitka. Wearing a dark mask I threatened the Lodhas that I will take back the *murgis* (chickens) from them if within a week all the children are not enrolled in the school, which also provides cooked Midday Meal. I have asked the BDO to make a special drive in this case and to send me a report by the 7th of this month. Before I left, I again told the villagers that if their children did not attend the schools benefits of other development schemes will also not flow their way.

We need to draw up a programme for extension work among the Lodhas owning land — even among those who do not own land — to improve their agricultural practices. Their skills in agriculture are rather rudimentary. The fields that we saw in Jhitka had not been prepared well, or laid out correctly, even the seeds had not been planted properly. They have merely dug up the fields once or twice and sown the seeds haphazardly, be it mustard, wheat or vegetables. Unless their agricultural skills and knowledge are enhanced they will never be able to utilise the land that they may have acquired or may have been given.

◎

23

Pursuit & Persuasion

◎

Six schemes for re-excavation of *sech bundhs* and water tanks had been sanctioned for Nayagram block and the work was supposed to start today. Last night the SDO informed me that there were some difficulties in the formation of the beneficiary and monitoring committees at the work sites. Therefore, I decided to convene a meeting with the Sabhapati, the Pradhans of the concerned gram panchayats and the local Member of the Legislative Assembly (MLA), who is apparently the one to raise certain objections. Supposedly he had mobilised local public opinion against the panchayats and, thus, stalled the implementation of the scheme.

We reached Nayagram at about 11.40 a.m. The SDO, Jhargram, the BDO, the Sabhapati, and the Pradhans of the three concerned gram panchayats were present. The MLA joined us after a few minutes. The meeting began and I asked the representatives what the problem was. The MLA's chief objection to the commencement of the work, which would employ several scores of unemployed people during this lean period, was that they had not received the guidelines. A little surprised, I asked him whether he had made any effort to contact the Sabhapati or BDO to whom the guidelines for the implementation of NFFWP had been sent as early as on 15 December 2004, in Bengali as well as in English. He acknowledged that he had not contacted either of them. I requested him to amplify on where the difficulty lay. He said that people did not know what was happening, they were in the dark, and so on. However, after discussion it was decided that work at one site could start today itself, and at the others from the next day, that is, on 9 January 2005.

Since out of the six schemes sanctioned, four are located in just one gram panchayat, Gram Panchayat no.12, I asked the BDO to select other schemes from different Gram Panchayats. Four schemes taken up simultaneously in one Gram Panchayat would merely delay all of them due to shortage of labour. Two of the villages in which the schemes had been located are also not in our survey list or in the VVI list. Therefore, these could be taken up in the next phase, after we receive the second instalment of funds under NFFWP. These schemes must be substituted immediately, that is by tomorrow, with two other schemes which may be implemented without more ado in two of the identified villages. I also read out to the assembled public representatives and the officials the list of villages that had scored more than 70 points on the VVI. There were 69 such villages in Nayagram — the highest number for any block in the state! Once I had read out the village names and their characteristics had been discussed, the panchayat members as well as the MLA agreed that the list had identified the poorest villages.

I made it clear that I wanted to see the work begin at least in one place today. After further discussion we decided to proceed to Keshardanga where an old tank was to be re-excavated. The Pradhan of the Gram Panchayat who had earlier mentioned that she had made all the arrangements for the re-excavation but a hitch had come up at the last minute, was also present. She offered to go ahead and make arrangements and left along with an SAE from the block. In the meantime, we decided to visit Srirampur, which is one of most vulnerable villages in the block and is on the route to Keshardanga. I requested the Sabhapati and the BDO to send the abridged Bengali version of the guidelines for NFFWP to all Gram Panchayats and to the MLA. These could be circulated even in the form of a letter from the Sabhadhipati and me. SAEs also need to be instructed that the re-excavation of tanks and *bundhs* that they are undertaking and the excavation of new tanks should not be done in a disorganised manner; the embankments should be properly dressed so that the next monsoon does not send the extracted earth on the exposed banks sliding back into the reservoirs.

I tried to impress upon those present that it was vital to start the work immediately so that landless and marginal workers residing in the vicinity of these locations are able to earn something before *Makarsankranti*, only a week away. Since most of the people in these villages are adivasis, it would mean a great deal to them to earn some cash before the festival. I also informed them that I would not hesitate to publicise the so-called objections to the work and the meaningless hurdles created locally if this happened again, even if I had to take up a mike and broadcast the scandal in villages, *haats* and markets.

Srirampur village is about 8 km from Baligeria, the block head-quarters. Leaving behind the *pacca* road immediately we took a *morrum* track, which further along merged with an earthen path that enters the jungle.

At about 2.10 p.m. we reached Srirampur; of its population of about 300 souls, 98 per cent belong to the Scheduled Tribes. Gorkhelar, about a km to the north, is also in the list of the most vulnerable villages (no. 291). I was disconcerted, but no longer surprised, to discover that in the primary school of Srirampur provision of cooked Midday Meal has not yet been started. The Gram Panchayat had not been able to appoint the cook and helper for the task and there was no SHG in the village to take up the responsibility!

The SHC at Tikrapara is only 2 km away, but the children here were not fully immunized. Due to the recurrent holding of Pulse Polio day, the polio vaccine had been administered to all the infants and children but several of the other shots were yet to be delivered.

I took a walk around the village. I noticed cement tiles being used for roofing in one of the houses — a promising sign. The inhabitants of this village are principally dependent upon *kendu patta*, sal leaves and weaving bamboo baskets. They own a little land but most of it is un-irrigated. Early marriage and early procreation seem to be common here also. I came across Bholanath Mahali's house, which was raided by elephants on 13 December 2004. In all probability, while rummaging around for grain or liquor the giants of the forests had wrecked the front wall.

Mahalis, a Scheduled Tribe, mainly depend upon weaving bamboo baskets and making other bamboo products for their livelihood — a perennial occupation. Bamboo work involves most adult members of a family. Normally the men cut and fetch bamboo from the forest; both women and men together split them into two before women slit the pieces into long, thin strips. Both women and men weave the baskets. Perhaps, it is only in tribal societies where women and men are engaged in the same kinds of work in the preparation of artefacts and handicrafts.

On specified days of the month the Mahalis carry baskets of various types and sizes to sell in the nearest *haat*. Large, loosely woven baskets, about 2.5 ft in diameter, are purchased locally by one Prasanta Das, a middleman from Tikrapara. He sells them in Tamluk to whole sellers who pack *paan,* betel leaf, in them for dispatching to various parts of the country. The loose weave of the baskets makes it ideal for packaging *paan* leaves because the ventilation secures their freshness even after a long journey to far-off destinations.

Almost every house in Srirampur has a well which, like the many others in this region, is often but a hole in the hard laterite, without any protection. Pre-fabricated sanitary latrine plates are standing against tree trunks waiting to be installed in toilets sanctioned under the TSC. I asked Bholanath Mohali, the owner of the house, why they were not being used. He told us that the plates had been supplied when SHGs were formed; however, they do not know what to do with them or how to use them! I requested the Sabhapati and the BDO to hold a meeting in the village as quickly as possible, discuss the hazards of defecating in the open, convince them about the importance of toilets and the convenience they offered, especially to women, and see to it that the plates are put to use. Although the Sabhapati nodded vigorously at everything I said, I knew it would be an uphill task.

Murali *khal*, a permanent stream with a broad bed, is about one and a quarter kilometres from the edge of the habitation. The villagers want a lift irrigation project on the stream to water the low-lying fields. There is no electricity in this village yet, and without electricity a lift irrigation scheme is just not going to be viable here. I explained this to them, and pointed out that instead low check dams can be constructed at several places on the perennial stream even from the funds available for augmentation of traditional water sources. We could also construct a number of *sech bundhs* or *dhal-bundhs* here, for the village is situated on the south-western rim of a micro-watershed that drains gently into the Murali *khal*.

We spoke with the people and explained to them about this micro-watershed and how the water from the upper slopes is draining into the stream and out of their reach. It may not be enough to prepare small check dams on the stream; what is required is to have a number of ponds at various points on this slope. Right now the land is lying dry after the paddy harvest. If tanks could be excavated here, the villagers could use the stored water for irrigation. That water is in short supply here even for washing and bathing became evident as we walked back from the river. Groups of young women going for a bath, with *gamcha* and little bottles of mustard oil in one hand and bundles of clothes in the other, passed us on their way down to Murali *khal*. If a large *dhalbundh* could be made upon the slope, girls would not need to trudge a mile just for a bath.

Adjacent to the village, below the road is a large section of fallow land not cultivated even during the *kharif* season. The area beyond the road, to the west, slopes down from the edge of a jungle and would serve as an extensive catchment area — an ideal spot for a large *sech bundh*. Fortunately, two of the owners of the land were part of a crowd of villagers. I put the idea of a *sech bundh* to those present, and under the blue sky the pros and cons of the proposal were loudly discussed by the assembly. After initiating the subject I had held myself back from the discussion. But sighting an overall consensus emerging from the hubbub about the suitability of a *sech bundh* on the identified piece of land, I asked the two owners present if they would be willing to give their land for the purpose of a reservoir. To our great relief they readily agreed.

By then two enthusiastic villagers had been able to bring over Dulu Tudu, who walked slowly with the help of a stick. He is the third owner of a part of the land which can be excavated for creating a reservoir. Since he is about 70 years old I suggested that he could be given an Old Age Pension. His neighbours clustered around him and after several minutes of intense persuasion Dulu Tudu also agreed. Following an intensive analysis of the site, its merits and demerits and acquiring the acquiescence of the land owners, I proposed that work may be started the next day. I was afraid that unless we struck the iron while it was red hot the owners of the land may back out. Fortunately, the proposal was met with a chorus of approval; they all agreed to start work on the morrow. As an added incentive, I also told them they will get their first payment on 13th of this month, before the *Makarsankranti*. I instructed the BDO to submit the proposal for this scheme immediately. Since we have developed templates for such schemes, preparing such proposals is no longer a time consuming process as it had been earlier.

On the way back we went around Bholanath Mahali's house damaged by the elephants and scrutinised it from the other side also. The flimsy roof and the weak walls had caved in rendering it quite uninhabitable. For the time being the displaced family was staying in their neighbour's house. I requested the Sabhapati and the BDO to provide an IAY house to the family. This family does not have much land, but moderate stacks of hay and paddy laid in their courtyard indicated that the yield this year had been reasonably good.

Some land adjacent to the village is being used for growing *babui* grass. *Babui* durries and mats are a few of the products made here. Pig-keeping is common to almost all families in this village. The pigs root around the houses and are fed leftovers, vegetable scraps, and anything else that the villagers can spare. At nights they are kept inside small cages adjoining the houses. From time to time, when the pigs are old enough for the market, *mahajans* from Kharagpur come and collect them. Rearing of chicken is also common here.

As we walked down the main track dividing the village, I noticed a wrinkled, old woman bent over with age walking along the road with the help of a stick. We stopped and I asked her where she lived. Budhi Rana, for that was her name, said that she lived down the road in Tikrapara with her grandson. I asked the BDO to include her name in the list of persons eligible for Old Age Pension for tribals.

The Mahali houses are of marginally better quality than that of Lodhas, with slight mud walls and straw roofs but without windows. Nevertheless, they do not achieve quite the same standard as the sturdily built Santal houses. Also, the walls and the roofs overhanging the narrow verandahs are lower and restrict ventilation. Mahalis also speak the Santhali language.

On our way back, as we crossed Murali *khal* I noticed that the stream lies at the bottom of the watershed with the two slopes of the long valley draining into it — little wonder that this is a perennial stream. Several springs bubble down these slopes. The slanting land adjacent to a spring is the ideal place to locate small but sustainable *sech bundhs*. Since the springs are often on private land, the owners may have to be persuaded to part with their land for excavating a tank. Though I have no doubt that these sites would be most successful as small reservoirs and serve as permanent sources of water for irrigating small parcels of land.

Vast areas on both sides of the red, sandy track are lying utterly vacant. In each long year, this area bears just one monsoon-supported crop. Only water harvesting reservoirs can change the colour of this land from a burnt red to a soothing green.

We reached the Keshardanga tank site at about 4 p.m. A few people had started work there after the Pradhan brought them over.

They have begun digging right at the wet centre of the heavily silted-over tank, which is about 50 m long by 50 m wide. The Pradhan, and the others collected there, told me that it was first excavated in 1970–1972. Persistently lashed by yearly rains over three decades, the undefended earthen sides of the tank had progressively given up and melted into it. Once re-excavated, this may prove to be a dependable reservoir of water for the *kharif* season and may also proffer succour to some winter crops. Twelve persons have started work today; only four of them are men. I requested the Pradhan to supervise the work and make sure that the excavation continues smoothly and the work does not halt.

The dependence of the people of this area on the forest is to be seen to be appreciated. Leaf, trunk, shoot, root, flower, and everything that the forest produces form the bases of the livelihood of the people. Therefore, it is necessary that the forest area that has been degraded here should be improved and protected. Given the reliance of the tribal population on bamboo and *babui* grass, cultivation of both types of grass should be taken up in a big way. Perhaps the key to providing sustainable livelihood to the local populace is a re-examination of the traditional sources of income of the adivasis. This can be done by studying the raw materials that they use, the implements and the skills that they employ, and the technology that may enhance their productivity — making improvements to all these aspects of the production process may be the key to an alternative development model for such areas. It saddened me to see that the sal trees in these parts of the forest had been partially replaced by eucalyptus. These new stands of the foreign species are neither as extensive nor as deep as in the parts of Chotonagpur that I am familiar with, but they are still an eye sore. A short-cut to afforestation, eucalyptus in sal land is an abomination.

Except during the four–five days beginning on *Makarsankranti*, when very few people will work, if necessary, there should be no break. If people wish to work during that period arrangements should be made for them to do so.

On the way back at about 5.10 p.m. when we crossed the Subarnarekha River on the other side, I noticed the fields immediately changed colour. On the Nayagram side of the river the fields are bare, but on the Keshiary side of the river they are green with vegetables and the seedlings for *boro* paddy. Nonetheless, after travelling a short distance away from the river into Keshiary, the countryside became as stark and arid as in Nayagram. Lack of irrigation in these areas has kept fields on this side of the river also bare.

The problem is not the lack of enough water but that it is not conserved, and we do not harvest it well enough to put it to use. Nayagram suffers from a shortage of water harvesting tanks, *pukurs*, *sech bundhs*, and *dhalbundhs*. Whatever funds are available have been traditionally divided among the Gram Panchayats. It has two effects: the money so distributed is normally utilised for construction of *kuchcha* roads, and whatever few tanks are excavated or re-excavated are small and shallow. Hence, water from the numerous springs and the rainwater that sweeps down the slopes drains into the Subarnarekha leaving behind heaving stretches of desolate red land.

◎

24
At the Edge of the Forest
◎

Accompanied by the DFO, Midnapore (East) Division, when I reached Tamakbari around noon, we found about 70 people working at the earthen dam. The excavation of this *sech bundh* started two days ago. It is right at the edge of the forest verging on Tamakbari *mouza*. At another site, further up inside the forest, one more *sech bundh* is being planned. The two are to be linked so that run off from the *sech bundh* deep inside the forest can be stored in the one lower down the incline at the edge of the forest where work is now on track. In some places the local labour engaged for the task has already dug to a depth of about 3 ft, exposing wet earth. This makes us hopeful that a perennial stream may replenish the water in this earthen dam and make it a regular source of water for the people of Tamakbari.

Resentment against the panchayat members has been brewing among the people of Tamakbari. Villagers came up to me and stated quite categorically that they did not want the panchayat to do this work; instead, it should be done through them by forming a beneficiary committee. I assured them that it could be done through the FPC or the local beneficiary committee, as the case may be. I have asked the DFO to start work on both the earthen dams simultaneously. Their original plan was to begin work on the *bundh* inside the forest after completing this one. However, there are 120 labourers in Tamakbari, and some of them can be more usefully employed at the other site.

Rameswar Kisku had some interesting facts to narrate to me at the second *bundh*. He is a trained Alchiki teacher and founder of an ashram in Tamakbari where children learn the Alchiki language. According to Kisku, he is a *sishya* of Pandit Raghunath Murmu, who is no more but his ashram runs in Rairampur in Mayurbhanj district.

He informed that a number of small organisations have taken up the task of teaching the Alchiki language to adivasi children in hamlets scattered across this region. The ashram he runs is duly registered as the Kherua Sari Saran Dharam Temakasha.

After going over the ground here we left for the second earthen dam inside the jungle. A low dam, well-worn by the elements, already exists there but its reservoir has not been re-excavated for a long time. Constructed around the year 1992 under the West Bengal Forestry Project, it is now silted and shallow and its bed is a nursery for weeds and grass. This tank is reasonably well located and the surface water flows into it from the forest further north-east. Apart from being silted, its embankment is also breached at several places. Still it holds about 3 ft of water in the pool close to the embankment.

Elephants are said to visit this place often and we could see their footprints at the edge of the water. Nearby, on the grassy bed, the DFO also pointed out dried elephant dung. A large herd had passed this way recently.

Dhananjoy Hansda, a resident of the village, had been away from Tamakbari when I last visited the village. He told me that there are a number of old people in Tamakbari whose names should be included in the list for Old Age Pension under the Scheduled Tribe Old Age Pension Plan. He gave me the names of three persons for the list: Bari Hansda, wife of late Dayal Hansda, Badrinath Hansda and Somi Hansda. Dhananjoy also informed me that the mini–kits supplied by the Agriculture Department, comprising seeds, fertilisers and insecticides, did not reach Tamakbari last year. I have noticed that such benefits seem to have a way about passing by tribal villages.

Agricultural extension is needed in this area. A meeting could be organised here by the Krishi Bikash Kendra or the block agricultural development officer and his assistants. Dhananjoy Hansda informed that a drinking water source was needed in Majherbasti of Tamakbari. Perhaps a well may be constructed from the special project for construction and renovation of wells sanctioned by the BCW Department. The site of the earthen dam is an excellent one. As I have noted earlier, the catchment area in these parts comprises the even sal forest bordering this site on three flanks; it forms a natural conduit flowing out of the forest into the reservoir. After the next monsoon the re-excavation of the tank and the strengthening of the dam are sure to create a large body of water. The plan also provides for two slipways for excess water and two field channels through which this excess water will go to some fields, adjacent to the forest, on the one side and on the other to the second earthen dam down the slope.

Segments of private *ryoti* land belonging to the adivasis border or intrude into the forest at various points along its periphery. At present the fields are lying fallow and until monsoon arrives there is no chance of their being cultivated. People from Tamakbari once again asked for new schemes, particularly a road and a culvert to connect them to the village of Rupsa. They are also interested in keeping goats, pigs, ducks, poultry, etc. Goat-keeping will be quite successful here because of the nearby forest, which would provide free fodder to the animals.

Land for an SSK building has been selected by the people of Tamakbari but funds are yet to be provided. We need to follow this up with the AEO, Zilla Parishad, Paschim Medinipur.

◎

25

A Fair in the Forest

◎

At 9.30 a.m. I left Midnapore for Nayagram to visit *Makar mela* held in Chandibila Gram Panchayat, Nayagram block. It is *Makarsankranti*, the most important festival of the tribals in these parts. Just as the Bengali community looks forward to the next *Durga Puja* right from the day the idol of *Ma Durga* is immersed, tribal communities in this region look forward to this festival the whole year. On our way out of Midnapore, as we crossed the bridge over the Kangsabati, I observed light sheets of mist swirling over the *ghats* on both sides of the river. Large crowds of the pious and the hopeful were taking holy dips on *Makarsankranti* before putting on new clothes. On the road we met a number of women and children walking towards the river with a small statue of Tusu on their heads. The idol, to which the past week they have offered *puja*, would be immersed in the river before they take their bath, and savour *til* and *pitha* on the banks of the river.

Passing through Keshiary, as we approached the golden sands of the Subarnarekha, I saw similar crowds, mostly of adivasis, on the river banks. We again met groups of women and girls crossing the fair weather bridge from either side. Little children hung on to red and orange balloons bought by indulgent parents. Although not all adults were clad in new attire, most girls and boys showed off their new clothes. Balloon sellers and vendors of sweets had set up shop on the sides of the bridge, on the sand banks in the shallow waters of the Subarnarekha. Some picnic parties had also arrived with blaring loudspeakers in toe. The banks of the main stream of Subarnarekha flowing past the Nayagram side of the river held the largest gatherings.

The BDO, Nayagram, was waiting for me at Kharikamathani *chourasta*. From there we turned right for the *Tapovan mela* which also lies in Chandibila G.P. In the middle of the thick forest beside a spring is a temple dedicated to Ram and Sita. Every year on 14 January, on *Makarsankranti*, in large numbers people from neighbouring Gram Panchayats, most of them adivasis, are drawn to this place to offer *puja* after the ritual bath in the springs. Wherever people congregate to celebrate some must gather to supply the means of celebration. Inescapably, a *mela* has grown up around the temple.

About 8 km from Kharikamathani, we passed Narda dam which has a reservoir spread over an area of about 5 sq. km Constructed several years ago by the Irrigation Department, bordered by thickly forested ridges, the water body has succumbed to extensive siltation. Under the creeping advance of reeds and tall grass the basin has shrunk. Masses of magenta-tinted water lilies overspread the surface along with the less pleasing weeds. Why cannot this reservoir be re-excavated under the NFFWP?

Turning right at Chandibila village we took a *morrum* track through the forest. A number of people, young boys and girls, men and women, and children in fresh bright clothes were returning from the *mela*. A few vehicles passed by us but most people were either on foot or on bicycles. Starting early in the morning, the *mela* carries on until late in the afternoon. Hence, by the time we headed towards *Tapovan* a lot of people were on their way back; mini-trucks full of people and trekkers returning from the *mela* clogged the narrow road. Balloons seem to be a favourite of children here as much as anywhere else. I saw a young father carrying a balloon and a small polythene bag full of *jelebis* on his way back home. He was one of the few people on the road who seemed to be carrying anything back from the *mela*.

As we neared the fair in the middle of the forest we could see a cycle stand set up on the side of the track among the trees: a quadrangle of thin jungle had been marked out with a *babui* rope tied to tree trunks, while a board proclaimed 'Cycle Stand run by an SHG'. To reach the temple one had to cross a stream, which gets its water from a spring. As we approached the clearing where the temple is situated, I noticed a man in a thin pullover and a saffron *dhoti* folded up to his knees, squatting in front of what appeared to be a shrine. This was Gangadhar Bhakta, a *pujari* at large.

On the occasion of *Makarsankranti*, Bhakta had set up a shrine at the foot of a thin termite-afflicted sal sapling, near the entrance

Plate 25.1 Off to the *mela*

of the clearing beyond the bicycle stand. His place of worship consists of a row of miniature terracotta elephants, with a few horses
thrown in for good measure, set up on a miniscule rectangle of a
ground plastered with red mud. A few pink and yellow flowers were
scattered in front of the idols. Nearby, a terracotta *dhup dani* and a
diya containing vermilion were also available to aid worship. This
was a *thaan* where on this auspicious day Gangadhar Bhakta was
offering the devout the chance to earn some additional good fortune
by offering *puja* to the local deity of the forest. Gangadhar Bhakta
had strategically located the shrine near the entrance of the clearing;
he knew well that the devotees were likely to have more money in
their slim pockets on their way in rather than on the way out.

A narrow footpath and a culvert of concrete and cast-cement
pipes have been built by the Panchayat Samiti across the bed of
the stream crossed to reach the temple. Known as Sita *nala*, this
is a perennial stream; the water flowed strong and steady at this
time of the year.

As we crossed the Sita *nala* we noticed a band of devotees near
the temple, loudly singing *bhajans* to the accompaniment of cymbals

and *dholaks*, while another group to the left of the temple was also doing the same — almost in competition. Some members of the temple committee welcomed us. After a few preliminaries, as they took us around the little clearing, they expressed their unhappiness that no effort had been made for development of this holy place. A *harikirtan pandal*, a round shed, had been built but one of its eight concrete pillars had recently been knocked down by irreverent wild elephants. During *Budhha Purnima* a four-day-long *kirtan* is held at the spot. A *samadhi* was also pointed out to us which, according to the members of the committee, is that of Valmiki, the author of the epic *Ramayana*, who according to the local tradition achieved *moksha*, salvation, here. Under an ancient Peepal tree stands a small temple. Through the low doorway one can see statues of Ram and Sita, with Valmiki standing behind them. In front of the deities presided a priest clad in saffron sitting cross-legged, who in girth and in the length of his beard resembled Valmiki.

Thus is located the very small temple, in a very small clearing right in the middle of the deep forest; there are three or four springs nearby, all flowing into the Sita *nala*. This could be transformed into a viable eco-tourism location. A number of mango trees around the temple, and an ancient tamarind tree, were in flower. A single well with a very narrow mouth is the sole source of drinking water to the pilgrims. The water, only about 6 ft from the surface, is sparkling clear. The open area is not very large and therefore, not too many buildings can, or should, come up here. Nevertheless, the Forest Department can certainly be asked to devise a plan for its development, which can be funded through RSVY. The waters of Sita *nala*, in which people are taking their holy dip, is quite muddy; but, perhaps, faith here does not recognise pollution other than that of the mind!

The *mela* is not a very elaborate one; indeed, it is quite a humble affair. There are no merry-go-rounds or Ferris wheels, not even the small hand-driven ones; neither are there other entertainments, such as a magic show, or games of chance that draw crowds. It is obvious that the people who make this respectful visit to *Tapovan* do not have much to spend. Therefore, their expectations from the *mela*, and the supply, are also limited.

I returned to the other side of the stream for a look at the wares on display at the *mela*. I had always found visiting *haats* and rural

Plate 25.2 Local sweets on sale

bazaars most instructive. In this *mela* the 'stalls' were actually plastic sheets spread in a clearing; *muri, ghugni, jelebi,* and other inexpensive sweets were on offer for a poor, rural clientele who cannot afford the expensive delicacies of the towns. The merchandise again underscored the limited buying power of the area. Nonetheless, stalls selling plastic toys, bats and balls, whistles, cars, and such like drew children and also women; these stalls were also cosmetic shops, selling such luxuries as *alta,* talcum powder, lipstick, and *bindis* along with toys.

On the way back to our vehicles we were walking behind two adivasis strolling arm in arm, obviously in high spirits. They were loudly singing a song expressing gleeful anticipation of their mother-in-law's death.

As we drove away along the strip of road cut through the sal forest past the returning throngs, I carried with me a feeling of disappointment. The current of gaiety, the ripple of cheer, and the mood of splurge that one associates with a fair, especially at festival time, seemed to have cagily evaded the *Makar mela* at *Tapovan*. The *mela* itself had little to offer by way of goodies or entertainment and the

Plate 25.3 The high-spirited twosome

mela-goers appeared to visit Sita *nala* for a holy dip impelled more by a sense of tradition than for celebration. To high-minded city-dwellers this may appear to be simple, wholesome merriment and fun, and my disenchantment with the meagreness of the fair may appear misplaced. Yet I suspect that the sieve of poverty drains festivals of cheer. Not even a shadow of doubt dims my conviction that the parents visiting this *mela* would also like their children to take a turn on a Ferris wheel or to laugh at the antics of a ventriloquist's puppet; they would, if they *could*.

◎

26

Unequal at the Margins

◎

From the *Makar mela* at *Tapovan* we headed for Junglekhas, which is the eighth most vulnerable village in this district.

We followed the road through the dense jungle and past a Santal village. Beyond the village was a *bundh* with another large reservoir that required re-excavation. Constructed in 1993 by the Jhargram Development Board with the help of the Irrigation Department, it has an extensive catchment area. Water from the large forest tract above and beyond feeds this reservoir. Two channels on either side of the *pacca* dam allow egress for excess water, the one facing the dam on the right side has a lock gate. These two channels irrigate large tracts of land totalling more than a thousand acres in the command area. I decided that the re-excavation of this reservoir should also be taken up under the NFFWP. It would be a massive project but it was required.

While I was taking a photograph of the dam from the side of a hillock, I got a text message from the AEO, Zilla Parishad, informing me that ₹4.54 crore had been sanctioned for the Special Lodha Housing Project. Truly, this was wonderful news. Although we had submitted the project proposal in late October, locating funds for it had proved to be an uphill battle. Several times we had been told that there are no funds for such a scheme, but running from one department to another I had persevered. Finally, my persistence had paid off and Pramila Sabar and 1,999 other Lodha families, possibly worse off than her, will now be able to live in a habitable house. Now there was a lot more work to be finished by March 2005.

On the way to Junglekhas I inspected the PMGSY road that was under construction from Dhankamra to Rameswar temple. Work was progressing at a steady pace and only the last stage of laying the metal bed and the black top remains. Rameswar temple is on the lower side of the right bank of the reservoir; at a little distance we could see the Subarnarekha. Built in the Odisha style, the imposing temple has *garvagriha* and *natyamancha* under the structure in the middle. Unlike most such temples it is not meticulously engraved or ornamented but stolidly constructed of stone blocks. Once the Subarnarekha flowed right in front of the temple, but now that its course has shifted a little further away only a thin channel lies immediately beneath it. One may wash one's feet in the stream by going down about 120 steps made of blocks cut from laterite stone. The temple is also constructed of this stone. Inside, lime-plastered walls and ceilings have been defaced by people fond of scratching their names in quest of immortality.

When we reached Junglekhas village, in Jamsola Gram Panchayat, in the afternoon the BDO pointed out a house which had been built with the funds provided from the Lodha Development Fund. It has pillars, concrete pillars. Not everyone has been that fortunate to get the funds to build a house. Mukund Nayek is the owner of a sagging hut. He is very angry that he has not been provided a house. Kusum Nayek's house is also a huddle. They could also be provided a house each. On the south-western side of the village is a tank reportedly excavated in 2002 by the Forest Department. Although water could have drained into this tank from the forested south-west, high banks probably force the flow to run past it and prevent such replenishment. Consequently, at present, the tank has very little water. Adjacent to the tank is the land Lodhas received with the *pattas* provided by government. It is an arid wasteland bereft of irrigation and yields nothing but thorny bushes. This is the problem with land given to Lodhas everywhere in the district. On some land that they received on the western side of the water tank, the Lodhas have planted *babui* grass with the fund supplied through the Forest Development Corporation. This is a regular source of income for them. However, the other lands lie totally barren.

All around the village the courtyards have small shrines presided over by terracotta elephants which the Lodhas worship as *Hati thakur*. Only today they have offered *puja* to little terracotta *hati thakur*s in different parts of the village, in the belief that if they worshipped him wild elephants would not attack their houses. We were also shown a *British Amoler Mondaler kuon* — 'Mondal's well

Plate 26.1 The Britisher 'amoler' well

of the British period'; once upon a time it had a parapet. Cut through the underlying laterite rock, the well is definitely very old and very deep. Since the *British Amoler Mondaler kuon* does not, however, have the vital parapet, I asked the BDO to take up its con-struction immediately.

Mangal Bhakta, a sturdily built man with bright eyes and a quick smile, owns seven to eight goats. Until a few days back he had 13, but taking advantage of the demand in the festival season just before *Makarsankranti*, he had sold off six. Originally, Mangal had bought bullocks from the Medium Term (MT) loan he had received three years back from the Scheduled Caste & Scheduled Tribes Development Corporation. However, since his hard un-watered land stubbornly refused to bear enough grain, and he also could not feed the bullocks properly, he sold the animals off and decided to buy goats. Due to the availability of an endless supply of fodder from the neighbouring forest the goats had thrived. Mangal is a most sensible fellow, and also among the few Lodhas who does not seem to be drunk in the afternoon. He has some land on which he has sown *babui* grass, and is also growing some papayas and other vegetables. Mangal Bhakta exemplifies that if utilised properly the Medium Term loan scheme can make a difference to the lives of Lodhas.

In the verandah of one of the houses lay bundles of long thin twigs. Upon asking the family what they were for, they answered that they did not know, but they got up to ₹50 for each bundle of a hundred twigs. Taking a closer look I found that they were basically *dantwan,* twigs used for brushing teeth, which after being cut into 8-inch pieces are sold for 25 paise–50 paise per piece at railway stations. In Midnapore they are available at the rate of ₹8 for 10 *dantwans*; three or four twigs would yield the number. This instance also illustrates the yawning gap between the earnings of persons who labour to supply forest produce and the middlemen.

The houses of the Lodhas here are like the houses of the Lodhas elsewhere — poorly constructed. Indeed, I think they are worse off. In many cases I find the walls are made just of uneven branches of trees and dry leaves. One well is also required in this Lodha *para* because the three wells in this village are all in the Adivasi para. The lone Mark-II tube well, set up only a year back, is not working. It should be repaired immediately. The nearest health centre, 7 km away, is at Chanabundh. A primary school is located in the Santal part of Jungle khas. The school building is among the best that I have seen in adivasi-populated areas. It has four rooms and is a completely *pacca* structure supported by concrete pillars. The AWC is also situated in the Adivasi para. I had observed earlier how public benefits appear to skirt tribal villages. The situation in Junglekhas confirms my belief that in the adivasi socio-political hierarchy the Lodhas are at the bottom.

We could identify three persons for Old Age Pension in the village: Sunil Nayek, Niranjan Nayek, who perhaps also suffers from a cataract, and Nolbon Nayek, who at the age of about 75 is the oldest man in the village. All three are Lodhas.

On the way back I stopped short at the sight of a hut beside the road. Brindaban Bhakta lives in the hut with his wife and two children; the family is landless. For their living Brindaban and his wife toil in other people's field and sell woven *babui* rope and the sal leaves they gather from the forest. Their white clay-washed windowless hut, about 15 ft long by 8 ft wide, built of packed earth and covered by a dwindling thatched roof, stands in a tiny com-

Plate 26.2 Solar power for Brindaban Bhakta

pound about 600 sq. ft in area. Although it was not very different than the average dwelling in Junglekhas, I was struck by the hut because resting atop the thatched roof, which itself was capped with a polythene sheet held down by a few terracotta tiles, was a solar panel. Brindaban Bhakta, a landless labourer living in an airless hut, had been provided with a solar light under the solar electrification scheme. The convoluted priorities of our rural development programme shone in this one image.

◎

The Lodha Housing Project

◎

Based on the experiences of my tours to the interior villages in the Junglemahals we prepared a project for the construction of houses for members of the primitive tribe, Lodha-Sabars. The objective of the project was to provide basic, low-cost housing facilities to some of the poorest of the poor, not only among our society in general but even among the weakest tribal communities.

A house is an attempt at permanence. Fundamentally forest dwellers, and given to their migratory form of life, Lodha-Sabars have never been builders of sturdy houses. The predilection for movement has also precluded the development of expertise in the construction of houses among the Lodhas. Although the Lodhas and other tribal groups, designated by them as 'Adibasis', live together in many villages, there is a striking difference between the adivasi houses and that of the Lodha-Sabars. The adivasis construct large, strong, often double storied houses made of solid, packed mud walls and roofs lined with tiles or covered with straw. Their houses have designated rooms: grain *golas* (storage containers), sleeping spaces and a separate kitchen. The walls are smoothened and mud-washed with specific types of coloured clay extracted from the jungle and streams.

Most Lodha houses, on the other hand, are one-room huts, rudely made and crudely covered. The thin walls are usually made of poorly prepared mud and/or bamboo sticks, which lack finish and polish. The roof is a covering of either straw or the leaves of date palms. These houses have no windows or ventilators, and wicker lamps have to be lit inside the house even during the day. Unlike the adivasi houses, the Lodha huts are as bare within as they are stark outside, with no shelves or built-in storage space. Most of the Lodhas' belongings, except for a few pots, consist of a few articles of clothing that are hung on a line stretched across the length of the hut. On an average a Lodha hut measures about 12–14 ft in length and 8–10 ft in width. This abject space the Lodha family shares with goats and hens — if they happen to own any. These houses are also bereft of sanitation facilities.

Paschim Medinipur district receives about ₹130 million annually for the construction of Indira Awaas houses for BPL families. At the rate of ₹25,000 per unit, only 6,500 houses could be constructed each year with this amount. Although by itself this amount and number may appear large, but when spread over 7,581 inhabited *mouzas* in 290 Gram Panchayats it becomes less impressive. Normally the Gram Panchayats divide the IAY houses among several villages in their jurisdictions — based on the clout and the munificence of the local panchayat representatives. Lodhas, who constitute less than one per cent of the population of this district, are not only a minority among a minority, that is the Scheduled Tribes, but their small number is thinly spread out within the 20 blocks of this district. They are neither politically active nor assertive. Hence, location of IAY houses in Lodha habitations is episodic at best, as in the case of Auligeria village, described earlier.

The only way a significant difference could be made to this problem of poor housing among the Lodhas was by targeting them with a special project. In view of the crying need for providing basic housing facilities to the voiceless Lodha-Sabar families of this district, a special project was formulated and submitted to the P&RD Department in the first week of November 2004. The sanction order for the project was received on 18 January 2005 from the P&RD Department.

The amount sanctioned by the government for the special housing project for the Lodhas was ₹45.4 million. This posed a bit of a problem since our target was 2000 houses and we had been planning to build houses at the rate of ₹25,000 per unit, as per the Indira Awaas specifications. This meant that either we build only 1816 houses or we reduce our cost to ₹22,700 for each house. Given the pressing need for houses, it would have been unfair to reduce the number; therefore we decided to explore how the cost could be reduced.

First, I consulted our Zilla Parishad engineering team. After much discussion, calculation and re-calculation, it was decided that since cement was a major item of expenditure we would try to minimise its use. While undergoing training in North 24 Parganas in the block, with the help of the local SAEs I had successfully designed and built Indira Awaas houses by using mud mortar for binding bricks and 'pointing', or covering the joints, with cement. I suggested this to the engineers in Paschim Medinipur; they agreed that it would work and the resulting building would still be a strong one. This would help in significant savings but not enough.

Our next line of action was to make the most of the local resources. Fortunately, Paschim Medinipur was a large district with several industrial units producing safe asbestos sheets for roofing, and one cement manufacturer. The companies were: Ramco Industries, Utkal Asbestos Limited, Visaka Industries, and Rashmi Cement. I decided to seek their cooperation. On 16 January 2005 I convened a meeting with the senior managers of the four companies explained the situation to them and sought their help. I requested them to supply asbestos sheets at a no-profit-no-loss basis, so that the low cost Tribal Housing Project for the Lodha and Sabars of this district could be effectively implemented for 2000 families. I also pointed out that it was also an opportunity for them to expand their network and publicise their products in the interiors of the district. The representatives of the companies were positive but wished to consult their superiors. On 19 January all three companies sent me letters of acceptance, which I gratefully acknowledged. This reduction in cost ensured that we would be able to meet our target of 2000 houses.

I decentralised the responsibility of implementing the project. From the district level we would provide the building plans, arrange tie-ups with the companies involved and provide the funds. The selection of beneficiaries and the implementation of the project was to be the responsibility of the Gram Panchayats and the Panchayat Samitis, respectively. However, I also made it clear that I would monitor the project on a daily basis. Guidelines were drawn up in detail and circulated among all Sabhapatis and BDOs.

It was decided that two houses would be made on a test case basis to find out how quickly the work could be done and what would be the on-site requirements of the project. The two trial houses were constructed in seven days (23 January 2005–29 January 2005) in Lohamelia Village, Jhargram Block. In the first phase of the project construction of 1565 houses began in 87 villages in 12 blocks of this district. The target date for completion of this phase was 25 February 2005. The remaining houses were expected to be completed by 15 March 2005.

On 27 February 2005, the then Chief Minister of West Bengal inaugurated the first cluster of houses under the project at Lohamelia village, Jhargram block and handed over the keys to the new owners — Pramila Sabar was the first person to receive the keys.

◎

27

A Glow in the Darkness

◎

On 19 January 2005 we began the process of identifying Lodha-Sabar families for the housing project. Accompanied by the Sabhadhipati, Paschim Medinipur Zilla Parishad, the Karmadhyakshya (Public Works), Zilla Parishad, AEO, Zilla Parishad, the District Planning Officer (DPLO), the Works Manager of Utkal Asbestos Limited, the Executive Engineer, the District Engineer of Zilla Parishad, and the SDO, I reached Lohamelia via Lodhasuli by 10 a.m. The aim was to initiate the construction of the first house under the Lodha Housing Project. We earlier had decided that one or two buildings needed to be built for the purposes of demonstration: to test the design we had developed and to show that it could be executed quickly.

We had decided that the first house to be built would be Pramila Sabar's. Hence, led by the *Upa-Pradhan* of the Gram Panchayat we went to her house. The SAE and his assistants then got down to work and the layout of the new house was measured on the adjacent vacant space and marked with lime dust. While the measurements were being made, I meandered next door into Dulu Sabar's backyard to find marks on the ground that indicated that he was planning to build a new dwelling beside his collapsing hut. The Sabhadhipati and I decided that instead of one we would construct two trial houses and, thus, included Dulu Sabar's house in the scheme.

To identify other beneficiaries we took a round of the village accompanied by the local Pradhan. The aim of this joint visit was to send an unambiguous signal to block and panchayat officials that the selection process should be transparent and must include the poorest. Our criterion was simple enough: any Lodha living in an uninhabitable dwelling must be provided shelter. Thus, we went on to identify 23 families in Lohamelia for inclusion in the housing project.

An interesting aside that came to our notice was the earnestness with which the recipients of chickens under the RSVY were taking care of them. Budhan Sabar's wife had received 10 chickens but only six had survived. She looks after her own chickens as well as those of her neighbours who had gone to work. Apparently the community has devised a system whereby individuals and families take turns to look after each other's livestock while others are away earning their living. By dividing time they are able to maximise their labour. Old ladies and children are also engaged in the task. The chickens had grown quickly and would soon be laying eggs. The Lodha-Sabars neither knew how to build a cage nor had the money to procure one. Hence, it was touching to find several families using their mosquito nets to keep the chickens safe. In one courtyard a fishing-net had been strung from the branch of a tree, its spread out edges weighed down by bricks; underneath, chickens busily fed from an aluminium plate.

Montipa village is approximately 2 km beyond Lohamelia. One has to go through Lohamelia and then follow, first, the earthen and then a notional track through a stand of eucalypti to come to Montipa, which lies between the forest and wasteland. Like many other Lodha villages similarly situated, it symbolises the state of the Lodhas.

Except for four, all the 17 houses in Montipa were in a terrible state. These 17 houses are going to be built anew under the Special Lodha Housing Project. Most of the families in the village have received *Patta* land. However, all of it is *danga* land and yields just one crop, when it does. From the RSVY fund a water harvesting tank has been constructed. It lies on the further side of the village on the slope below the forest. The houses themselves are almost inside the forest. One has to walk along narrow paths from one to the next. Somehow, this village did not find prominence in the VVI. This is probably because even the census workers did not bother to visit the village.

The following day, after visiting other work sites in Jhargram, I reached Lohamelia well after six in the evening. Darkness had fallen but with the help of a torchlight we made our way to the house of Hari and Pramila Sabar. Upon reaching their homestead I found Hari Sabar digging one side of the foundation all by himself! I asked him why he was working so late. He told me that during the day he had gone to the jungle to collect sal leaves. Upon his return, finding some portion of the foundation

Plate 27.1 Pramila Sabar's house under construction

incomplete he decided to complete digging the length before calling it a day. It was a stirring sight, especially since most people tend to dismiss Lodhas as incapable of hard work and responsibility.

We then visited Dulu Sabar's house next door where the second house is to be built. The foundation excavation had been completed there and Dulu Sabar had also participated. Their neighbours told me that the beneficiaries had themselves been working very hard throughout the day — as Hari Sabar was doing past 7 p.m. on a dark winter evening.

◎

28
Two Villages

◎

Due to the concentration of government establishments in the district Sadar or headquarters, it is expected that the Sadar sub-division and block would be among the more prosperous areas in the district. To my surprise, in Paschim Medinipur this was not quite true. My visits and the findings of the VVI showed that the Sadar sub-division and block were among the most backward.

The Pradhan of Manidaha Gram Panchayat was very agitated; grumbling, he asked where we thought would the poor Lodhas get ₹7000 to deposit with the Panchayat Samiti before work could start on their houses! I was quite as astonished as the SDO, Sadar. In late afternoon, accompanied by the SDO, I had reached Manidaha Gram Panchayat and was talking to the Pradhan and the Zilla Parishad members of the area. Yesterday the Sabhapati and the BDO had visited Inchilachak and Sarengasol, two villages in this same Gram Panchayat with a concentration of Lodha families. They had gone to identify the beneficiaries for the Special Lodha Housing Project.

We asked the Pradhan who had told him about such a scheme. He said that yesterday during her visit the Sabhapati had stated as much. She had also made it clear that until each of the beneficiary families deposited the amount she will not be able to begin building the houses in the village. We assured the Pradhan that there was no such stipulation, that the Sabhapati must have misunderstood the circulars, and that the entire cost of the house would be borne by the government. Nevertheless, I asked the SDO to make inquiries into how this 'stipulation' had been slipped into the arrangement!

As we proceeded to drive past the Gurguripal eco-tourism park, I commented on the thickness of the stands of sal and the relative richness of the undergrowth. The Pradhan told me that the forests had begun to regain their shape ever since the FPCs were formed in the early 1990s. Earlier numerous trees would be cut and smuggled out, but the FPCs had made a big difference. Since the villages comprising an FPC had all its families as members, gradually a sense of ownership of the forest had grown among them. Instead of being encroachers upon the Forest Department's jurisdiction, the people had become active stakeholders.

After crossing Nichubhadulia village, a tribal habitation, I sighted the tank being excavated under the RSVY. We stopped to inspect the work being executed by the Soil Conservation Department. Thirty workers were engaged in the excavation of the tank on a plot of land donated by tribals. The Soil Conservation Department is one of the agencies I was able to involve in the execution of RSVY earth-work schemes. Their manner of operation was to excavate smaller, shallower tanks that would serve to store water for a part of the year to irrigate small plots fringing the tank. This was a tank costing only ₹35,000 and the 30 people engaged for the task work in rotation. In this way all the families get a fair share of the work. This is the integrity of a tribal village.

As the sun was dipping over the highest sal fronds by the time we reached Asnabandhi village, we went directly to the tank being re-excavated there. From the high banks of the tank I could see that it was a fair-sized pond with two levels — a deep central square section about 35 m by 35 m that holds some water until late spring, and a shallow periphery about 45 m wide by 45 m long and 10 m wide that is fully submerged only after the occasional bountiful monsoon. A few straggling date palms bravely standing on the bare red embankment confirmed the scantiness of water through the year. There does not appear much scope for a re-excavation project worth ₹150,000, the sum allotted for this purpose. Work has begun but today there are no workers at the site. I asked a few inhabitants why there was no activity today. Since there was no plausible reason, I asked for the job worker — a local resident. It turned out that the local FPC had been given the responsibility for this scheme and its secretary was present. I told him that other FPCs were doing a decent job and we expected the same here. I also made it clear that if they did not make much progress by next week I would either withdraw the sanction or give the work to the gram panchayat.

Asnabandhi is a completely tribal village of about 40 families, all Santals. Sturdy mud-walled houses capped mostly by four-*chala* straw roofs are scattered around the narrow *morrum* road that runs through the village. Thick clumps of bamboo, thorny *ber* trees, mop-headed toddy palms, and even tall thin eucalypti rear above the clearings in which most huts stand. In one such clearing, glowing golden in the mellow late afternoon sun, a new earthen house was under construction. Forever fascinated by local construction techniques, I decided to have a closer look.

By the standards of the villages in the area, the house was reasonably large — about 25 ft long and 12 ft wide. Built entirely of mud, the upward tapering walls had just about cleared the lintel level. Even from a distance I could see that the elongated rectangular structure had been divided into three rooms set in a row, a large one on each side almost squeezing the smaller room in the middle. But something struck me: this house was not quite of the pattern common in the Junglemahals. Not only did it have two doors, as against the usual single entrance, it had large windows set in the wall in *each* room on at least two sides. As I approached closer to the house, the new walls appeared to be made of bands of packed mud differentiated by slender cracks. One could make out that they had been built layer upon layer, with today's still-wet 12-inch-thick layer at the top, the darkest brown. Intrigued, I walked into the construction to have a closer look and talk to the builders.

A few words with two of the half a dozen workmen revealed the story.

Brought to these forested areas by the seasonal demand for masons, the team of six builders, specialists in the construction of earthen houses, was from Murshidabad. They were working simultaneously on a few houses in adjacent villages. This was not the normal ploy employed by masons in urban areas, to engage and keep in suspension three or four work sites, but was necessitated by the nature of the construction. Preparing the mud, a mixture of the available red earth, clay and straw took a day — watered and blended at intervals to ensure consistency and cohesive strength. The following day the prepared mud would be rolled into balls to be pressed and patted down on the previous layer of the wall until they formed a new, flat layer about 12 inches thick. In a single day only one layer can be completed because it is then left to dry for one or two days. Only when the topmost layer was dry could the next one be laid. At the lintel level, rafters of sal logs were arranged across the parallel walls, and on top came the framework for the

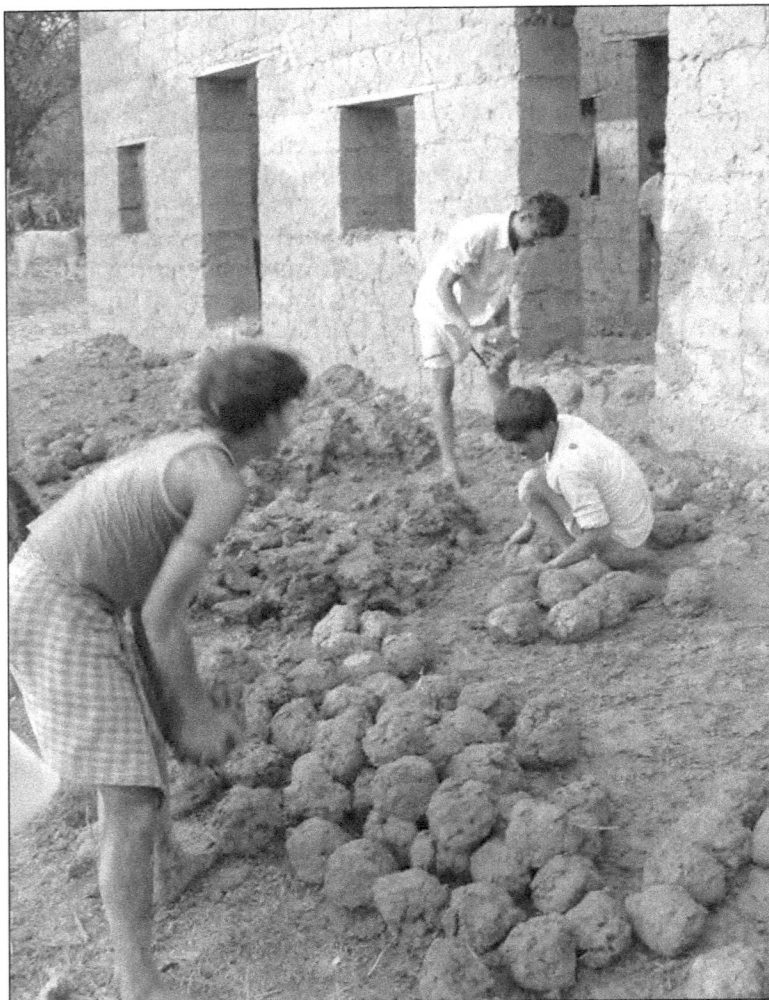

Plate 28.1 The building material

sloping roof of either straw GI or sheets. Thus, building one house could take up to 90 days and interruptions were not uncommon. The product, the new house, would be a comfortable habitation, its thick walls keeping it cool in summer and warm in winter.

I had long been convinced that in these areas this is the way houses under IAY should be built. Nonetheless, three factors had thwarted my earlier attempts in this direction: first, the bias in administrative and panchayat functionaries against building *kuchcha* mud houses under IAY; second, the shortage of skilled masons on the scale required; and third, taking this path would require much greater work and supervision. Far more convenient to distribute the amount among the beneficiaries and let them build the small brick huts. The perception that small, dark *pacca* brick tenements were preferable to the spacious mud houses is built into the system. And what is more, without reference to local preferences, even in the decennial census, houses are classified accordingly!

Houses here are made of mud, layer upon layer upon layer. Many of them are double-storeyed, and evidence of the good yield this year lies stacked in the courtyards. Dogs of this village are, perhaps, a good sign — signalling that the people here have enough to feed pets. Not that the poor do not keep pets, I have come across dogs even in the poorest Lodha villages.

Kalo Mandi's house is a reasonably spacious double-storeyed structure. Built by adivasi workmen long back, the packed mud walls are 18 inches thick with a broader plinth which provides a narrow ledge along its length. Up to a height of about 4 ft, the outer walls are carefully plastered with black earth. In the forecourt some women of the house are boiling broken rice and paddy husk for feeding the cattle. On one side of the large courtyard, newly harvested paddy is painstakingly heaped high in two stacks shaped like small huts with sloping tops — to let unexpected rain to slip off instead of soaking the paddy. It is obviously a 'well-off' family as apart from some land they also own several heads of cattle and a number of chickens.

Kalo Mandi's house is an exception to the rule in Asnabandhi. As we walked about the village, I came upon Bideshi Hembram's wife in front of her house. It is probably the poorest house in the village, so poorly constructed that I mistook it for a Lodha house. Thin saplings stuck in the ground provide the frame of a wall, which has then been haphazardly patched together with inexpertly mixed mud. The straw roof cries out for repair, as do the sun-cracked walls. Hardened chunks of mud, with nothing to hold them together, have fallen off the walls, laying bare the rude saplings or leaving ugly gaps exposing the darkness within.

Across Bideshi's courtyard, overhung by a large *ber* tree, live an old couple, Bhigu and Saraswati Mandi. Their condition demands that they be accommodated in the tribal Old Age Pension scheme. Their house is also not any better than Bideshi Hembram's hut. They keep a few chickens, some pigs, and also a dog. Holders of an Antyodaya Card, the couple has been given only 15 kg of wheat in the last two months. Their ration card told me that on 24 December 2004, the day after they received the Antyodaya Card, they had got 15 kg of wheat from the ration shop in Nayagram. The BDO must enquire into why this has happened and send me a report.

Saraswati is wrapped in a single piece of once-white *sari* that at once also becomes a shawl covering her torso against the January cold. Most other women in the village follow suit; their, usually, colourful *saris* are also tightly draped around them for warmth. Shawls are uncommon among the women, while older men, such as Bhigu, have in deference to the approaching night wrapped themselves in a shawl or a rough woollen blanket. Younger men and boys are also, by and large, without sweaters, although some of them have a woollen scarf wrapped around their neck — their only concession to winter. Among the younger girls too sweaters and shawls are not much in evidence. Also striking was the near absence of silver jewellery on the vast majority of the women I came across — significant because silver bangles around their wrists or anklets normally represent their savings.

In this village I did not come across a single sanitary latrine. Somewhere along the road the TSC had lost its way.

◎

29
Work in Progress
◎

On the way to the nearly complete re-excavation site of Kumar *bundh*, we stopped at the AWC at Choto Pelia, the same one that had caught my attention on 24 November last year. Things had changed slightly since our last visit. The then roofless AWC now has a shining GI sheet roof and the walls have also been repaired — although not quite as well as I would have liked. Yet, instead of 12, 45 children are present this morning. Food, out of stock on the day of my previous visit, had been supplied in the meantime and partly explained the large attendance — including a few pregnant women. The Anganwadi worker, Lakshmi Hembram, and the helper, Rupali Hansda, were also present. In a gleaming new weighing scale suspended from the rafters supporting the verandah roof, they were weighing a two-year-old child, Mamoni Murmu. Now the main difficulty is the absence of a separate kitchen shed for the AWC, and to secure the regularity in supply of food articles.

I checked the registers and found that some teaching material had also reached the AWC, which is also meant to provide pre-primary education to the enrolled children — one of the most widely neglected aspects of this 30-year-old project. Over the years the emphasis on supplementary feeding as part of the ICDS project has grown, overshadowing the other services that the AWC is designed to provide; although in West Bengal, as in some other states, these centres have also played a role in the immunization programme. The Anganwadi worker assured me that apart from nursery rhymes children were also being taught the alphabet. I did not mention to her that none of the children were carrying a slate.

From the AWC we drove to Kumar *bundh*, reaching there at about 10.30 a.m. Even from a distance I could see the long row of date palm trees. When the work had begun they had stood tall on the low *bundh*; now they are almost drowned in the earth piled neck-high around them, with just the fronds visible like headdresses of comic book African chiefs. Finishing touches were being given to the re-excavated area; hence, only about a dozen labourers were engaged at one end of the site. The half-moon-shaped reservoir of the *sech bundh*, reclaimed from the creeping jungle, is about 120 m long and about 10 ft deep at the deepest point — 3900 man-days of work have gone into creating it.

We walked across the reservoir checking the conical pillars of earth left standing after the digging to indicate the quantum of earth removed. It is a definite marker of work done, and forms the basis for calculating the wages in a contractual arrangement. I wished it were a sunny day but the sky was overcast and a cold breeze nipped at our earlobes. Most of us officials were wearing at least a jersey or a thick sweater with a scarf around our neck for good measure. As we walked across I could not help notice that most of the workers, male and female, did not have any warm clothing on. Indeed, two of the men digging earth at the southern end, save for *lungis* hitched half-way up, worked bare-bodied. Their bare feet, of course, were no cause for surprise.

Plate 29.1 Kumar *bundh* — work in progress

After inspecting the bed of the tank and surveying it from the farther side, I proposed a slight modification to the plan. The northern side of the tank could be further excavated to a depth of another 3 ft. This was important because that is the end where the outlet for water is located. Through this outlet, water persuaded by gravity would be carried by field channels to the fields in the command area on the arching slopes beyond. The field channel, an important component of this scheme, is also being dug. Hopefully, the additional work would be finished in another week.

From Kumar *bundh* we proceeded to Bansberh to inspect the excavation of another old *sech bundh* being taken up there under the NFFWP. We went through the village where poultry units were distributed on 28 November 2004. Most of them had survived, although in nearby Tesabundh the mortality rate had been quite high — up to 30 per cent. After trekking through the fields we reached the Upar Bansberh *bundh* at the edge of the forest. Quite similar to Kumar *bundh*, this old reservoir was also created on the top of a slope at the edge of a forest and overlooks a large chequered slope of paddy fields. The significant difference is that the upper slopes of this *sech bundh* border the thick forest and a channel of a

Plate 29.2 A field channel for the overflow

nearby stream empties itself into its silted reservoir before flowing out from the southern end. The stream is a natural feeder of the tank, bringing down the collected precipitation from the extensive forest beyond.

The work on the Upar Bansberh *sech bundh* has been progressing quite well; the until recently congested, the weed overrun bed of the tank is now about 6 ft deeper. As in the case of Kumar *bundh*, the northern side, where the outlet is going to be, is yet to be dug out sufficiently. Of course, the work here is not as far advanced as the Kumar *bundh* but a large number of labourers are engaged here. Most of the activity centred on the field channel where about 50–60 persons were engaged. Fearing a scarcity of water for their fields, the people of Tesabundh further down the slope were objecting to the re-excavation of this *bundh*. Nevertheless, the amount of water flowing down to their lands is not going to be seriously affected. About 300 m further down another *bundh* is being built on the stream that issues from the Upar Bansberh *bundh*. The Forest Department is implementing this scheme under the RSVY. We went on to inspect that *bundh*.

Work was underway on the almost finished dam on the far bank of the stream, flanking the forest. To reach the other side we walked on a thin embankment built upstream. Dinanath Bouri, the beat officer of Kantapahari beat was present at the work site. Work on this *bundh* had started on 2 January 2005 and the pace of work has been quite satisfactory. The project aims to create a check dam on the stream to store the water that flows through the forest into the Upar Bansberh *bundh* and beyond. The dammed channel is only about 25 ft wide. However, the *bundh* was not created by deepening the stream. Instead, the barren forest land, adjacent to the stream at that point, was deepened to expand the reservoir, while simultaneously providing material for the embankment to block the stream. Due to the perennial spring upstream the reservoir thus created would certainly store a fair volume of water. Although the quantum varies from one season to the next, throughout the year water seeps from Upar Bansberh *bundh* and flows down this channel. This check dam will help store the water here and recharge the ground water, while the excess flow runs out through a small channel into the stream beyond the dam. But the spill-way was missing. I have asked the beat *babu* to make sure that a spill-way is developed on the northern bank of the stream to direct the overflow into the natural channel beyond.

When we reached the new *sech bundh*, the workers were taking their mid-day break. Almost all of them were adivasis. In groups of two, three and four, men and women squatted on their haunches on the ground, where a few minutes ago they were wielding pickaxe and spade. These implements and the woven bamboo baskets, used by the women to carry chunks of earth dug up by the men, also rested beside them. A few couples could also be seen sitting together with an aluminum food carrier and a plate in front of them. I walked among them, ostensibly to scrutinise the digging, but actually trying to see what the workers were eating.

Most bowls and tiffin boxes contained *pantabhat*, a little cabbage or potato leaf *saag* and salt on the side. The meagre vegetable appeared to feature on the meal as a token, a reassurance that this was a complete lunch. The actual meal was the heaped moist rice with salt and an occasional green chilli to thrill the taste buds. Some people were not eating, just sitting and quietly resting their bones; even though, like the others, they had eaten in the morning, they would now eat only after work in early evening. Two meals a day: all that this employment generation programme can ensure in these parts.

We walked across the fields down the slope towards the road until we finally met the stream again at the bottom of the micro-watershed. Due to the re-excavation of Upar Bansberh *bundh*, and the creation of the check dam just inspected, the conservation of water in the upper reaches will certainly receive a boost. The field channel that they are digging at the Upar Bansberh *bundh* will also carry water almost over 1 km down to the fields adjacent to it, and the excess water will again drain out into the stream at the bottom of the slope.

From Lalgarh or Binpur-I Block we crossed the fair weather bridge across the Kangsabati. The temporary wooden bridge is built over a broad but shallow river each year, after the waters of the monsoon have drained into the Bay of Bengal; this year the bridge has been constructed by a private party. The contractor is paying a rent of ₹12,000 per year to the Panchayat Samiti for setting a toll point on it. The Panchayat Samiti, that has fixed the value of the toll to be charged, has not spent a paisa on constructing the bridge; until last year its annual expenditure on this project was ₹500,000–₹700,000. This is a model that should be followed elsewhere in the district also. The bridge is important because it connects two parts of Binpur-I Block. In the large tracts of land on the opposite bank of the river potato is grown. The fair-weather bridge on Kangsabati makes facilities, such as the Lalgarh *haat* and market, the block headquarters and the BPHC, accessible to the people of the five Gram Panchayats on the other side of the river.

> *Work progressed in the remote villages identified through the Baseline Survey and the VVI; the movement of the Maoist extremists also continued. By now it was evident that they had two main targets: the police and the local leadership of the CPM. The last two attacks had been against the police and the government. Late in the evening of 5 February, Anuj Pandey, the local committee secretary of the CPM in Dharampur, under Binpur-I Block, was shot at, though he escaped unhurt.*
>
> *In mid-2009 television viewers across the country saw the double-storeyed pacca house of the same Anuj Pandey ransacked and destroyed by the enraged people of the area.*

◎

30
Of Houses and Homes
◎

The winter sun peeping over the horizon found SDO, Jhargram, and me on the road to Belpahari via Jamboni. Hamlets swaddled in bluish ribbons of smoke, drifting from the morning *chullahs*, emerged from pre-dawn shadows. We passed along a jungle of naked trees standing ankle-deep in fallen leaves; it was the time of the year when nature sheds its old garments before putting on new.

Although the sun was not yet fully up, already a number of people, mostly women and children, were busy sweeping the dried leaves into piles before packing them into sacks to carry them back to their homes. Pushed by young boys, a few bicycles, with bulging sacks sagging over both sides of the seat, passed us. In the seasonal sequence, at this time of the year dry leaves are an important source of fuel for people in these parts; it reminded me of some southern blocks of this district where pacing across harvested fields I had often come across paddy roots with lengths of stalk left standing — to be dug up when dry for fuel. The poor cannot afford to let anything go waste.

Warming sun rays were breaking through the screen of trees behind the village when we stopped at Sangram. The nearest house being constructed, about 30 m from the road, belongs to Haripada Sabar. The four walls have been erected up to the roof-level; the roof has to be laid and the cement pointing of the brick joints on the outside remains unfinished. Pre-fabricated concrete posts meant to support the narrow verandah in the front have not yet been delivered. Haripada's wife Kachi is cooking food on a hearth in front of the house-in-progress.

Thirty-two houses are being constructed in Sangram and 41 in Jugibundh. Many of the other houses in the cluster coming up in Sangram have reached the same stage as Haripada Sabar's house.

Most of them are being built in the space adjacent to the original hut. Such is the shortage of homestead land among the Lodha-Sabars that some of them, such as Haripada Sabar, have had to demolish their original huts to provide land for the new construction. In such instances, until the new construction is complete the family must, perforce, sleep in the open or take shelter in a neighbour's ragged tenement.

As we moved around the village inspecting the work we came across Srikant Sabar, the doubter in the village. Srikant, who lived in a thatched crumbling mud hut pock-marked with holes, had grave doubts about the quality of both, the houses and the work. A small group had also collected. Always interested in feedback from local inhabitants at a work site, I stopped to listen to them. With expansive gestures and emphatic shaking of his shaggy head, Srikant complained that although we were building houses of brick, mud was being used as mortar; further, he felt that the house was too small.

I asked the other villagers present if they had any complaints. Apparently, they had none. Then, as had been done earlier by the SAE supervising the construction here, I explained the following details to Srikant and the others: less than ₹22,500 had been sanctioned by the government towards the cost of each house; the house had been designed by engineers in consultation with Lodha-Sabars and would be strong, airy and well-lit; within this amount it was not feasible to use cement mortar for binding the walls; and even though mud mortar was being used, cement pointing of the joints on the external surface would protect the mud mortar and reinforce the joints. Neither was Srikant satisfied nor did his head stop shaking. Finally, I pointed out that our intention was not to force a new house on anyone. If Srikant, or anyone else, was so pessimistic about the fate of these houses and did not want one, he was free not to accept it. We were sure that there would be Lodha families in other villages who would be happy to have a new house. At this, Srikant's head stopped shaking and he meekly protested that that was not what he meant. I noticed a few grins among the dispersing group.

The health centre that serves this village is at Barsole, about a kilometre away. The local primary school is nearby, across the road from the village. I was told that the AWC functions in the shade of the primary school; like so many AWCs it has no building of its own — a fact that never fails to gall me. The helper, who is from this village, had appeared then. I asked her how the AWC was running. She reported the obvious: the children have to sit in the open and the food is also cooked outside. The food supplies are in the helper's safekeeping; for this I could not blame but only thank her. Her only request was to construct a building for the AWC.

In our round of the village I was confronted with the same abject poverty that marks Lodha-Sabar villages in the Junglemahals. Tumble-down, crudely pieced-together huts made of mud, bamboo and straw, without any windows and often not even doors; the single room is an unlighted shelter for the night and a place to keep their meagre possessions; a few lean-tos covered with torn tarpaulin sheets or date palm fronds propped against one side of a few huts provided space for a kitchen. In front of a few houses I noticed a few calves tied to short posts. It transpires that Lodhas here buy young calves cheap and after rearing them for one or two years sell them at a profit. I peeped into a few huts and saw what I had grown to expect — a line on one side of the hut on which a few old articles of clothing were slung, a rolled palm leaf mat or two leaning against the far corner, a bucket and a few other steel or aluminium utensils. That was it!

A few of the huts had a narrow verandah with a *chullah* at one end. But most people cooked their food on earthen stoves in front of their houses. At this early hour, rice, the filling staple, was cooking in aluminium *handis* whose bottom halves were plastered with a thin layer of clay to prevent them from getting permanently blackened.

Subhendu Sabar's house had been recently re-thatched with bright new hay; inside the one-room hut I confronted its expected starkness. Nearby is another small mud hut that is crowned not with straw but with layers of palm fronds. In the sunny front yard of the house, next to a stack of asbestos sheets, Rabi Sabar, a man of about 50, and his wife and daughter had sat down on the newly swept earth for the day's meal of rice and vegetable curry. They had three deep aluminium plates, three small steel bowls and one steel tumbler of water between them. In the centre lay a small rectangular earthen vessel that held salt and a few red chillies. Rabi Sabar's new house is also coming up nearby but I do not know when his family will eat better.

Plate 30.1 Rabi Sabar's family has their morning meal

In all there are 65 families in Sangram; it is a 100 per cent Lodha-Sabar populated village. Most of the people engaged in the fields are daily wage labourers. Very few own any land. A water harvesting tank is being constructed on the land of Peon Sabar in Sangram village, under the RSVY project by the Minor Irrigation Department. The rectangular tank will be 40 m long and 20 m wide and 4 m deep. It would take at least another month to complete the work, because the workers are not digging mud but hard red gravel or *morrum*. Intermediate layers of lateritic rock render the work especially difficult. The site has been well-selected: in the leeward side are fields green with wheat and potato irrigated by shallow tube wells. The number of people on the rolls at this site is about 150, but these days about 100–110 people are working here. At about 7.35 a.m., when we reached the edge of the work site we were met by an unforgettable sight.

Under a powder blue sky that merged into the fresh green of the distant fields beyond, at the far end of the sectioned, boulder-strewn, red expanse of the half-dug tank, we could see the arcing rise and fall of a single pick-axe. It was too early for most but Guiram Sahis

Plate 30.2 Guiram Sahis, alone at work

had reached first, so what should he do? In the cool of the morning draping his loose shirt on an earth pillar in one corner of the tank, hitching his faded *lungi* up to his knees, and tying his chequered *gamcha* tight around his head to pre-empt sweat, he began his day's work. The lone pick-axe rose, and fell.

◎

31

Pukurs and *Bundhs*

◎

Our next stop was at Jugibundh village where 42 houses were being constructed for Lodha-Sabars. Tuku Sabar's new house is being built on the site of their earlier one, since dismantled. Their sparse belongings lie under a shed of dry date palm leaves nearby. Tuku Sabar and his wife have decided to place a window on the front wall of the new house, at their own expense. Another house under construction, in which the owner is also contributing, belongs to Suchitra Sabar. She has decided to strengthen the base of the walls with laterite boulders. Nearby is the house of Lala Sabar and his wife Milki Sabar, who are having their morning meal of rice, a bit of vegetables and fried potato leaves. They have finished digging the foundation but the bricks have not come yet. A quick tour of the two *paras* in Jugibundh, where the two clusters of houses are coming up, revealed that in one *para,* although the foundation of most houses has been excavated, work has come to a standstill due to the shortage of bricks. I have asked the BDO to check and ensure that the bottleneck does not persist.

There is a large *pacca* well with a protective parapet in Jugibundh. Constructed two years ago, half full of leaves and branches; it has been lying idle for the last one year. Apparently, there hangs over it a dispute over who should clean the well, the Gram Panchayat or the Panchayat Samiti. Since neither has accepted the responsibility the villagers decided not to use the well; instead, they have dumped more leaves and branches into it! It has not struck anyone in the village that they — the users of the well — could very well take up the responsibility for cleaning it. This is the flip side of the development process.

Jugibundh, larger than Sangram, is a prosperous village with a mixed population. Children of this village attend the same primary school as the children of Sangram, which lies across the road in Sangram; it was too early in the morning for me to visit the school. Mahatos own most of the cultivable land around here. The BDO told me that this year the mini-kits supplied in this area under the RSVY have been instrumental in some crop diversification. The water-guzzling *boro* paddy and potatoes sown earlier have been replaced by wheat and mustard, which have taken up much of the area. However, mini-kits of new crops alone are not enough. As I wandered around the stretch of wheat and perky mustard, I thought perhaps too much water was being lavished on the new crops. In several fields water stood inches deep. The steady splutter of diesel-powered shallow tube wells pumping water indicated the source. The change of crops must be followed by a whole variety of inputs, including skills and knowledge, and the farmers should be again and again made aware of the specific requirements of wheat cultivation. This misuse of water needs to be corrected. I have asked the BDO to contact the ADO in this regard so that extension activities could be carried out.

From Sangram and Jugibundh we moved on towards Belpahari Block. At a distance from the road we occasionally saw sacred groves surviving in the land cleared for cultivation. In these groves Santals and Mundas offer prayers in the months of *Poush* and *Magh*.

On the way we stopped at Kukrakhupi in Dharsa Gram Panchayat, within Jamboni Block, where a large water harvesting structure is being excavated under the NFFWP. The proposed *sech bundh* is well located, half-way up a gentle slope that loses itself in the forest. As this land is vested in the government there is no dispute related to the ownership or use of land, and consequently the tank is being excavated. It is assuredly going to be a public *sech bundh*. Some portions of the work-site have been excavated to a depth of about 3.5–4 ft, while the shallow parts are about 3 ft deep. Although bathed in the early morning sunshine, the unfinished tank was a picture of desolation. Among the conical measurement pillars lining the length of the dug up area, red boulders lay strewn and the harsh excavated *morrum* was piled along the sides. Progress here is frozen because the workers had struck an unyielding layer of boulders and lateritic rocks. Several members of the beneficiary committee of this scheme were present at the time. We had a quick conference on the spot.

From the beneficiary committee I learnt that there were two chief difficulties: first, the layer of rock, which was not amenable to pick-axes and spades; and second, the low rate sanctioned for digging the earth — as they were digging not earth but rocky *morrum*, which it took greater effort and time. I told the BDO and the SAE that as far as the first problem was concerned, small explosives may be used by a trained team to blast through the layer. Once the layer is broken the second tangle could be unravelled by digging according to the Minor Irrigation Department's separate schedule of rates for excavation of earth and for *morrum*. I tried to impress upon the block officials, and also the beneficiary committee, that I would very much like the work on that site to resume the following day. I also shared with them the reasons for my insistence; with the onset of summer, merely weeks and days away, the longer the work was delayed the more difficult it would be to negotiate the laterite. Moreover, late February, March and April are the leanest period of the year for landless labourers and marginal workers, as very little agricultural work is available. Haltage of work at this site would affect those very vulnerable segments of the population to whom this project was meant to provide work.

Arun Kanti Baid was the person in-charge, or leader, of the beneficiary committee. He is an educated youth, and earns his living by tutoring children. I was astonished to learn that he tutors 40 children on a regular basis. He gives tuition sessions in the morning and evening, charges ₹40–50 per child each month and teaches all subjects. Many of his pupils are children of the workers at this site.

Leaving the harsh landscape behind, we drove into the swelling, thickly-forested areas of Belpahari Block, the north-westernmost extremity of the district. On the way we passed children, women and even old men sitting in front of their houses making *babui* rope. These days the rope sells for about ₹10–12 per kg. Once the rough rope has been woven a major task is smoothening. This is done by looping a length of the rope around a tree trunk or a round wooden post and pulling alternately at both ends so that the coarse rope is buffed into the smooth final product. Sometimes a sickle, a bullock-cart wheel or even a stone is used to chafe the rope into final shape.

Our first stop in Belpahari Gram Panchayat was Nainagara *bundh* where the re-excavation of an old *sech bundh* is under way. About 150 people armed with pick-axes, shovels and bamboo baskets were at work, and their pace was brisk. The reservoir, about three acres large, extends lengthways between the road and the forest. From the heaps laid on the inclined banks of the *bundh* it is evident that a large quantity of stones has been dug up, but now labourers have struck earth. A spring has been unearthed in the north-eastern corner of the tank from which water is trickling out into the *bundh* — always a happy sign.

As I talked to a few workers it became clear that the beneficiary committee for this scheme is dormant; representatives of the community have not been involved in overseeing the work. I have asked the SDO to ensure that a meeting of the beneficiary committee should be held within the next two days. Provision has not been made here for either drinking water or a crèche. These should also be arranged immediately. Although work on this site started on the 10 January, in the interim period only a few labourers were engaged here. Last payment was made only yesterday. A muster roll is being maintained but payment is being made on a group basis — which can facilitate leakage. I openly informed the beneficiary committee, and also the workers present, that they should not accept group payment but only payment on an individual basis. Some labourers also came up and requested that measurement should be done twice a week and accordingly payment also be made twice a week. I asked the SDO to examine if this was feasible. Although the scheme is not more than 2 km from the block headquarters, the BDO has not found time to visit the scheme in a while!

Almost beside the road, a kilometre further along at Asthajuri, within Belpahari Gram Panchayat, another *sech bundh* is being re-excavated. The beneficiary committee for this scheme was formed by the local villagers when the work started here about three weeks back. However, the membership of the committee was not pleasing to the Gram Panchayat, which refused to ratify it. I instructed the BDO to ensure that the beneficiary committee was formed in consultation with the Gram Panchayat immediately. If he was not able to convince the Gram Panchayat, the SDO should come over and resolve the deadlock.

The *bundh* is located on the lower slope of a gently rising ridge. Young acacia and eucalyptus trees have replaced the Sal and other local trees on the hillocks overlooking the reservoir, but at least the denuded forest has been partially revived. Although in the centre of the tank a pool of ankle-deep water survives, most of the tank bed has been encroached upon by gravelly silt, weeds and bushes. Today the workers were trying to carve out the northern and southern sides of the *bundh*, which is also full of stones. About 60 persons are at work here, although normally 100 people are engaged. Here too no arrangement has been made for drinking water. I directed the SAE to immediately engage one person for this purpose; I have emphasised in several review meetings that the NFFWP schemes provide for such an arrangement at each work site but information, especially information that may benefit the poor worker for whom the scheme is meant, trickles down much too slowly.

For the inhabitants of Asthajuri village, as for the people of other villages in this area, the nearest *haat* is held in Belpahari once a week on Wednesday; they depend on it for purchase of articles of daily use. Although they are supposed to receive their wages on Tuesday, in time to make their few purchases in the *haat*, the payment is irregular. Weekly payment on Tuesday must be ensured. The local Gram Panchayat representative who is meant to oversee the work here is also supposed to ensure timely payment. Obviously, he does not find time to discharge his responsibility. To my horror, I found that the money for the weekly payment had, indeed, been handed over to the panchayat member yesterday. Apparently, instead of arranging for the job worker to make the payment under the supervision of a block employee, the BDO had yielded to local pressure and permitted the Panchayat member to take charge of the money for payment of wages! This was most irregular and should be stopped immediately. The workers also grumbled about the low rate of wages. I explained to them at considerable length that payment could be made only on the basis of the quantum of work done, and, therefore, the beneficiary committee must become operational to ensure that not only do they receive payment on time but also the wages they deserve. They could not expect adequate payment if they do not work enough in a day. Further, they needed to increase the pace of the work on the *sech bundh* so that it was completed before summer sets in — it becomes too hot to work in the sun, and the earth is too hard to dig. Certainly they understood the importance of the re-excavation, how they stood to gain from a deep reservoir to store the monsoon bounty that would otherwise drain away swiftly into the hill streams taking the valuable topsoil with it. The land on the other side of the *bundh* belongs to Asthajuri and its people. Hopefully, come winter a significant part of the cultivable land would be able to bear a second crop.

When we prepared to leave, I called the SAE, Anjan, and his job assistant Janmenjoy to our vehicle. I rebuked them for the lapses in the two schemes, and asked them to ensure that payment was made on time, water carriers were engaged immediately and beneficiary committees on the two sites were also formed without any further delay. I also asked the BDO to explain as to why these flaws have been allowed to persist in these schemes even after almost a month of their commencement.

The point raised earlier by the workers about being paid on the eve of the local *haat* should also be conveyed to all the BDOs, so that payment date is scheduled in each Gram Panchayat, to the extent practical, with reference to the local *haat* day — especially in the interiors where there is no *bazaar*.

◎

32

The Damned Dam

◎

*An important destination on this day-long inspection tour today was
Khandarani dam, about 8 km from Belpahari Block headquarters, near
the tri-junction of Paschim Medinipur, Bankura and Purulia districts; an
area where the LWEs were becoming increasingly active. Some time ago
the Chief Secretary had told me that he had heard of a dam which had
been almost completed and then abandoned at Khandarani in Belpahari
Block. Supposedly, it had been taken up by the Zilla Parishad, but before
it could be completed had become mired in a legal tangle created by
an overzealous forest officer. If completed, so the Chief Secretary had
been informed, it would be a major source of irrigation to cultivable
land owned by the inhabitants of several villages. The Chief Secretary
wanted me to find out if the information was correct, and, if so, whether
the forsaken project could be salvaged. Back in Midnapore I had made
inquiries and found the story to be substantially accurate.*

*In view of the irrigation requirements of 13 villages in Bhulabeda
and Banspahari Gram Panchayat of Binpur-II Block, the Zilla Parishad,
Paschim Medinipur, had proposed the construction of a small dam
over the Khandarani khal in 1995–1996. The scheme was taken up at
Amlasole mouza in 1996. Work on the scheme continued intermittently,
according to the availability of funds, for more than three years. Then, in
March 1999 — by when ₹98.91 lakh had already been spent — it was
halted by the DFO, West Midnapore division. Curiously, until August
2000 no written direction was given to the Zilla Parishad by the DFO,
Jhargram. Between August 2000 and May 2004 the matter was taken
up sporadically by the Paschim Medinipur Zilla Parishad. In May 2002
the Range Officer, Bhulabeda Range, lodged a complaint in the Belpahari
Panchayat Samiti against the Zilla Parishad contractor for attempting
to resume the work. The Paschim Medinipur Zilla Parishad had taken
up the matter again in 2003 but the tangle remained unresolved.*

Plate 32.1 The incomplete dam

Six km further along the narrow state highway, climbing and dip-ping with the ridge on which we travelled, we turned southwards. Another 2 km through the sal and nettle-fringed track brought us to the watercourse, which further upstream was sought to be dammed. Leaving the shallow, pebbled bed muddy behind us, we drove through thick forests before crossing Barihati Village, a hamlet comprising about 30–35 families of Mundas and Santals. Although situated in the forest, *ryoti* land belonging to the tribals surrounds the village — now empty of crops. If the dam had been complete, shallow canals would have slaked the thirst of these fields in Barihati and nearby Sinduria. In a few minutes we were at Khandarani dam.

Since our vehicle had stopped in the lee of the dam, we climbed up the bushy incline to reach the upper rim of the reservoir. As I gazed across the reservoir, my first impression was of its beauty. Skirted by low-lying sleepy greenish-brown hills, a curving expanse of water flared out into a calm lake reflecting the pale satin blue sky above as it came up against the 75-m-long concrete dam. However, turning towards the concrete structure evoked a sense of dejection.

The concrete dam was almost complete but it was not yet functional, for neither the locks to the channels that would supply the feeder canals, nor the canals were ready yet. The pity of it!

To learn what had transpired in this desolate part of my district, I did not have to wait long. I spotted two persons taking a dip in the reservoir and turned to them. Rupen Munda and Birsa Munda informed me that in the 1970s, at this very spot, the Forest Department had attempted a number of times to make an earthen dam across the perennial stream that forms this reservoir. However, successive monsoons had washed those dams away. A few years ago, the Midnapore Zilla Parishad, with the help of the Forest Department, had constructed the concrete structure across the channel. Before it could be completed a new Forest Officer had been posted to this division and the work was stopped. Although work had been initiated on the left side — from where a first stretch of a canal had been excavated to carry water to Barihati village and irrigate the 100 acres there — the construction was incomplete. The locks that would have regulated the flow of water had also not been allowed to be built. Time and again the local villagers had requested the Forest Department to permit the completion of the dam, but it had not come through.

The area of the reservoir is about 150 acres. In the middle there is a small island on which dark stumps of drowned trees remain. Weathered, black tree trunks with vestigial branches also protrude from the shallow reaches of the lake. The two villages of Goalberia and Aguibil with untilled *rabi* land are positioned upstream of the dam. They too were interested in its completion, for then lift irrigation schemes could supply water to their fields. In fact, some *ryots* of Goalberia stood to lose land due to construction, but even they had made it clear that they had no objection to the expansion of the reservoir.

As Rupa and Birsa Munda, and a few others who had arrived in the middle of this wilderness, poured out their grievances, I could not help reflecting what a wonderful tourist spot this would make! To the right of the lake rises the Korasheni hill crowned by a small gleaming white *Shiva mandir*. The lake, a natural basin, nuzzling in the lap of low hills is a fine place for birds to nest. I could see cormorants and other waterfowls near the banks. Yet the local population is dependent upon little other than the one crop of *kharif*, paddy.

As we stood talking, a jet flew past shrieking overhead, reminding us that we were in the 21st century. Or, were we?

Prompted by the Chief Secretary, I had taken up the issue of the incomplete dam in November 2004. By January 2005 several senior officials of the Forest Department had visited the blighted project site. Towards the end of February 2005, before leaving the district, emphasising the importance of the project and enumerating the benefits that would accrue to people and forests in its vicinity if completed, I sent a reminder to the Forest Department urging the revival of the Khandarani Project.

The dam was finally completed in 2009.

◎

33

A Beautiful Valley,
Disturbed and Disturbing
◎

From Khandarani we took the road from Odolchua to Kankrajhore and proceeded towards Mayurjharna via Simulpal. As described previously, the LWEs had disrupted the construction of this road a couple of months back. Now the earlier earthern track was being re-laid under the PMGSY. Work has begun again and I met the contractor Dushmant Giri on the road. He told me that he faced several obstacles. For one, local politicians were insisting that no machine but only manual labour should be utilised for constructing the road. The villagers working on the road had also informed him that the LWEs had indicated that only the culverts and causeways should be constructed not the road. Regardless, he had continued working. Giri also said, and I found his statement credible, that there are no security personnel on the route — I had not come across a single police patrol in this area.

Construction of the road has altered the picture of the route. When I had first come here several months ago I had driven on a narrow, winding rocky track that led from Odolchua to Kankrajhore and beyond. Now from Odolchua to Kankrajhore there is a wide 7.5-m-broad road, at places nestling along the rocky hillside. Apart from facilitating developmental work, the road has also opened up the valley and provided job opportunities to the local population. This truly picturesque area could also be nurtured very easily for tourism purposes. Yet we must wait until the LWE problem is resolved, and basic development takes place.

At about 12.30 p.m. we reached Amjharna, or almost. We had to stop a little way outside the village because earth was heaped high

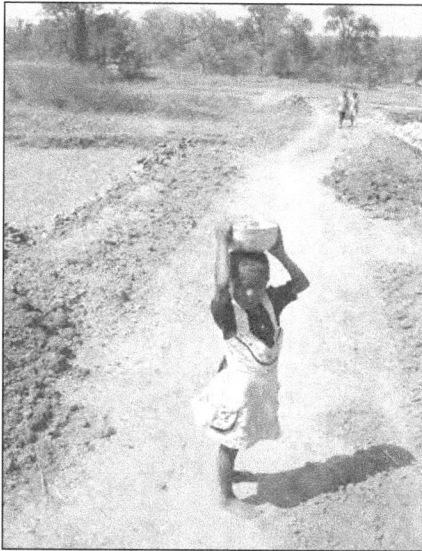

Plate 33.1 Father's precious help

all across a road that was under repair. So we decided to walk. The road to Amjharna has been widened and, when complete, would be able to support even heavy vehicles. As we approached the village, we came across a tiny girl, not yet four years old but bearing the responsibility of an adult. Clad in an old black and yellow tunic, the bare-footed little angel walked alone ahead of us, her extended arms determinedly clutching at a large brass bowl on her head. The glistening bowl was two-thirds full of *pantabhat* and contained a smaller bowl which held some boiled beans. When asked where she was going, the little one gazed quizzically at us — as if wondering, 'Do these strangers understand nothing?' — before telling us what we knew: she was carrying lunch for her father who was working in a nearby field.

Our primary destination was the water harvesting tank being constructed under the RSVY at Amjharna. About 14 people were engaged at this site. This scheme was taken up at the very outset of the programme. However, because we had insisted upon using local labour the number of labourers available here has been limited. Amjharna, after all, is a village of only about 35 households. Literally the hardest aspect of the scheme has been a massive quantum of rock, which had to be unearthed, broken and cleared while digging this tank. The positive facet was that they have been able to strengthen the sides of the tank with the same blocks of rock.

Trilochan Mura is the owner of the land where the tank has been excavated but the benefits, of course, in terms of the agreement for provision of water, will go to the farmers who own land in the vicinity. Trilochan Mura suggested that other smaller schemes may also be taken up, especially since there is a perennial rivulet that runs through the slender, tree-verged vale. Apparently at Amjharna there is a site for building a *bundh* near the Akasani hills that could be taken up by the Forest Department.

The MHU visits Amjharna regularly on Tuesday; to avail of the facility sometimes very sick patients also come to Amjharna from neighbouring villages. Amjharna Village itself is populated mainly by Muras, or Mundas, who, since they own much of the cultivable land in the locality, are certainly better off than the Lodha-Sabar inhabitants of the area.

Plate 33.2 The makeshift umbrella

As we stood in the brilliant sunshine talking to Trilochan Mura at the work site, I caught a sight that, whenever recalled, shall always fetch me a smile. Emerging from the forested hillside, a short distance away, two young men were walking towards us. The younger, scarcely more than a teenager, cradled in his arms a transistor that was belting out a new Hindi song; a red *gamcha* wrapped around his middle, he wore a red T-shirt and sported a blue baseball cap as protection against the sun. His elder companion, also with a red *gamcha* around his waist, wearing a yellowed vest, was without a cap. Instead, in one hand he held aloft a short branch from a teak tree like an umbrella, its large leaves protecting him from the harsh sun!

Babui grass is one of the main crops harvested in these parts. Most houses have large stacks of the material standing next to them, over 10 ft high, covered with tarpaulins. An old man sitting outside his house, cutting his fingernails with a blade and listening to a tune on the radio, told me that a *mahajan* give ₹4 per kg for dried *babui*. Nearby, in the shade of the house two water buffaloes chewed their cud. A few goats tied to a bullock cart bleated for replenishment of their fodder, while chickens scurried around. Beside the stacks of *babui*, a few women were squatting on the ground tying dried bunches of the grass into orderly bundles for storage. I noticed that one of them was a frail old widow — her silver hair dishevelled, her rumpled white *sari* drawn up over her knees, struggling with a bundle; I could not help wonder if her's was an age for such toil. Returning to more manageable issues, I asked the SDO to check if an SHG was working here; if not, one could soon be formed. Then we could easily provide a storage godown-cum-shed for the dried grass; the tribals cultivating or gathering *babui* would then get a much better price for their labours.

The Panchayat Samiti has built a road up to Trisima village for ₹50,000. A large number of people here have also come forward to work in the project. The houses are mainly built of mud and locally extracted stones with baked red terracotta tiles on the roof. Most homesteads have a small kitchen garden attached to them supplying seasonal vegetables — tomatoes, brinjals and beans. Brinjals are a perennial favourite in these parts. In the valley, on the banks of the fast-flowing streams, banana also flourishes, and as we drove along I saw several fine clumps of banana plants with generous amount of leaves.

Plate 33.3 For a bundle of *babui*

The trees are preparing to shed their leaves, but before they are entirely lost the foliage is turning golden, brown and red. The hillsides are a mosaic of burnt, rich colours, across which sunshine sashays from dawn to dusk like a painter possessed!

There is a well at the entrance of Amjharna, which is the chief source of irrigation as well as drinking water for neighbouring houses. It was cut out from almost sheer rock about 25 years back. It needs a parapet and a platform. In Amjharna and Amlasole water is never a problem. I found a number of small water bodies at several levels on the slopes, and there is a scope for creation of more such small tanks and *dhalbundhs*. However, most of the land around these water bodies was lying fallow. There is a need for intensive extension work by the Agriculture Department in these areas. The training camps should be held and new crops introduced here, such as vegetables, pulses and oilseeds. There is tremendous scope for various *rabi* crops.

Our next stop was Amlasole, where we first visited the primary school. For some reason the school was not being held today; no one is around to illuminate us with the reasons — no teacher and not a single child. In front of the primary school two additional classrooms are to be constructed, the foundation for which has already been excavated. A hand pump has also been set up there, as I had promised. However, how does the DO ensure the running of a primary school in the remotest part of a disturbed district if the teachers play truant, the parents do not demand accountability, and the primary education administrative machinery does not follow up?

Precisely on the northern side of the primary school, a new water harvesting tank under the RSVY has been excavated by the Minor Irrigation Department on Manasi Munda's land. It is almost complete and has come up quite well. Again I noticed springs that were lying unutilised or were being used for cultivating, of all things, the resource intensive *boro* paddy. Without agricultural extension efforts, farmers here are unlikely to make the most of the advantages nature has bestowed on them.

We also visited the water harvesting tank next to the primary school. Work is still on but basically the final dressing is being done. I visited another tank, into which ground water is seeping, further down the valley, next to the stream flowing through its centre. This is going to be a sizeable storage tank; however, the sides are yet to be strengthened. An average of about 15–20 people are working here. They are all from Amlasole. Since they do not own any implements, Lodha-Sabars who work here have also been provided with pick-axes and spades. The third tank being excavated a few hundred metres upstream with the help of Zilla Parishad fund amounting to ₹50,000 is smaller; it has not been completed. This is most distressing because it is superbly located right beside the stream; in place of a dreary excavation site, we could have been looking at a pond. The work here needs to be expedited.

On our way back we stopped briefly at Kankrajhore. In the centre of the village a signboard has been put up publicising that the MHU visits every Wednesday. I also saw the primary school in Kankrajhore; two additional classrooms are to be constructed and the foundation has been laid.

The slopes of Amjharna, Amlasole and Kankrajhore valley are covered with *babui* grass. For the Forest Department it is a source of headaches, since villagers are constantly trying to clear the forest and plant *babui* grass. Most of the land on which the grass is being grown, especially forest land, is basically encroached upon and cultivated by force. Those inhabitants who have been in the game from a little early are reaping the rewards, whereas others — especially the Lodhas — have been left out in the cold.

◎

34
The Santal Families' Robinson
◎

One morning in late February, I called up the Chief Secretary on the telephone to tell him that the most of the first lot of chickens distributed in vulnerable villages in November 2004 had survived, had even started laying eggs, and that we were trying to tie up the collection and sale of eggs with SHGs. However, when the Chief Secretary came on line, I blurted out, 'Sir, the chickens have started laying eggs!' Normally a severe looking man who seldom smiled, the Chief Secretary burst into laughter.

Accompanied by the SDO, Sadar, I left the headquarters at 7.40 a.m. for the Keshpur Block Office. When we reached there at about 8.10 a.m., I found Nurul Islam, Karmadhyakshya, Paschim Medinipur Zilla Parishad, the BDO and the Sabhapati of the Keshpur Panchayat Samiti waiting for us. From there we proceeded towards Rasunchak, which, according to the VVI, is the seventh poorest village in this dis-trict. That Keshpur Block, agriculturally the most prosperous and heavily cropped block in the district, should have such a village was a little strange.

Retracing our steps towards Midnapore, we turned left at Panchamichak to take a broad 20-ft-wide mud and *morrum* road. We passed through Panchamichak village, which sends a large number of labourers to Midnapore town. Most of the rickshaw pullers in Midnapore town also come from this village. They leave for Midnapore early in the morning and hire a rickshaw from their owners on a daily basis. The owners get ₹20 at the end of the day, and with the rest of the day's earning, about ₹50–60, the rickshaw pullers come back to Panchami. Most of the population here is Muslim; they speak Panchami, which is basically a mixture of Urdu, Hindi, Oriya, and Bengali. It is the kind of language that we hear in parts of Contai sub-division, especially in Contai-II Block.

The road here is very broad and connects three Gram Panchayats. Given its importance, it could have been taken up under the PMGSY. There are a large number of ponds in this part of Keshpur that supply fresh fish to Midnapore. Understandably, local fish, as opposed to the frozen consignments from Andhra Pradesh, are much in demand in the town. A Zilla Parishad member told me that a large number of ponds have been excavated in this area and water from these is being used for cultivation purposes also.

We went by Gopalchak, which is also high on the list of vulnerable villages, across the *khal* that divides Gopalchak from Jamua, another village high on the list. Gopalchak is primarily a Lodha village, whereas Jamua has a large Lodha *para*. Both sides of the road are green expanses of *boro* paddy interspersed with a few fields of wheat. Kograhaat, where we stopped and parked the vehicles, is a tiny market with a few shanty shops.

In the early morning Kogra Primary School, a long one-room *pacca* structure with a *pacca* floor, also serves as the local Anganwadi. Both, Gita Rani Patra, the helper and the Anganwadi worker, Kakali Rana, were present. Since the children are also taught here — rare in most ICDS centres — about a dozen children, mostly girls, sat cross-legged on the floor on used sacks with slates and thin sticks of chalk. Each of them carried a deep plate or a single unit stainless steel tiffin-carrier in which they would receive their food, to be served at about 10 a.m. The register reveals that 99 children are enrolled here. Of the names of adults noted in the register, four neo-natal mothers out of 11 and four pregnant women were present. Four-year-old Lata Panja, with close-cropped hair and wearing a short pale green frock with a green *bindi* to match, recited a poem for us.

About 100 m down the narrowing road we turned off into the fields sown with groundnut and *til*. The road to Rasunchak ends here. I could see the village, about a kilometre away, from the road itself — an island of soaring bamboo groves in a vastness of fields through which the sloping roofs of a few houses are visible. To Rasunchak, which lies right in the middle of a stretching expanse of fields, there is no road, not even a tread-defined pathway. As we approached the village, from a distance I noticed that from the green fields near the road-side we were moving towards a stretch of sun-baked brown beginning to crack under the fierce new summer sun, a brown expanse that surrounds our destination.

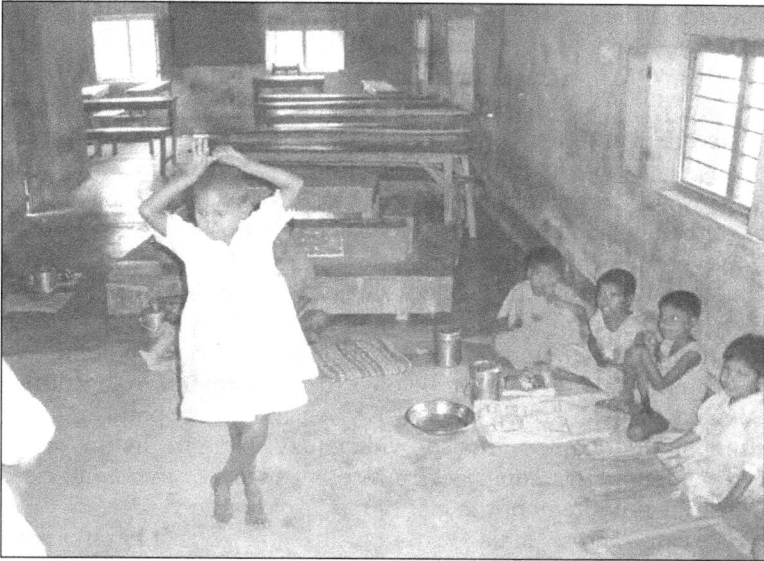

Plate 34.1 A poem recital in an Anganwadi

The village is a cluster of 23 houses, all occupied by Santal families. I was informed by the panchayat member accompanying us that most of them are landless labourers. A very few own small parcels of land. Kangsabati River is about 3 km away, and apparently this low-lying land slopes towards the river. During the monsoon this area, now dry and broken, is often flooded. Why can we not have some water harvesting tanks in these parts?

Groundnut had recently been sown here, but in a few fields slim sprigs of *til*, flax, sown earlier, were springing up. This land does not belong to the Santals. The panchayat member accompanying us told me that we could see tin roofs and that tin roofs are a sign of a developed village. I pointed at the lone tin roof in Rasunchak. The panchayat member responded by informing me that three families in the village have been provided with IAY houses. I walked on across, what to all appearances was, a cricket pitch prepared on the hard fissured earth.

At the nearest corner of the village we came across an ICDS centre being conducted in a small shed. The tattered straw roof, exposing a section of the bamboo frame beneath, sags wearily to one side straining the supporting bamboo posts. The floor of the shed is a raised, uneven platform of packed earth. The register tells me that 77 children are enrolled in this Anganwadi but only 16 are present. I wondered! Pushpa Tudu is the Anganwadi worker posted here and Rekha Das the helper. I am struck by the absence of any plates — something that one finds in most Anganwadis. The Anganwadi worker tells me that the exhausted stock of food has not been replenished for some time. I asked the SDO to make a note of it and ensure immediate resumption of supplies. The SHC for the village is at Pakuria. It is called Dhobagora Health Centre.

In the centre of this island of Santal hutment is a pond. Indeed, the houses are all built on the surrounding banks of the pond — a *pukur par* village. This *pukur* belongs to one Netai Das from a different village; he also owns land nearby. All around the pond are thick clumps of tall bamboo that provide gauzy shade to the houses. A few coconut palms, some jackfruit trees, and one or two simul trees break the monotony of the giant grass around the village.

We came across Sitala Hembram sitting in front of her hut with her granddaughter. Wrapped in a white sari, matching the unvarying silver of her hair, Sitala Hembram is about 65–70 years old. She should be a fit candidate for Old Age Pension. I wanted to know if her name had been included in the list prepared by the Panchayat Samiti or not. The panchayat member, the local member of the ruling party, had a list; he showed me his diary and triumphantly pointed out her name in a list of nine candidates waiting for a vacancy. Sambhu Hembram, who is also about 65–70 years of age, was squatting in his courtyard smoking a *bidi*. In reply to my question he told me that they had been living here since the time of his father and grandfather. Amit Mangal Hembram, his son, is a daily labourer. These days, he and others like him from the village, are working in the fields of *til* and groundnut. They get ₹36 and 1.5 kg of rice for a day's labour!

Twenty-two families in Rasunchak own land totalling about 5–6 *bighas*, that is, about 2 acres. Unless the owners can save enough money to pay for the shallow tube well water, these fields yield just one crop. Some of the houses have recently been re-thatched with the fresh straw from the *kharif* crop. The dwellings here are really of poor quality, many with mere polythene sheets protecting the roof. The houses are squat, mud-walled structures with long roofs sloping over the narrow earthen verandah to protect the dwellers from the scorching sun and lashing rain. Most of them are *chaar chala*, roofs that slope on four sides. Doors either comprise some bamboo staves nailed together or even a piece of patched sacking. Tuki Hembram, a grey-haired resident of Rasunchak, tells me that during the monsoon water climbs up the side of the embankment around the central pond, and people perch on bamboo *machans* to wait out the flood. This is one of the poorest Santal villages that I have seen. I have no doubt about the efficacy of the VVI in identifying and ranking villages according to the level of vulnerability.

Modest stacks of paddy, covered with faded electric blue plastic sheets, await threshing in the constricted mud-plastered courtyards of some houses. Most of the houses comprise a slim L-shaped verandah and one room. The verandah basically serves for keeping their possessions, such as trunks, cycles and some *nagaras* (drums). Dhiren Hembram is about 50 years old. He and a few others in Rasunchak weave small baskets of bamboo that is available in abundance all around the village. However, these are not sold in the market but are for personal use only. Unfortunate, because this is something that could also supplement their income.

On the eastern side of Rasunchak, in the verandah of a hut enclosed by a bamboo lattice, I found two 15–16-year-old boys bent upon a turquoise sari ornamenting it with elaborate *zari* designs. One of them, Durga Mandi, told me that last year he had learnt this work in Mumbai. After they work on it the cloth is sent out to Kolkata and then to other metros. On one side of the verandah five more boys were busy at the same task on a different sari as a radio played Hindi film music. Fifteen-year-olds Lakhan Mandi and Putu Hembram are also engaged here. Payment to these boys is made on a contractual basis. For completing one sari they get ₹300 to ₹500, depending on the intricacy of the work. Harun Khan, about 16 years old, is from Kumari, a neighbouring village. He is the link between the people who bring the orders, the sari, and the *zari* here, and then take away the finished products to the markets. Although I tried, I was unable to determine the prevalent rate of labour, the wages the boys receive for a day's work. The panchayat member pointed out to me the 'road' that links this village to Kumari — a narrow, winding 3-ft-wide pathway, built of raised earth following the *aals*, that probably turns to soggy mud during the monsoon. The Panchayat member wanted to take credit even for this!

A little later I met Kanai Hembram who also works in the *zari* workshop. He confided that the skilled boys get ₹9 per hour. When available, they get work for 12 hours in a day. Normally, in a month they manage to get three weeks of work. There is no electricity in this village, but in the verandah-workshop a tubelight powered by batteries has been installed by the middleman. The *zari* workshop started only about a week before the last *pujas*. Earlier it was being done in Baharagora, several kilometres away, and the boys from the village had to go there every day. No proper road to Baharagora exists and during the monsoon communication was severely disrupted. Therefore, they had requested the middlemen to start a workshop in Rasunchak so that they could work here itself. I feel that a training programme for this trade could be started here, especially for young boys and girls.

There is a small pond next to a house with clumps of banana plants around it. Since its inhabitants virtually own no land, this is a very poor village indeed. Greenery is at a premium and the land between the huts is dry and hard. Unlike other Santal villages, in Rasunchak there is no sign of tiny kitchen gardens tucked away behind houses or of flowers to brighten the home. It is as if the Santals of this village are cut off from their roots.

Upon checking Sita Hansda's Antyodaya card, I found that of the 22.5 kg of grain as ration to be issued on this card she was getting only 5 kg of rice. Another Antyodaya card belongs to Gunadhar Tudu who claims that he is not getting the ration that is due to his family. Earlier they had been given only 5 kg of rice, but last month they had all gone together and quarrelled with the ration dealer, after which, against the cards of five persons, they were issued 15 kg of rice. I told them that they must go in a group, and, if necessary, quarrel to get the full quota of 17.5 kg of rice and 17.5 kg of wheat per month.

Sabitri Hembram is sitting with a child on her lap on the protective earthen platform surrounding her house. We examined her health card; although the child on her lap is about one-and-a-half years old she is again pregnant. So far she has received two shots of tetanus, one tetanus booster and only one dose of iron. She has not received any ante natal care. I also checked the health card of Archana Hembram, daughter of Sudhi and Ram Hembram. Like Sabitri she too carries a one-and-a-half year-old son on her waist. Archana until now has only received two shots. Although clad in a

Plate 34.2 An expectant mother with her child

bright green sari and bright red blouse, she appears to be not more than 16 or 17 years old. She has never attended a school.

Of the more than a dozen children I came across in Rasunchak I saw only one boy wearing a pair of rubber slippers.

Only after the visit, while walking back to the vehicles, we learnt that Rasunchak was once a de-populated mouza. *About 60–70 years ago the land owner, a small local landlord, had brought four Santal families over from the north-western part of the district and settled them around the* pukur. *They were provided with huts and were engaged in his field on a regular basis. Gradually these four families grew and some other Santal families also joined them. Since the area is low-lying and prone to waterlogging, and even flooding, they all settled only on the banks of the large water tank. It is tempting to call Rasunchak an oasis, but an oasis connotes wellbeing — far removed from the tiny habitation of despair. Rasunchak is a barren island in the main stream of rural agricultural prosperity, that is Keshpur. It is an island occupied by uprooted people, wrenched away from their environment, from their culture, from their chief source of livelihood and tradition — the forest.*

◎

35
East of Eden
◎

In the afternoon of 9 March the Chief Minister held a video conference with all DMs to review the progress of developmental work in the districts. The Chief Secretary and other senior secretaries to the government were also present. Before the Chief Minister arrived the Chief Secretary spoke with us briefly. His message was simple — whichever government, wherever it exists, is primarily for the poor. The focus of its attention is on those people who cannot take care of their needs and requirements, not those who can take care of themselves and are well off. Most of us do not have to worry about drinking dirty water, about going hungry or about our children not receiving higher education. It is our duty to see to it that the basic services the state provides are available to the people. It was not possible to pin down one or two things that the DMs and ADMs should look for when visiting the identified vulnerable villages in the state. The visits would elicit priorities. But employment generation through the various programmes should certainly be our first concern. If at the time of leaving the district we were also able to say that so much employment had been created during our tenure, our stint as DM would have been worth it.

Although we had received detailed directions to reach our destination, we nearly passed by Atsangra and stopped at Khatranga, a large village lying virtually across the road with a population of over 2000 people. So tiny is Atsangra that even in Khatranga it is not very well known. According to Census 2001 it is a *mouza* populated by only 39 persons. The most vulnerable village in Kharagpur-II block, Atsangra ranks 28th in the district.

We spied the hamlet, a few adjoining clusters of huts surrounded by sky-serrating bamboo and a variety of trees which, mostly leafless at this time of the year, seemed even taller. The ever-fresh green of the banana plants, flourishing on the banks of a pond at one side of the cluster, reflected on its muddy water. No doubt, for this group of huts this was the main source of water for a variety of chores; two hand pumps standing at the entrance of their house meant for public use were also their source of drinking water.

The people here seemed to be fond of social forestry, or at least were not inimical to it. Not only were both sides of the *morrum* road lined with eucalypti, even the evenness of the green fields was broken by small clusters of trees. Many of these were relatively young; probably because the older mature trees had found their way to the market. Happily enough, as we approached the habitation on the mud track leading off the *morrum* road, in the village itself I saw several sturdy Shishu and Shisrish trees which had survived the greed of wood traders. The fields to the north of the habitation were lush with the *boro* crop, but we soon learnt they were not part of this village.

About 30 m away from the *morrum* road stands the first clutch of mud houses, the residence of two brothers Shyamapada and late Kalipada Soren. Haphazardly laid one-roomed huts, made of mud and crowned with carefully trimmed thatch roofs, crowd around a courtyard worn smooth by use. Although their overall neatness is reminiscent of the nobler Santal houses in the Jangalmahal area, these are humbler. Somehow, the native dignity that characterises even the smaller adivasi houses in Jhargram is absent from these dwellings. Among the things lost in the uprooting of these people from their forest homes are traditional skills and technology. The Santal families own very little land: between the two brothers and their grown-up children there is less than 4 *bighas* to plough. Bereft of the resources that their fellows in the Junglemahal garner from the forest, their only option is to sell their labour. A van-rickshaw standing next to one of the huts indicates the occupation of its resident.

Basanti, Kalipada's widow, and Laxmi Soren, Shaktipada's wife, were busy this morning. In large aluminium vessels set upon two separate earthen stoves, that seemed to have grown out of the courtyard, they were boiling paddy that would convert to par-boiled rice. From time to time they would feed the gaping black maws of the stoves with the fuel of the season — fallen dry leaves and straw. In one shed were enclosed a few pigs. Three or four tethered goats nibbled at some leaves left for them on the ground, while chickens

Plate 35.1 Preparing par-boiled rice

pecked away furiously nearby. Next to the small stacks of hay in the frontyard there was a *tulsi* plant. No vegetables were grown in the strip of land surrounding the huts either; the chickens, perceived an easier source of varied income, had defeated earlier attempts in this direction. The families did not rear any fish in the pond; it was not an activity their years in this part of the district had yet equipped the Sorens even of the newest generation.

Talking to the women I learnt that Basanti Soren's husband had died in Midnapore some time back, but the reason was not clear. From Basanti's hesitant words I gathered that he had gone there for the delivery of their daughter-in-law and there were some problems, after which he somehow died in a *jhamela,* row. My desire for information was not strong enough to blind me to the muted pain the memory was causing the widow, so I dropped the topic. Though I did learn that at present the son and the daughter-in-law were away at the latter's father's house in Jikulia, in Debra Block. Basanti's son, she told me, had one daughter and one son. The daughter's age was about 10 and the son about 11 years old.

Two children — siblings — had followed us into the courtyard. In response to my query Namita Soren, aged about 14, smiled shyly and said that she did not go to school but helped her mother at home. Sujan Soren, the boy who was younger, studied in class-III in Gadgachi School. Clearly, even in Atsangra it is more important for boys to attend school than for girls!

As we walked towards the next cluster of houses, one of the villagers told us that Kalipada Soren did not die in any *jhamela*. In the month of *Agrahanya* he had, indeed, taken his daughter-in-law to Midnapore for the delivery of her child but the doctors had advised a Caesarian section. Kalipada had not been able to arrange the money required for the operation; in despair he had hung himself from a tree near Midnapore Sadar Hospital.

A pond separates the two other clusters in Atsangra. This pond between the homesteads is owned by eight brothers all related to each other, but not all of them stay in Atsangra. Houses here, as in Rasunchak, are not of as good quality as in the Jhargram area. One of the clusters is occupied by the Mandi brothers, Suren Mandi and Sonaram Mandi; their houses stand next to each other. Sonaram's house, closer to the road, is double-storeyed and a reasonably well-constructed mud and straw structure. A shallow pump-set squatted in his courtyard. Sonaram Mandi owns 1 *bigha* and 5 *kathas* of land. Around his homestead, enclosed by a nettle fence, there is land enough for a kitchen garden, but there was little evidence of any attempt towards turning the land into a productive vegetable patch. He revealed that earlier he had planted a few *lau* creepers that the chickens had ravaged, so he did not plant anything again. The pump-set, which he used to rent, is lying idle; it broke down some time ago and he does not have the money for repairs. Hence, this *boro* season he could not use the machine to cultivate his fields either. Sonaram has fallen back upon working as a labourer in others' fields. I was a little taken aback by the low expectation of these people from life. Perhaps, persistent adversity beat them into believing that not much is to be obtained from this hard world.

The other brother, Suren Mandi, has two sons, Gorachand and Trilochan, who must be about 18. Gorachand Mandi and his wife, Teesta, married five years back and have a son about six months old. They have named him Sonaram. I examined the infant's health card and was relieved to find that he had received all the immunization doses due so far at the local health centre at Popura, about a kilometre away. In all, the father and two sons had 1 *bigha* and 15 *kathas* of land. The two sons, apart from helping their father in

Plate 35.2 No need to lock this door

their field, also work as labourers. Trilochan told me that right now there was no work to be found. The wages in this area vary between ₹32–₹50 in cash plus 1 kg of rice and two bowls of *muri*.

In Atsangra there are four Santal families and one Mahali household. The last clutch of huts in the village belongs to an extended family of Mahalis, who are basket weavers. An old couple, Shambhu and Rebati Mahali, live here with their son and daughter-in-law, Bablu and Sumitra Mahali. The condition of the houses was much poorer than in the other two clusters; thin rudely-built walls with mud plastered over bamboo, rotting thatch roofs that have weathered several scorching summers and lashing monsoons. Significantly, the houses here have doors with bamboo sticks loosely tied together to form a sagging panel — the type that brazenly declares that it has little to safeguard. Only a tall, generously spreading hibiscus bush ablaze with crimson blooms lights up a corner of the otherwise brown courtyard of Shambhu and Rebati Mahali's house.

On a fence nearby leaned a new prefabricated concrete plate, meant for the latrine but serving no other purpose than as a statistic of our sanitation campaign!

During this season the Mahalis are not engaged with their craft of making bamboo baskets. Taking advantage of the paddy harvest and available straw, they were trying to repair their houses before the onslaught of the monsoon in a few months. This Mahali family also owns a small *pukur*, on the banks of which grow thick clumps of bamboo — the raw material of their trade. Most of their income in other periods of the year comes from bamboo products. I asked Rebati Mahali if Atsangra comprised only these five houses that we had already visited. She laughed and said yes, there were not even eight houses in Atsangra ('Ath' means eight in Bengali). This is one of the smallest villages among the most vulnerable villages that I have visited, but not the bleakest. The main problems here are not only of unemployment and lack of irrigation, but more fundamentally of landlessness. Since the families here own small parcels of land, even if irrigation were available it would not benefit them directly. How does one solve the problem of land? Should we not look at alternative income generating activities based on new skills or, perhaps, animal husbandry?

Less than half a kilometre away, along the *morrum* road lies the village of Gadgachi, ranked 1090 in the district in terms of vulnerability. As we walked towards the village, it became evident that its material condition was reasonably better than what we came across in Atsangra. The population is also mixed. In the village we met Putul Rani Ghorai, the Panchayat Samiti member from this area. We requested her to accompany us and show us the village.

Our first stop was the Gadgachi Primary School, a long building with green-washed walls and a sloping tin roof. A narrow verandah, on which the three main classrooms open, ran the length of the building, to which a newer fourth small room had been added at the farther end. Opposite the new room was a Mark-II hand pump — in working condition. At one end of the large open field in the front, two swings and a see-saw rested in anticipation of the labours that the day would bring when the school is filled up with children. What I liked most was the volleyball court with the net occupying the ground. This obviously is the centre of young life in the village — of boys, anyway. The panchayat member and the other villagers

I met at the primary school had no complaints against it. The four teachers attended the school regularly and Midday Meal was being served to the children.

As we walked around the village talking to the residents, we came to the IAY house that belonged to Sarojini Mahali. Set in the shade of tall, leafy bamboo in a corner of Gadgachi, it was a ten-year-old one-room hut with mud walls and GI sheet roofing; although still standing, it cried out for repairs. The once open verandah had been enclosed with a screen of thinly split bamboo sticks; the bamboo door was shut and secured with a tiny rusted lock.

The second IAY house that we inspected belonged to Biswanath and Panmoni Soren. In the midst of a cloud of bamboo shavings Panmoni Soren sat busy splitting green bamboo sticks, with a curved handle-less iron blade, into half a centimetre thin strips to weave baskets. Her husband was away working in somebody's field for the day's wages. Behind their house was a small pond, probably excavated to provide a platform for their homestead. Putul Rani Ghorai told us that the homestead on which their IAY house is being built had been *khas* land, probably vested. Until the house was built the couple had not owned any land of their own.

This IAY 'house' was constructed only about six months ago: with 3 ft high 'walls' of packed earth, eight concrete and three wooden pillars in the middle to support the shining GI sheet *chaar chala* roof, and giving a free run to sunshine, wind and rain throughout, it was a shed masquerading as a house. The walls had never been completed. Panmoni Soren informed me that they had not been give the money to build the house, as was the rule, but that someone was doing the work for them. That 'someone' turned out to be the local committee secretary of the leading political party. He had taken the 'responsibility' of constructing these IAY houses. Obviously, the responsibility was weighing too heavily on his shoulders because the work was certainly not worth ₹20,000! Although I felt like raving and ranting at the Panchayat Samiti representative, controlling my anger I asked the BDO to conduct an inquiry and send me the report within a week.

On the way out of the village, we passed by a grand Peepal tree under which *gram devata*, the village deity, was worshipped. This was but a small raised area on which lay two pink hibiscus flowers. As we were about to leave the village, a young man of about 35,who had accompanied us on our brief round of Gadgachi, came up to me and said, 'Sir, this is the first time a DM has visited our village since independence'. I could not be sure whether this was meant to be a complaint or a compliment.

It was strange to find these tiny adivasi villages scattered among the vast villages in the prosperous western side of the district; strange, until one recognises the pattern.

◎

36
A Tale of Two Villages
◎

On 18 March the Ananda Bazar Patrika *published a news report titled,*
'Panchayater naam suhunley-i chotey jan gramer manush' — '*Villagers*
get angry even at the mention of panchayats'. It was a leak.

Some time back, in one of my periodic reports to the government
I had conveyed the disillusionment of the people in the Junglemahals
with the local panchayats who had failed to live up to the expectations
of the people. The news report, quoting extensively from my letter, had
made the point that this was one of the reasons for the rise of the Maoist
extremists. The next day the paper followed up with a report on one of
the remote villages in Binpur-II block; this time the villagers, underlin-
ing their neglect, stridently echoed the sentiment.

Accompanied by the DPLO, I left my headquarters for Nayagram
block. At about 8.45 a.m. we crossed over the fair weather bridge
across the Subarnarekha. This was time for a tiffin break for the
labourers who had been digging sand from the river bed and load-
ing it in boats and trucks since dawn. In the raised sandy middle of
the river, groups of men and women sat having rice and vegetables
in aluminium bowls. A line of young women and girls, women in
sari and girls in bright frocks, carrying collected fuel wood from the
Nayagram side were approaching the bridge. They must have gone
into the forest at least two or three hours back and now they walked
back with both arms clasping long bundles of thin sticks and twigs
over their heads. Soon we had left the Subarnarekha behind and
were travelling through an undulating landscape.

At about 9.15 a.m. we reached Nayagram block office. The SDO
and the BDO were present. We stopped there for about 40–45 minutes to review the progress of work under diverse programmes, in
particular under RSVY and NFFWP. It appeared that work had not

begun in any of the Gram Panchayats. The BDO informed me that the dispute over the composition of the monitoring committees for each scheme has proved a major hurdle. There is considerable conflict among panchayat members over this issue, especially in Jamirakhal Gram Panchayat. In fact, most other programmes are also at a stand-still there. The local branches of political parties are creating all kinds of obstacles and are refusing to allow the executive assistant and the job assistant to supervise the work. This knot has to be untied. Although the situation is not quite as bad as in most of the panchayats, the work in this area was also held up. Therefore, we need to send an ultimatum to all that until the work is begun in all the places by the end of the coming week, money allotted will be withdrawn and no further allotment made. I was prepared to transfer the Jamirakhal allotment to the Panchayat Samiti so that it could be administered and implemented from the block.

In Singdoi village houses are being constructed for Lodhas under the Special Housing Scheme. The SDO told me that people here do not want the honeycomb windows that had been planned for the rear wall of the house. Their principal fear is that the window would allow ghosts to enter the house! Therefore, the best efforts in favour of ventilation are also likely to be stopped.

The workers engaged in the excavation of a tank here complained that the ground is very hard, and there was rock at the bottom of the pit. Some of them protested, '*Haat phete jachchey*', 'Our palms are cracking'. With great seriousness I went up to them and with some deliberation scrutinised their palms. Then, looking up I asked, 'Koi? Phaata haat to ami dekhte parchi na,' 'Where? I can't see any cracked palms'. Everyone laughed and the surliness that had threatened our exchange evaporated. By now their gnarled hands had seen too much to be defeated by rocky laterite. But the workers had made a point about the hardship of their work; and I recognised it.

Despite the rocky nature of the land considerable progress has been made on the large tank, which is sure to serve as a water storage tank. The workers though are aggrieved that the payment is being made late. I asked them on which day the local *haat* was held and they told me that it was on Friday. I directed the BDO to ensure that payment is made on every Thursday without fail so that people have money in their hand before the day of the *haat*. To break the laterite rock workers are using explosives, which is not really permitted but, in the circumstances, cannot be helped.

On the way we met Sitaram Soren — the man who had had one too many to drink early in the afternoon of my previous visit, and had threatened that he would build a *bundh* on his land to stop the water from going down to the proposed large tank. I asked him whether he was still planning to build it. His short reply was a sober, 'No. It is for our village.' Apparently, it was still too early for his drink.

From Srirampur we moved towards Metia in Jamirapal Gram Panchayat. Jamirapal lies to the south-east of the block headquarters. We left the state highway and moved to a raised *morrum* road for the Gram Panchayat headquarters. Our targets were Metia and two other villages nearby which comprise three of the most vulnerable villages in the district. Along the way, squatting in the shade of trees were groups of women selling *hanria* in aluminium pots. The morning meal is accompanied, and sometimes substituted by those who can afford it, with *hanria*.

About 3 km from Metia village I saw a youth on a bicycle wearing a *lungi* and a white T-shirt with the blue and red 'Tommy Hilfiger' logo emblazoned across his chest. I am certain that Tommy Hilfiger could not in his wildest of dreams have imagined that in such a destitute part of the world there are people sporting his T-shirts, albeit pirated.

The raised *morrum* road bisected extensive dry stubbly fields lying fallow in the *rabi* season due to the absence of irrigation. I do not know how irrigation can be provided to such areas. The plain to our left slopes gently towards the Subarnarekha, not more than 4 km away. On the western side the ground is undulating and, therefore, offers greater opportunities for harvesting surface water. But there are no such *bundhs* in sight.

Metia is a set of houses strung along the road. We stopped at the first house; it belonged to Bhano Mandi, a man in his late or mid-50s. I asked him how long ago had he built his house. When he was very young, was the reply. His parents had come from near Baligeria in search of livelihood. One can make out these houses are of relatively recent vintage because the road defines their existence. Almost all the houses in the village are along the road. The quality of the houses is poor, low mud walls and long sloping roofs, unlike what we find even in the northern parts of Nayagram block. Somewhere along the line during this migration they seem to have lost some of their skills in construction of houses. I could not find a single double-storeyed mud house in Metia village.

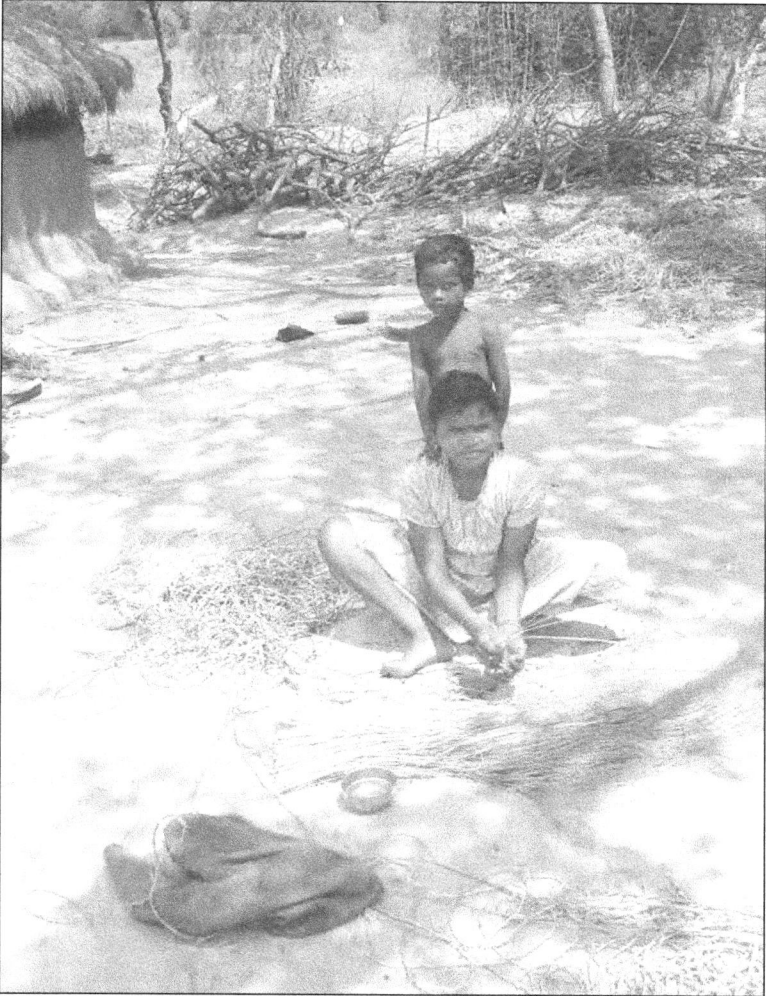

Plate 36.1 Shakuntala Tudu at work

At the far end of the village we talked to some people. With her little brother looking over her shoulder, a 12-year-old girl sat in her courtyard weaving strings out of *babui* grass. Nearby, washed paddy was spread out to dry on a plastic sheet. The small girl was Shakuntala Tudu. I asked her why she was not in school, but she was too shy to reply. Haren Tudu, her father, then emerged from the house. There is a small pond in the rear of their hut, dry and empty.

There is one tube well in the centre of the long habitation and one small pond in the rear of the village about 300 m away. Another pond is located about a kilometre away. The people of this village use these two ponds for bathing and washing. However, right next to Haren Tudu's house, under a cluster of tamarind trees, there is also a disused well with a parapet — full of rotting leaves and twigs its water is unusable. I have asked the BDO to renovate the well, deepen it a little and put a shed over the top.

Ram Besra and Banshi Hembram, two aged men are the neighbours of the Tudu family. Since this area was empty, the Besras shifted to this site about 20 years back. Most of the inhabitants of Metia either settled down here or were born here in the last 50 years. The older residents remember their parents bringing them here from different parts of Nayagram or localities nearby. Except two families none of the others have any land and many of them go to earn their labour to Egra, a small town about 20 km away across the Subarnarekha. For men the rate of labour here is ₹30 and 200 gm of puffed rice per day. Women get even less.

Thus Metia exists, a veritable labour camp that has risen beside the road. In urban and semi-urban areas, huts built along the road indicate a certain degree of prosperity. To the contrary, in rural Bengal it is a mark of landlessness of the residents — be it refugees from the neighbouring country, migrants from other states or districts or, as here, migrants from another part of the same district.

In the neighbouring village of Kusumkuria there are two *paras*, Uparpara and Nichapara (upper and lower localities). Uparpara, also known as Uparbasti, is inhabited principally by adivasis, mostly Santals. Uparpara has 20 houses. Most families here keep pigs and chickens. They take care of each others pigs and chickens in the same system followed in the Jhargram area. The inhabitants of Uparpara, many of whom are old, own little land and depend mainly upon wage labour. The younger population journeys for work to nearby villages and towns. Dalhor Hembram, a feeble old woman over 70 years of age, sits on her low *charpoy* in the uncertain shade of a tree next to her tiny straw-roofed hut. She is a deserving candidate for Old Age Pension for tribals.

A hand pump in the centre of Uparpara is the chief source of potable water; it stands in a muddy pool. Some women informed me that the hand pump needs to be repaired; to get the pump working one must first pour some water into it from the hole in its cover.

Plate 36.2 Mahi Besra shelling tamarind

The hand pump also sorely needs a concrete floor around its base to prevent contamination. I also came across a well in the frontyard of the panchayat member from this area. Constructed by the Gram Panchayat, it is a ring well without a platform or a parapet.

Mahi Besra, a young mother, was shelling tamarind on her raised mud verandah in the shade of an overhanging straw roof. I stopped by to ask her how much did she sell the tamarind for. She said ₹5 per kg. A tall well-grown tamarind tree in her frontyard is the benefactor. In a year sometimes when the yield is good they take about 50 kg from the tree; during other years the yield may go down to 30–35 kg. She earns a maximum of ₹200–250 in a season. In the market in Midnapore tamarind sells for ₹45 a kg!

A few stacks of recently harvested wheat lie in Sitamani Hembram's courtyard. A middle-aged woman in her early forties, Sitamani's right leg and foot are swollen due to filaria. Her two small bare-bodied sons are sitting beside her scraping with their fingernails and eating the sweet orange flesh of the *bel* fruit. She recounted to us how sometime back a large portion of her crops was destroyed by elephants. In one corner of her frontyard Sitamani

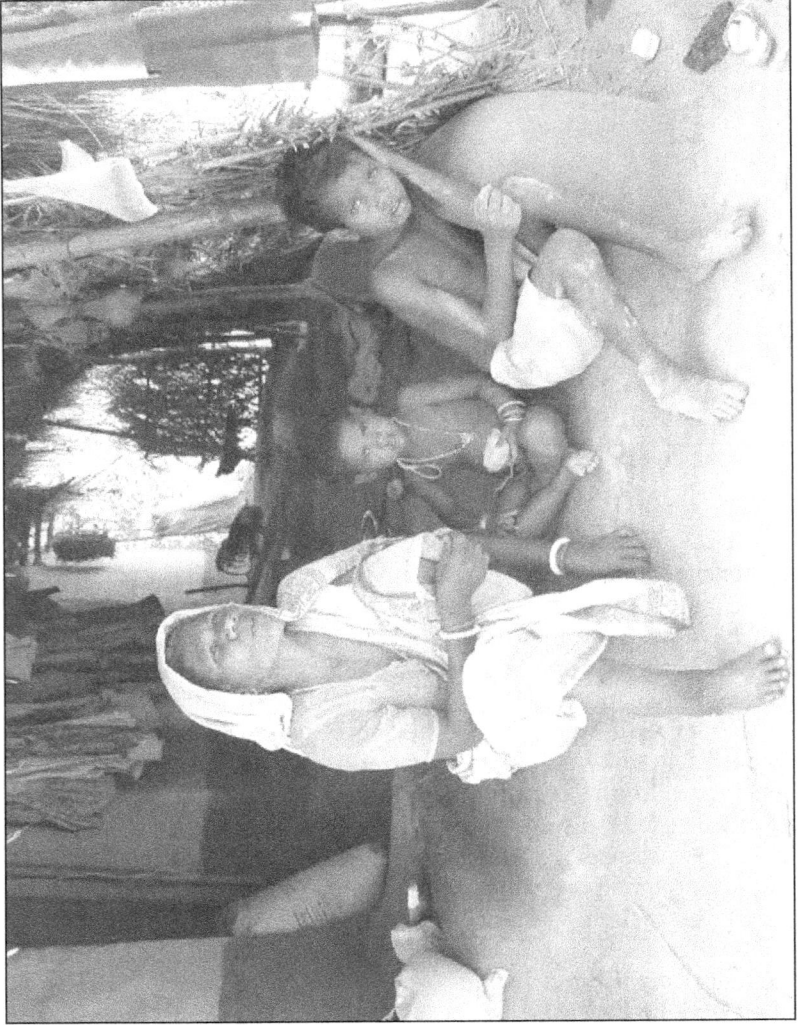

Plate 36.3 Sitamani and her children

Hembram is brewing traditional *mahua* liquor in an improvised still: sealed with mud, three aluminium pots sit on top of each other on an earthen stove, with the distillate flowing through a tube into a plastic cotainer on the side. I asked her how much did she sell the *mahua* for. She told me ₹12 per 330 ml bottle. 1 kg of *mahua* flowers yield about three litres of *mahua* liquor.

Further down the lane we came across a house under construction, a double-storeyed structure in brick and concrete with fancy window shades. It belongs to one Subal Hembram who works in the Revenue Office in Chatinasole under Gopiballavpur-I Block. The only *pacca* houses I have seen in these poor villages are owned by either teachers or government employees.

The narrow stream separating the adivasi populated Uparpara from the Bengali Nichupara does not quite indicate the difference in the lives of the two sets of residents. On the other side, several houses of its Bengali residents are two-storeyed and appear relatively prosperous. These are houses that belong to people who own land, cattle and goats. Even the vegetation is different. Uparpara has a thick cover of trees and bamboo; tamarind, bel, ber and other trees that have sprung up wild abound. On the other side of the *khal* there are fewer trees; jackfruits, palms, mango and other fruit bearing trees have been planted and nurtured.

Pradip Mahapatra, who was also weaving *babui* rope, told me that about 40–45 families live in this *para*. The government has sunk some hand pumps and a public well has also been dug. But the overarching difference between the two *paras*, Adivasipara and the Bengalipara, is land: of the total 245 families in Bengalipara only five are landless. Pradip's house is in the more modest part of the village; huts here are small and share a courtyard. He owns some land, which is the main source of his livelihood. In the courtyard of his house, his wife is frying fish in a cast iron *kadahi* over an earthen stove that is almost level with the ground.

Nearby, in the forecourt of a neighbour's house, where a widow lives with her daughter, son-in-law and grandson, *dal* and vegetables are being cooked. Further along, in front of Rabin and Rikta Mahapatra's house a ladyfinger and potato curry simmers on the stove, while Rikta prepares to cook spinach. In the neighbouring house I think cooking has been completed; for rice — the last to be cooked so that it may be served steaming hot — has just been taken off the hearth. Near most houses are large caches of dry leaves,

Plate 36.4 Fish curry for lunch in Nichupara

stored in a net; painstakingly collected dry leaves comprise the main fuel in this season. A glance at my watch told me that it was almost 1 p.m. No wonder lunch was being cooked in every house in Bengalipara. In the Adivasipara I had not come across any signs of preparation for lunch. For the residents there, who must travel a distance to encash their labour, the first of the two principal meals is taken early in the morning.

As I took a photograph, a pregnant woman in red standing under a tree called out, *'Hain nao, ebar tolo,'* 'Yes click, now take a picture.' With a glowing face she posed; I obliged.

The fields in Nichapara were plush with wheat, which was being irrigated by shallow tube wells. Since most of the land is owned by the people of Bengalipara, i.e., Nichapara, I asked them whether they could identify any spot where a *sech bundh* could be made, or where a *pukur* could be excavated. There was a spot between the Adivasipara and the Nichapara which would make for an ideal *bundh*, but the owner of the land was not willing to donate it. There is a primary school at the entrance of the village at Uparpara (also called Uchupara by the Bengalis). The primary school is a two-room *pacca* building without any toilet or water source. Since the school was open for just half a day today, it was closed by the time we reached. Bengalipara also has a tiny grocery shop and a flour mill.

Beyond Kusumkuria lies Jouka village. It is also an adivasi dominated habitation laid along the road. The road itself is on a narrow ridge, which separates cultivable land on both sides. The adivasis must have settled here long time ago near the land where they found employment. Soon we crossed a few large *sech bundhs* — and at least two streams, which, to my eyes, begged to be dammed. There is enough water in this area but hardly any attempt to hold on to it. Funds from the Hariyali Project (a central government watershed development project) are sitting idle in the Gram Panchayat, unutilised despite entreaties and admonishments. Perhaps the first step would be to conduct a water survey. I have asked the BDO to identify the spots between Metia and Kusumkuria where check *bundhs* could be constructed across the stream. We could even go in for one concrete structure or a series of low concrete structures.

The distinction made by the panchayat between Bengali and adivasi groups is all too evident in this village. In the Adivasipara, which incidentally is home to the local panchayat representative to the Gram Panchayat, there is only one hand pump and that too does not work properly. On the other side of the *khal* in Bengalipara there are three government hand pumps and a well. The road too is well constructed and repaired.

Plate 36.5 Some houses in Nichupara

The further away adivasis settle from their native area in and around the forests, the more likely they are to be the labelled workers of local land owners — big or small. They are people colonised in their own land. Brought and settled in distant parts, these adivasis provide manual labour to local land owners. I had asked Ram Besra and Banshi Hembram of Metia where they had migrated from. They had said, 'From very far off. You would not know, so far off.' When I persisted for a name, Banshi had told me they had come from the vicinity of Baligeria — less than 15 km away! For them a kilometre is a long distance; 15 km separate worlds.

◎

37
A Moonlit Visit
◎

As we drove towards Gurguripal, our destination, to visit work sites in the neighbourhood, the sun was on its way down but the road had come alive with the familiar signs of evenfall. Women walked by with gleaming brass pots of water balanced on their head or carrying dry dung cakes heaped in woven bamboo baskets, often holding on to a frisky child with their free hand. Men sat on parapets of culverts or outside tea shops sipping creamy brown tea from small glasses, between puffs of *bidi* or cigarette animatedly discussing myriad affairs. Small herds of short cows and packs of smaller Bengal Black goats common to this region also made their way home.

Shortly we stopped at Gurguripal, outside the entrance of the extended water conservation area. The wooded entrance was now framed in a massive gateway of concrete. The heavy beam at the top, over 12 ft high, is quite unnecessary and actually a wasteful expenditure. I had not quite bargained for this type of 'development'. I told the ADFO as much, but it is a fait accomplis. Construction and upgradation of the road leading into the park is also complete; the track has been widened, raised and topped with *morrum*. A drainage ditch about 3 ft deep accompanies both sides of the length of the road. They plan to plant ornamental foliage beyond the drain, which will itself function as a water retention trench. Along the banks of the reservoir a number of newly erected clusters of concrete pillars caught the eye. Upon enquiring I was informed that large concrete umbrellas would eventually cap these pillars to create picnic points for visitors! Suppressing a shudder, I requested the Additional Divisional Forest Officer (ADFO) to at least replace the concrete tops with opaque corrugated fibre roofing. They would cost much less and perhaps not weigh so heavily on the vision.

Row-boats and pedal-boats for tourists to rent out for a row around the lake have also been procured, and the ticket counter would be ready in another two weeks. One rest-shed with two toilets each for ladies and gents has been constructed a little off the road. Across the road at the point where a monsoon stream crosses it, a causeway has also been built. Further along, around the edge of the lake land has been levelled for planting a garden. I wondered whether they were making the place much too ornamental; people would visit Gurguripal to savour wilderness not the calculated prettiness of an urban park.

After a round of Gurguripal we went further up the state highway towards Dherua to see the earthen dam built on a *jhora* at Berapal.

The jungle thrives on both sides of the stream upon which a fair-sized earthen check dam had been constructed less than 50 m from the road. In the gathering dusk as we climbed up to the top of the dam my heart gave a tiny leap. The curving stream bed beyond, widened by innumerable gushing monsoons, had been inundated and formed a swelling expanse of water. Lower branches of some trees and shrubs kissed the muddy water that had climbed up the shallow banks. I spoke to the few people who had gathered there; Paban Singha, a 60-year-old resident of Berapal, and Joydeb Adak, who is the leader of the local FPC (representatives of two coexistent hierarchies — traditional and modern) were more vocal than the others. According to them, this was an excellent choice for a *bundh* for it would result in a renewal of the water sources for three villages, Belpara, Berapal and Gurguripal that lie downstream, across the highway. Three hundred acres of land cultivated by these villages is likely to benefit from this *bundh*. A slipway had been made on the higher side of the dam so that excess water may drain out into the stream further down.

Members of the FPC who had collected there were also spontaneously appreciative. The old man Paban Singha could not stop smiling, but then neither could I! This is a gem of an intervention that will not only help recharge water in the area, but also provide vital irrigation water for fields lower down across the road. We need more such schemes around the forest throughout the district. Indeed, once the next monsoon clothes the earthwork with grass, the earthen dam will be beautiful. The local people are already looking forward to picnics at this site in the coming winter.

The light was failing but the enthusiastic ADFO told me about the progress of work at Asnabandhi. Since I could not resist the temptation, in the darkening evening on a red road through a green forest, we drove on towards Asnabandhi.

On the way I learnt that the Upar Bansberh re-excavation work has also been going on quite well and local villagers were happy with the result. By the time we reached Asnabandhi darkness had fallen. At the village we picked up Subal Mandi, the head of the FPC who is executing the re-excavation project at the first work site. The *dhalbundh* being created is on land sloping down from the forest and has a huge reservoir. A good amount of laterite boulders had been dug out and laid on the banks of the tank and I was amazed at the amount of work that had gone in the making of this reservoir which was already about 6 ft deep. On the forest side, just beyond the tank, is an embankment about 2.5 ft high which the villagers have raised to hold the water. This would actually defeat the purpose of a *dhalbundh* by preventing water from up the slope to flow into the tank. I suggested this to the members of the FPC, and they agreed that this *aal* should be removed and the water should be allowed to flow down into the tank on the western side which will not have an embankment. On the other three sides there can be a 3-m-high bank. The tank would provide a vital supply of water throughout the year. Although we were armed with torches, a glowing moon provided enough light for our inspection.

We walked across the field on the glistening white *aal* to the pond in the middle of the Asnabandhi village. Since I last visited it on 25 January, considerable progress had also been made on this re-excavation site. The earth measurement pillars eloquently testified that the tank bed had now been deepened by about 6 ft in two stages. The centre of the pond is now about 10 ft deep from the ground level. Water has begun to seep into the pond; disturbed water-fowl began swimming away from the light of our flash-light into the dark.

The FPC had made rapid progress since my last visit, when dismayed by the lack of progress I had threatened to withdraw the fund. About 70 people work here and on the forest *sech bundh*.

In fact, work is being done on alternate days at the two sites. The Forest Department has also put greater pressure to meet the deadline of 31 March. The FPC members have worked harder than ever, sometimes in double shift and even late into the evening with the light powered by a generator. Seven weeks back the work had not even started.

◎

38

Maharajpur . . .
'What's in a Name'?

◎

Large potholes appear on the *morrum* road and jar the vehicle. Despite repeated exhortations and reminders, what the Panchayat Samiti is doing with the SGRY funds, if it is not using these for repairing such *morrum* roads which form the main means of communication in the interiors areas, remains a mystery to me. So I asked my companions. Both the Sabhapati and the BDO of Salboni Block, who were accompanying me to Maharajpur, between them could not think up a satisfactory answer to my question.

The area to our left was open undulating scrub land that merges into the forest. About 300–400 m away to the right were some hamlets woven in a tangle of bamboo clumps. Buffalo-drawn carts with huge iron wheels 5 ft in diameter are common in these parts. The land lay fallow after the *kharif* harvest. Although almost all houses in these parts have mud walls, but most have replaced the straw roofs with asbestos or GI sheets.

Mangal Tudu's house, at the periphery of Maharajpur village, is a set of huts with a tiny courtyard in the centre. The main hut has a tin top; the courtyard is about 10 ft long and 10 ft wide. On one side of the courtyard, Kabita Soren and Kajal Tudu sat in the shade on a strip of palm mat making sal leaf *thalis*, plates. Two neat piles of selected and sorted sal leaves, all nearly equal in size, lay near them, while between them was a small bunch of fine neem twigs, stripped of leaves and dried. They were breaking the pin-thin twigs into short two-inch lengths with which they stapled the sal leaves together, glossy side facing upwards, to form circular plates. The going rate for sal plates, used during weddings or any other social occasion, was about ₹60 per thousand plates. One woman may sew

Plate 38.1 Making sal-leaf plates

about 500–700 sal *thalis* in a day. But before that, everyday at the break of dawn, they must leave home to collect sal leaves from the forest, returning at about 8.30 a.m.–9.00 a.m. with bulging sacks balanced on their heads, in time for some *muri*.

Haru Tudu told me that there are 25–26 houses in this village, all of Santals. The nearest primary school is at Chandabila.

In Maharajpur an SSK is held under a shed with a floor of raised earth below a straw roof propped up by roughly hewn wooden posts. It has walls only on three sides, made of large dry palm fronds tied one on top of the other in threes; the SSK has no blackboard. Fortunately, there is a Mark-II hand pump nearby. The land for the SSK has been donated by a widow, Makhan Mandi; thereafter, little progress has been made towards the development of its infrastructure. Funds should be provided immediately for the construction of a permanent building for the SSK with toilets.

According to Murmu, the inhabitants of Maharajpur have received *Pattas* for about 52 *bighas* of land. As a result most people here own small plots of land while some still have no land to call their own. The doors also tell their stories. I came across a house whose courtyard was deserted and the door shut and bolted but not secured with a lock. Although tin, GI sheet or asbestos have replaced the straw as in other nearby villages, the houses are a sorry sight. Under the overhanging roofs round pots are hung to house pigeons. I asked one of the ladies whether they ate the pigeons, and they all raised their hands in abhorrence, 'No, no, they are only pets'.

I met Kali Soren carrying a load of sal-leaf plates over one shoulder to her house. Her silver hair is tied at the back and she wears a faded red petticoat like a skirt with a neatly folded green shawl draped over her bare breast. Most women in this village do not wear blouses but drape their *sari* over their left shoulder to cover their torso. Slippers are entirely absent.

The little used kitchen is seldom part of the main house. In front of each house there is a tiny kitchen shed with its roof made of palm fronds. In a few houses rice had already been cooked, but in most preparations for the evening meal had just begun. In the earthen verandah of her house Sambhu and Churamoni Soren's daughter Panmoni was cutting vegetables for the evening meal — the stem of the pumpkin creeper and potatoes. The door of their house is made of bamboo sticks tied together without any provision for a lock. On one mud-plastered wall of their house I find sketched in charcoal a credible dinosaur. By its side is the legend in Devanagri script, 'Daneshbar'.

Standing alone on one side of the village, Mani Tudu's house is among the most pitiful that I have seen. Long years of relentless beating of sun and rain have eroded the red mud walls and

Plate 38.2 Dinosaur

battered down a small room on the side. The palm frond roof supported by a failing bamboo frame has large holes to which the Relief Department's lone tarpaulin is unequal. Gnarled walls and a yielding roof, yes, but the widow's house does not even have a door! Beside an unlit earthen stove Mani Tudu stood in front of her house, a picture of abject poverty.

Plate 38.3 Mani Tudu's house

I asked the Sabhapati why she could not be selected for an IAY house — I was not reassured by his evasive answer. Lakhan Mandi and Bangi Murmu are two persons who were allotted funds for IAY houses in 1992. Before that and since then, in over 23 years, no one has received an IAY house in Maharajpur village. Bangi Mandi's house is about 15 ft long and 10 ft wide. I do a mental estimate of the one-room structure: the mud walls may cost no more than ₹2000, three concrete pillars and the front verandah of raised earth another ₹500, about ₹4000 for GI sheet roof, and another ₹1,500 for the wooden truss and the door. A total expenditure of no more than ₹8000. In 1992 the amount allotted for each IAY house was ₹16,000. Where did the rest of the money go?

One of the blessings bestowed on the village by the panchayat is a ring well built around 1987–1988. A twisted alluminium bucket with a length of rope tied to it sat next to the well, confirming that it was still in use. But without a protective parapet, let alone a platform around it, the concrete ringed opening at the ground level is a public health disaster. I peeped in to find the water about 25 ft below teeming with frogs, leaves and branches. I shuddered to think of what all must flow into it with the onset of each monsoon. Why cannot we build a parapet around the well?

We did not see a single house in Maharajpur that has a sanitary latrine.

We walked around the periphery of the village. The villagers told me of a *sech bundh* at the north-eastern corner of the village. As we headed towards the *bundh* I noticed a young girl holding a child on her hip gathering kindling in a bamboo copse. The mother was wrapped in a red *sari* and had a crimson *bindi* on her dark forehead; her 18-month-old daughter wore a red frock. Together, in the gathering evening they made a pretty picture; its sweetness, nevertheless, was robbed by the distressing certainty that the smiling mother could not be more than 15 years old. She did not remember when her daughter had received her vaccines nor did the infant have a health card.

A group of children had collected by then. Chatting with them I found out that they attend the SSK, which runs more or less regularly. As they posed for a photograph, I noticed a tall girl in a bright blue chequered frock wearing a startling pink *bindi* standing self-consciously at one side. I grimly wondered how long it would be before she too changed into a *sari*!

A public dug well is located next to Sukhchand Soren's house. It has water at the depth of about 30 ft. A large well had also been dug in the village by the panchayat a few years back, but its mouth, about 8 ft wide by 8 ft long, had not been bound in cement. After two or three seasons the walls of the wells built in the laterite belt collapse. In these areas wells should be paved with laterite blocks almost till the bottom and a protective parapet of brick and cement should protect the opening.

Trilochan Murmu lives in a mud house with the roof patched with a tarpaulin. Just back from work, on the way he had bought some sweets. Trilochan looked on as his wife gave his two small sons sitting in the threshold of the hut a *rasogolla* each with a slice of bread — a treat. Chickens were making their way back to the court-yard and the goats are already tied up. Mud pots and aluminium utensils were being put on earthen stoves to cook rice.

Pathmoni Soren was feeding her son; his aluminium plate held rice and some vegetables, no *dal*. She is the widow of late Sambhu Soren and lives all alone in a small house with a tin roof. Most houses in Maharajpur do not have large stacks of hay in front of them; the piles that I saw in a few courtyards were unpretentiously small. This is certainly not a grain surplus village.

Sombari Tudu, Moni Murmu and Mangli Murmu are three women in the village who seem to be suffering from cataract. Sombari Tudu is over 60 years old and wears glasses. She told me that she has cataract in her eyes. Since every year under the Blindness Control Programme operations are performed in government hospitals,[1] I asked her why she did not get it operated. Her answer: because it cost money. When I explained the process of enlistment and the schedule of surgery and post-operative care, and stressed that all this was entirely free, Sombari Tudu would not believe me. She had never heard of such a thing! So poorly are government programmes publicised that even 20 km from the district headquarters people do not know about them!

Jaya Soren, whose photograph I took, had had too much *mahua*. She wanted me to take more photographs of her. I could hardly say 'No'.

Kharam Murmu followed me to the vehicle and asked me for my address. I told him but I was not sure that the old man was sober enough to remember. I asked him to repeat the address and he said, *'Ekta kagaj hole likhe nitam, na hole shala mane thakbe na'*, 'If I had a piece of paper I would write it down, or else i'll bloody well forget it'. So I wrote it down for him on a sheet of paper. But I am not sure if he can read.

We left Maharajpur at about 6.00 p.m. The sun had set and the sky overhead was turning to a stunning glossy grey as the orange and pink faded over the horizon. Darkness was falling. As we drove by unlit hamlets, in grey courtyards we could spy aluminium pots glimmering on blazing earthen stoves.

The principal problems of Maharajpur are characteristic of most vulnerable villages in this part of the distict. The tribals own very little land, and that little is also not very productive. The uncultivated land in Maharajpur is Patta land distributed to the adivasis under the land reforms programme. At this time of the year, their land is lying hard and barren. Why is it that invariably adivasis seem to have received the poorest of the vested land distributed? Are they the beneficiaries of land reforms, or has it rendered them victims of statistics?

Most of the inhabitants are marginal farmers and several of them are landless. Their difficulty is compounded by the fact that the land does not retain much moisture. Additionally, there is hardly any source of irrigation. The lone water harvesting structure is the sech bundh *excavated under the water shed project, upon which two other neighbouring villages also have claims. The farmers of Maharajpur get a small proportion of water stored in that* sech bundh. *Therefore, other than the single* kharif *crop that they cultivate during the monsoon, they grow a few* bighas *of potatoes, and that is about all.*

The villagers' dependence upon the forest is evident from the fact that women from every household go into the jungle early in the morning and return with sacks of sal leaves, which in the late morning and afternoon they sew into sal plates. But each day one person can earn no more than about ₹40 selling sal leaf plates. And this is not a perennial activity either.

There is also a terrible lack of awareness about basic facilities and priorities. There is a primary school in neighbouring Chandabila. But the parents of Maharajpur prefer to send their children to the SSK held under a tiny shed made of log poles and palm fronds. Forty-five children are supposed to be enrolled there. But I am not sure how many actually attend on a regular basis. Minimal health care is about 3 km away in the Health Sub-Centre. Outreach camps do not seem to be held regularly. Even immunization is incomplete in this village. Drinking water is another area of concern since most of the village is dependent on a lone tube well, very recently set up, near the SSK about 50 m from the road. The houses in Maharajpur and Unchapara do not have an independent source of water other than the contaminated well in the middle of Majhpara. That the incidence of child marriage is very high, is small wonder.

Intoxication, addiction to local liquor appears to be a serious issue. Most of the people that we met earlier this evening, i.e., most adults, had already had a few glasses of mahua that I could smell on their breath. Even the women are not untouched. The loquacious Jaya Soren who insisted that I take a photograph of her could thank the mahua for her high spirits. There is little else in Maharajpur to prop up the spirit, for even water for bathing and ablution is scarce.

On the way back, Sudeep Mitra, DPLO, told me that today he had again heard what we had heard elsewhere too. Two sentiments had been muttered by some villagers during our visit: one, that they were not going to vote for anybody, 'Kauke bhote diba na, kono labh nei'; and, the second was 'Era sab emni asbe aar chale jabe. Karo aslei kono labh nai' — 'Won't vote for anyone. There is no use?' and 'They will just come like this and go back. Whosoever comes, it will make no difference to us!'

Note

1. National Programme for the Control of Blindness was launched in 1976 to reduce the prevalence of blindness, particularly if it is caused by cataract. It aims to bring relief to those afflicted by cataract and glaucoma by developing infrastructure and capacity to combat these ailments. Fully funded by the Central Government, the programme reaches out especially to the weaker sections who cannot afford cataract surgery, by enlisting the aid of NGOs and other community based organisations working in tandem with the governmental health care system.

◎

39
Life at the Peripheries
◎

Tiakati is ranked 53 in the district on the VVI. According to 2001 Census Tiakati has an area of 75 hectares, largely unirrigated, and a population of only 24. Female literacy percentage is reported to be 8.33 per cent, while 33 per cent of the total workers are marginal workers. It is also located across the undulating fields from Tamakbari, the most vulnerable village in Sadar Block, but falls in Manidaha Gram Panchayat.

The clear summer morning brightened the landscape as we passed through the congested areas just outside Midnapore town and turned towards Dherua. Villages were awake. Women led cattle off the road, to tie them down in stubbled fields. Beside the road, people with plastic bags holding their accessories for the day — such as a tiffin box, water bottle and perhaps a small hand towel to contend with drenching perspiration — waited for public transport to Midnapore. Cyclists on way to work pedalled hurriedly past to get into town; others with either full or empty gunny bags tied to their bicycle carriers also passed by; goats and cattle were being led out into the empty fields or towards the edge of the forest; women patted *gunthe,* into shape and slapped them on to the concrete sides of railway crossings, on parapets of culverts and bridges; a man who must have started work early in the morning was on his way back with two large sheaves of newly harvested wheat over his shoulders.

A little past Manidaha Gram Panchayat office, which stands directly off the state highway, we turned right at Rupsa village to take a mud road in the next village past the Dobra culvert. It gave me some happiness to see the culvert across the little stream. Instead of jumping across the stream at Baramchatti village to the Tamakbari side, or the other way round, people can now just walk across the culvert. However, to get to Tamakbari one would still have to walk on a feet-broadened *aal*; it will be a while before we have even a *morrum* road beyond the culvert to that village.

Instead of stopping at Tiakati we passed through the village, a huddle of huts, towards its north-eastern outskirts, because I wanted to inspect the water harvesting tank being excavated there. To its northern side, a *khal* formed by natural drainage leads from the forest into this reservoir. This is a wonderful site for a water harvesting structure, right adjacent to the forest with sal trees standing guard west of the tank and the embankment on its eastern side. The *khal* is actually a gully that extends deep into the forest and serves as its natural drainage point with the water flowing down, now, into the newly excavated reservoir. An excellent site — to me a sight, if not of glory at least of satisfaction. I am increasingly convinced that we must have more and more of these kind of *bundhs* all around the edges of the forest throughout the district.[1]

Two persons were at work at the site. Sanatan Mandi is from Tiakati village while Bhuban Mandi from Barhamchatti village 2 km away. Bhuvan is the only Santal that I have met who has grey eyes and sports a goatee. A *lungi* was tied half-way around his body. He told me that 25–30 people worked here everyday. After the recent rains the reservoir is half full. Two levels have been excavated, i.e., to a depth of about 6 ft. Now water has to be pumped out so that the work may resume.

Sanatan Hansda and Dulal Mandi are two young boys who had come with Sanatan Mandi to work at the site today. They were carrying *kodal*s for digging and were preparing to start work on a section at the southern end. They told me that they get ₹60 per day for their labours. Both stopped studying after the sixth standard, which they attended at Gurguripal High School. Although I knew the answer, I asked them. The inexorable reply came, '*Gharer abastha bhalo noi*', 'Conditions at home are not good'.

The forest *mouza* is known by the name 'Tiakati' but the knot of houses, which is also known as Tiakati, is actually Uttar Barhamchatti or North Barhamchatti. Dulal Mandi told me that there are no hand pumps in the village and in the coming summer months drinking water is likely to become a problem once again. As we entered the village I saw a group of six women headed for work. They stood framed against a clump of bamboo: five women and a girl in a red frock, accompanied by three little boys and a baby on one hip. Five of them carried the tools of their work, two knitted bamboo baskets each, containing the aluminium container with their lunch in it, while one of the women balanced an aluminium *ghada* on her head, presumably the day's supply of drinking water for the group.

The youngest of the three boys, who could not yet be four years old, resolutely held on to a small *kodal* slung over a shoulder. With stinging irony he reminded me of the glossy UNICEF and government publications proclaiming the Rights of the Child. I stopped and talked to the group. The children were too small to be left at home. They are not in an Anganwadi because the nearest one is several kilometres away. The 15-year-old girl in the red frock has not been to school, ever.

As we turned towards the village, I noted that the quality of the houses is not as good as in Jhargram, Binpur-I or the Jamboni area, although the better off houses appeared to be reasonably well-built, again of packed earth with straw roofs. In front of one hut I checked the health card of Mangal Hansda, born to Parbati and Kartik Hansda on 15 February 2005. The SHC is at Chandra, as is the PHC, about 4 km away and that is where they go for their immunization. The mother had received all the doses of iron, Tetanus-I and II. However, the child now almost two months old had not yet received polio drops, only the initial BCG shot on 19 March 2005, a month after his birth! Kartik and Parbati Hansda live in a cruel caricature of a house with walls of bamboo sticks holding a sagging tattered roof of ageing brown straw. The rear wall of the house is made only of dry, curling, palm fronds marked by ragged gaps. Why cannot Parbati and Kartik Hansda be provided a house under IAY?

Babli Hansda, the widow of Palton Hansda, is the recipient of an IAY house. Built about four years back, with walls of mud and a roof of GI sheets, it is about 22 ft long and 8 ft wide. As houses go, it is basic but a dependable shelter from the elements. Babli Hansda does not have any land or any other source of livelihood except her labour. She has a daughter about 13–14 years of age, Champa, and a son, Babu, about five. Champa Hansda is a physically handicapped girl. She needs to be checked by a medical team; it would enable her to receive an identity card for the physically handicapped, and the few attendant benefits. Both Champa and Babu are suffering from malnutrition. I also met Ria Hansda, daughter of Ram Hansda, who appears to be a hunchback. Rabi Hansda is another physically disabled person here. I wonder if they have the cards or even know about them.

Plate 39.1 The tired bridegroom

There was a wedding last evening of Tutu Hansda's daughter in his house. By local standards it is a largish house. The thick earthen walls have been freshly plastered with a mixture of clay and cow dung and the straw roof has been refurbished and neatly trimmed. A rude canopy of straw supported by four green bamboo up-rights, in which the night-long marriage ceremony was performed, stands empty in the courtyard glistening with the same *lep* of mud and cow dung. At one corner of the house, on the protruding plinth rest two tribal drums, while black goats feed on sal leaves nearby. I found the *jamai*, the new son-in-law, in a bright white *dhoti* and a vest, sleeping on a bare reed mat under a tree, his head pillowed on one folded arm — a picture of exhaustion. Through an open entrance to the house I noticed children sitting cross-legged on the earthen floor inside eating off sal leaf plates. As usual, I unashamedly edged to the doorway to take a closer look at the feast. The two children had just then sat down to a mound of rice and a bowl of dal, with salt on the side — in the house of celebration!

Near Tutu Hansda's home stands another poorly constructed house of bamboo and mud. Srinath Hansda's house is about 18 ft long and 8 ft wide; in the place of a door hangs a hand-woven mat of palm leaves. Anaath, Srinath Hansda's son, is lounging outside one of the doorways, eating *muri*. Srinath is apparently not very happy with him because when I asked about his son he said '*Aar bolen na*', 'Please do not ask'. Chotu Hansda lives next door in a similar hut; it has, however, a door made of bamboo staves.

I met Nabin Mandi and Dhananjoy Mandi, two old men who appear to have cataracts in their eyes. An eye screening camp was held last month in Chandra but these two did not attend; they did not know about it.

The best house in the village belongs to Bijoy Murmu. It is a large double-storeyed, white-washed dwelling made of brick and cement with shining GI sheet roofing. A motor-cycle, under an electric blue polythene cover, stands on the wide verandah. In front of the house is located the only well in the village. It is a ring well with a 4 ft diameter but no platform around it. It was funded by the panchayat. This is the way the benefits of government schemes are appropriated by the wealthy even in tribal societies. Bijoy Murmu, the owner of the big house, is actually a maker of *cholai,* illegal liquor; that is the source of his fortune and the influence that he wields on the panchayat.

Badrinath Mandi and his wife Suti Mandi's house lies a little outside the village, on edge of the forest. They settled down here about a year back and built a mud house with a tin and bamboo door, which is tied with a rope to the door frame when they go out. Badrinath and his wife were at home and so was their three-year-old son Tuli. Tuli Mandi was eating something from the aluminium cover of a pot. I asked what it was. Suti Mandi told me that it was *kurkut*, red ants, which they collected from the forest yesterday. Ground on the stone sill along with onions and salt, Tuli was eating the red ant savoury with watery rice.

Collection of sal leaves and making of sal plates is a common occupation in Tiakati. All the families here are engaged in it. In the sal forest nearby I could see a few women and children collecting sal leaves. Most adults, however, work as agricultural labourers. The wage during harvesting in the nearby fields comprises ₹30, two seers of rice and 200 gm of *muri*. During harvesting women and men get the same rate. But at other times men get ₹5–10 extra and also more to eat. Goats and pigs are also kept by those who can afford them. Here too, people asked me about improving the condition of their road — an earthen trail to their village that turns into a course of mud during the monsoon making communication difficult.

On the way back I stopped at the SSK that lies in the middle of the two habitations; the door of the one-room building was stolen some days back. I asked the few onlookers present why they could not take care of their school. They said that the Pradhan and the panchayat members were not allowing them to use the building for teaching Alchiki to their children; and SSK classes were not held regularly. The main resentment is against the Panchayat's refusal to let them use the building for teaching their children in their own language. This movement for learning Alchiki among the tribals of this area is strong and I do not see any reason why their aspirations should be thwarted in this manner. It only serves to breed a simmering resentment among the Santals. They have a right to learn their mother tongue; if they are not allowed to do so in their own village they will learn it elsewhere, as has been happening even in nearby Tamakbari. Indeed, now children from Tiakati go to Badarpur, about 4 km away, to receive Alchiki lessons.

Since two panchayat members were also present, I asked them to hand over the key to the FPC who would look after the building and also use it. I also asked the BDO to follow up with the Pradhan.

Women of Uttar Barhamchatti get their potable water from a nearby spring. At Dakshin Barhamchatti or South Barhamchatti village, I met a group of women and asked them where they wanted a new well located. The panchayat had decided to dig a well in the land of Ajay Mandi, at the far end of the village. The women vocally opposed the decision because many of them would have to come from the other end. They wanted the well to be located beside the malfunctioning hand pump in the centre of the hamlet. I agree, and that is where the well is going to be. One woman, Tuli Mandi, asked me whether there was any chance of getting widow pension. I asked her to apply through the panchayat to the block office. I also asked the SDO and the BDO to try and see that she gets the pension. No one gets widow pension or disability pension in this or the other half of Tiakati village. Baha Mandi complained that the ration shop is apparently issuing only 500 gm of rice per child every month — the amount due to them each week!

The bicycle is the main mode of communication and transport in most of the tribal areas of the district. It is the vehicle for transporting, among other things, family members to the *haat* or *bazaar*, pregnant women to the hospital, children to the health centres, milk in large aluminium cans slung on the either side of the rear wheel to the market, wood scrounged from the forest, large sacks of sal leaves, and dry leaves for fuel purposes. Dhiru Pati, a vendor of ribbons, ringlets and toys who moves around villages to peddle his wares, uses one too. A bicycle is the first sign of 'affluence' among the poor, including in the indigent adivasi hamlets in hilly areas.

On the way back from Tiakati I had an appointment with the Regional Manager, Punjab National Bank, who had requested me to inaugurate the building of a farmers' club in Bhatpara village, which the bank branch at Chandra had adopted. I checked and found that this was not one of the identified 1424 most vulnerable villages in the district. I chided the Regional Manager about it, since we had requested all banks to focus on the vulnerable villages first on a priority basis. Although he was apologetic he stated that the selection had been made in consultation with the Gram Panchayat, the Panchayat Samiti and the BDO. Bhatpara is a relatively prosperous village of 128 families most of whom are Scheduled Castes. Bhatpara has a primary school, an AWC and other amenities. However, the population of Scheduled Castes in this part of Midnapore is not the worst-off, the tribals are; the bankers and others must also realise this.

After the function on the way back I decided to go to the Tamakbari earth excavation site. I am sure that I will meet more angry people, but I must see what has happened to know why payment had been delayed by over a month at this site. I felt like withholding the BDO's pay for a month.

At about 11.30 a.m. we reached the water harvesting tank site at Natunbasti. My friend Rameswar Murmu was present. I asked him how the work was progressing. He informed us that the excavation was not going well since the workers, after the initial payment, had not received any wages for over a month now. 'That is why we asked you not to give this work to the panchayat', Rameswar Murmu remonstrated. People have not been getting the payment in time, therefore, they have not come to work. Less than 20 persons were engaged in the excavation today. The new well at Natunbasti had come up but, according to Rameswar and others present, the earth has not been filled right next to the rings of the well and, therefore, the encircling platform is likely to crack and break. An examination revealed that the villagers' fears were not unfounded. Moreover, the platform is only about 3 ft wide.

Next we visited the earthen dam being re-excavated by the Forest Department about 150 m away. The work there was also carrying on slowly. Today there are only 4–6 labourers at this site. On the western side a depth of about 9 ft has been reached, but on the eastern side, that is, the catchment area side, it is much less, only about 4 ft deep. We will have to check whether this is going to be a series of steps or the slope will be a gradual one. I asked the DFO and the ADFO why so few were at work today. Sanjoy Hansda, the paymaster, told me that this was because the measurement of the completed work had been done today and the payment had been made.

As I walked around the *bundh* being re-excavated, I beheld a sight that clutched at my heart as will its memory. On one bank of the *bundh*, within sight of the few workers struggling with the hard red earth, a few leafy sal branches about 6 ft high had been lodged in a small mound of earth. The thickly clustered leaves, now dry and curling, cast a thin shadow on the leeward side. In this slender shade of the dry branches protected from the glowering sun — if not from its heat — on an empty yellow plastic sack lay a baby, naked but for an amulet on a string around her waist — asleep.

In our part of the country this is the adivasi worker's 'creche'!

◎

Note

1. Before I left the district in April 2005, after consultations with the Conservator of Forests and the DFOs in the district, and then with the Chief Secretary, I forwarded a plan for the same. I do not think it saw the light of day.

40
A Twice-Told Tale
◎

The *morrum* road that we turned onto from the National Highway ran through open empty fields. On both sides we noticed a few large tanks and plantations of eucalyptus and bamboo. The social forestry scheme appears have taken roots in these areas.[1] Any upland area or any land that cannot be used for paddy cultivation appears to have been utilised for planting trees.

The BDO was waiting for us when we reached Alikosha village, which is also the name of the Gram Panchayat. In the mid-morning glare from the *morrum* road we could make out Kamia across the stretching green, an island of trees and barely discernible huts in the middle of a sea of paddy. The surrounding villages comprise a *boro* growing irrigated area. How has the island of tribals, identified by the VVI as the sixth most vulnerable village in the district, come to be located in this sea of relative prosperity?

The first inkling came as soon as we set off towards our destination; from the *morrum* road in Alikosha not even a footpath wends its way towards Kamia. We walked across the fields along the raised *aals*, which, as in Tamakbari and Rasunchak, also serve as pathways. Fields of green-gold and golden-brown paddy bend under their own weight on both sides. Some harvested paddy also lay in sheaves on the still moist earth, drying in the warm April sun. Shallow tube wells seem to be the main source of irrigation in this area.

As we approached the village I noticed a *than,* a small, usually raised, demarcated place of worship, at the corner of a clearing. Small terracotta horses and elephants clustered around a terracotta icon, under a rude low shed made of 4 ft tall bamboo stakes with a thatch covering; according to the greying Sukna Mandi, it was dedicated to *Shib thakur*. The village itself consisted of a few houses built around a pond with clumps of soaring bamboo and some trees giving it the aspect of a large grove.

Kamia comprises two habitations set apart by about half a kilometre of paddy fields. There are seven families on the banks of a small *pukur*, and four residing on that of another pond a few 100 m away. Sombari Mandi, Sukna Mandi's wife, came out of their hut. She was wearing an old but bright green *sari* over an orange blouse. A thin silver chain around her neck, silver earrings, and thin silver bangles are all her wealth. I noticed that she also wore the red and white *shankha-pola*, bangles that all traditional married Bengali women wear. Is this what joining the mainstream means? However, Sombari's thin frame and her care-furrowed brow proclaimed her anemic condition — physical and material.

Sombari's daughter-in-law, who appeared to be a few months pregnant, was having her morning meal of rice with water and a bowl of vegetables. I asked her why she ate so late, for normally the morning meal is taken at about 8.30–9.00 a.m. She pointed at the stacks of hay next to the manual threshing machine and the threshed paddy spread on the mud-plastered courtyard. Since she had been busy threshing the paddy this morning, her food had gone cold.

Sukna and Sombari Mandi have one son and two daughters. Shaktipada Mandi, 16–17 years old son, is married. Shaktipada said that he had just appeared for the *Madhyamik* examinations and planned to learn computers. Paora Mandi is the second child, a daughter. She is about 15 or 16 and has never been to school. Mani Mandi, the youngest child, is about 6–7 years old. She is studying in the second standard of the primary school at Alikosha. Sombari lives in a single-storeyed structure with mud walls and a sloping, low two-tier straw roof that protects the vital verandah from the incursions of the monsoon. Sukna Mandi has his own hand pump in front of his house. Another one has been set up by the panchayat at a corner of the pond. The hand pump provided by the panchayat is a regular old style one without any platform. Located at the edge of the *pukur*, it must be susceptible to routine contamination.

As we were talking to the Mandis, I noticed a few people come and sit down near the entrance of the village in the shade of the trees. I walked over to them for a chat. This was a group of five labourers, two men and three young women; the youngest of the latter would have looked well in a school uniform. They had been working in the fields harvesting paddy, for which they had taken a

Plate 40.1 Lunch break

contract. The five were a family. After their morning toil under the strong sun they relaxed squatting on the bare ground in the shade, the men with their shirts off, and a transistor radio nearby playing a Hindi song through the static. As they were about to begin their meal, quite unashamedly, I peered into the large aluminium bowls to see what they were eating: rice kept fresh in some water, a little green vegetable (some kind of spinach) in a small bowl, and two pinches of salt on a leaf. It was easy to divine that the mainstay of their food was the heaped, wet rice spiced with salt. They carried water in old mineral water bottles. After a few words, since I could sense their discomfort at my intruding presence, I left them to their much needed meal and earned moments of respite.

Gurbari Mandi and Ratan Mandi have a hut on the far side of the *pukur* in Kamia. A hand pump stands in one corner of the courtyard; it does not have a circular cemented platform either. However,

I notice that instead the enterprising owners have placed a pre-fabricated toilet platform, provided under the TSC programme, under the hand pump to prevent the formation of puddles. A half-built hut stands on one side of the courtyard. Their present home is a pitiable structure with one small room covered by a sparse straw roof and an obviously un-lockable door made with bamboo sticks nailed and tied together. Next to the house is a small vegetable garden fenced with rude sticks. Gurbari and Ratan own a few goats and little else.

Old Jyotiram Mandi stays on the third side of the *pukur*, in a house with only half a roof. Apparently built under the IAY, now it is in ruins. Jyotiram Mandi's wife Fulmani Mandi was drying her few clothes and a few dusty blankets on a wobbly *khat* in the backyard.

We moved on to the water harvesting structure being excavated by the Agri-Irrigation Department under the RSVY. It is a square and the sloping sides descend in three steps to the base. The work is approaching completion and they are laying a polythene lining on the bottom to minimise seepage. I was told that in the earlier stages about 100 persons used to work here everyday; today I saw around 25. The embankments, stretches of piled earth dug out of the new pond rising up to 12 ft, need to be firmed. Sukna Mandi, on whose land the *pukur* has been excavated, should be helped to plant fruit-bearing and fuel-wood trees on the banks of the new *pukur*; the trees and plants will strengthen the embankment of the pukur and also supplement his income. With some satisfaction I saw water beginning to seep in through the western flank of the pond.

The new pond is being built between the two hamlets adjacent to Kamia. We walked over to the other habitation — Annageria. The other half of the revenue *mouza* Kamia comprises four huts in different stages of dilapidation covered with polythene sheets and straw, built around a *pukur*. The central *pukurs* in Annageria and Kamia main are both vested and partly owned by a large land-owner. One hand pump serves Annageria, but without a platform it nestles in the perennial muddy puddle at its base; at least the hand pumps can be secured with a platform! Of the four families in Annageria, three belong to the Bhumij community and probably related to each other through common grandparents. All four of them claimed to be landless and I did not doubt them. They work

Plate 40.2 New tank at Kamia

as labourers in the fields around them and till a morsel of land on the bank of the *pukur*.

The nearest SHC is about 2 km away at Jamuna village; earlier it was at Charda. I asked for the health card of Lata Singh born on 13 March 2005 — less than a month old. She is the daughter of Basanti Singh and Ajit Singh of Kamia. The mother has not taken a single shot of tetanus or iron, or had received any antenatal care during her period of pregnancy! This is just unpardonable. One dose of polio was administered to the child on 23 March 2005.

On the packed-earth verandah of a hut, under the low, sloping straw roof, I spied three women and a girl in a pink printed frock having *muri* with tamarind *chutney*. Apparently they had had their main meal earlier in the day and were taking a short break from work. Between them, on a swaddle of blankets on the floor against the wall, lay a chortling Bapi Singh born on 1 December 2004, I examined Bapi's health card. In this case the mother had been given five out of eight shots. The second tetanus shot was due. But the child, although almost five months old, had not yet received anything other than the polio vaccine!

Some immediate steps needed to be taken in these two habitations of Kamia village are: provision of Mark-II hand pumps with platforms, in place of the traditional hand pumps that are in use at present; ensuring health care by holding a meeting of the health workers of this village; provision of poultry, pig-keeping or duck-keeping units; and provision of other income generation schemes including social forestry, especially cultivation of fruit-bearing shrubs and trees.

Kamia is the twice-told story of a village settled by a local zamindar about 50–60 years ago. Two or three Santal and Bhumij families were plucked out of red laterite — from where they do not know — and transplanted in the rich alluvium of the plains. They were settled around pukurs in the middle of the fields to ensure that they could supply their labour to the landlords' land without let up. Since then households have grown, and now a total of 11 families of about 100 people has congealed into the village of Kamia — an island of poverty amidst a sea of plenty. In all its history Kamia has received one IAY house; today that is the shabbiest house in the village!

◎

Note

1. Social Forestry Scheme envisages the development of forests in unused, barren and fallow land in and around populated and less populated areas of the country. The aim is to reduce the pressure of human population on natural forests by planting various species of fuel-wood and fruit-bearing trees in areas such as beside roads and railway tracks, the banks of rivers and water bodies, and community owned land.

Epilogue:
At the Heart of Darkness[1]

◎

Paschim Medinipur district has been identified as one of the 150 most backward districts in the country by the Planning Commission of India. Yet that does not necessarily mean that the district is uniformly backward. If the district were divided into two almost-equal halves by drawing a line from the north-eastern extremity to the south-western corner, we find that the picture alters.

It is generally known that the western and north-western parts of Paschim Medinipur comprise some of the most neglected and backward areas of the district. All the blocks of Jhargram sub-division, major parts of the three blocks of Medinipur Sadar sub-division (Garhbeta-II, Salboni and Medinipur Sadar blocks), and small portions of the three blocks of Kharagpur sub-division (Kharagpur-I, Kharagpur-II and parts of Narayangarh blocks) fall in this area. It is not surprising that this hard, undulating lateritic shelf that tilts towards, and then merges, with the eastern and south-eastern deltaic plain, is not only forested but also home to a majority of the adivasi population of this district. There are notable disparities between the two halves of the district, particularly in the income and literacy levels. Rainfall in the western half is also less than in the rest of the district. Nineteen blocks of this district, most of them falling in this half, are also designated as Integrated Tribal Development Project (ITDP) Blocks. Overall the western and north-western half of Paschim Medinipur District is more vulnerable than the blocks lying in the alluvial deltaic plain in its eastern and south-eastern parts.

The Deepest Shadows

By almost any yardstick contrived to measure development, a large number of villages in these blocks fail to fulfill the basic criteria. It would, again, not be surprising to find that most of these villages are predominantly populated by adivasis. Without wasting time on the parameters of development let us examine some common threads that weave these habitations into an unsightly tapestry of backwardness.

In these villages, most of the land owned by the adivasis, including land received by *Patta*, is either poor in quality, *danga* (upland), or un-irrigated or both; many of them do not own any land and depend only upon their labour for existence; almost every household is dependent upon the forest for vital supplementary income — on sal leaves, *babui* grass, *kendu* leaves, herbs and roots, etc; and, though this may sound trite, middlemen buy the forest produce from the adivasis at a pittance and sell at unimaginable margins (Example: adivasis collect and sell shelled ripe tamarind at ₹5 a kg, and collect, stitch and sell sal leaf plates at ₹60 per thousand plates; in Midnapore, 1 kg of the same tamarind sells for ₹45 and thousand sal leaf plates for ₹400, i.e., at 400 per cent and 660 per cent higher rates, respectively).

In these villages, overall literacy rates are much lower than the district average, and female literacy plunges even more sharply; the abysmal levels of literacy blindingly reflect on the almost 100 per cent incidence of child marriage, and girls who are mothers *twice-over* before they are 17–18. In uncommon instances, if a primary school is located in a village, it is unlikely to have the full complement of teachers or children. In the last few years SSKs have appeared in or near several of these villages but whether they are meant to serve the children of these villages or the panchayat appointed sahayikas, who come mostly from outside the village, is no longer a matter of conjecture. Many of these villages lie at the end of a footpath that turns to mud in the monsoon; other than bare feet, bicycle is the only form of transport — *even for women on their way to the health centre for delivering a baby.*

Houses in most such villages are of poor quality; not because adivasis lack house-building skills but because the surplus necessary for constructing a strong house — the right type of earth, paddy straw, bamboo or sal logs, and labour — is beyond their reach annually. Yet despite the wealth of straggling, palm-leaf patched, lock-less if not door-less, huts, IAY houses are rarities in these villages. Ordinarily known as the 'control', the local ration shop usually provides kerosene oil, sometimes sugar, infrequently grains, and generally stocks frustration; the modified ration dealers do ensure that the adivasis deposit their ration cards with them for 'safekeeping' and, undoubtedly, for perfect accounting. Although basic healthcare facilities (at the SHC level) appear to be functioning, for grievous ailments inhabitants of these villages habitually rely upon semi-literate quacks, whose shops may be found at the nearest *bazaar*, instead of government doctors.

This litany of wretchedness is endless . . .

Exploring the Reasons

Why has the situation come to such a pass? Despite no major locational disadvantages, and in spite of several natural advantages, why is this area backward and the people vulnerable to hunger and unable to avail of the benefits of government programmes? Why is the adivasi a stranger in his own land?

Some cogent reasons may be as follows:

Alienation

The adivasis in this area are yet to be assimilated in the 'mainstream', social or political. Bengalis and adivasis co-exist with a constant recognition of each other's otherness — voiced continually, strongly, and often derisively by the former and tiredly accepted by the latter.

The established educational backwardness of the adivasis may be traced to the inadequacy of schools in this area. The number of schools may not necessarily be few but they do not take into account the sparsely populated and scattered villages that characterise adivasi areas. Moreover, the number of teachers and their attendance is a matter of concern.

The low literacy levels among the adivasis may also be due to the fact that the adivasi child has to struggle in school, under unsympathetic teachers, with a new language, Bengali. It is worthwhile to note that in most adivasi villages *the old and the young* understand and speak very little Bengali. Culturally, interaction between the two groups is limited; although adivasis participate in the major festivals of the non-adivasis, the latter are not to be found even at the fringes of adivasi social events, except to laugh at them.

Indeed, the points of contact between the adivasi and the non-adivasi are two: (*a*) the market — for labour or the *haat* for agricultural or forest produce, and (*b*) elections. In the first instance, however exploitative, transactions are guided by mutual interest. However, the adivasi has increasingly awakened to the fact that elections are not an exercise in fulfilling mutual needs but the elaboration of only one-sided interest; the 'others' need their votes but give little or nothing in return. That is why even government officials visiting a village, mistaken for public representatives, meet with responses such as: '*Ek ta-o bhote debo na*' (We won't give you even one vote), '*Aabaar bhoter jonye eshecho!*' (So you've come again for our vote!), '*Ekhane karo ashle kichu hobe na!*' (Doesn't matter who comes, nothing will happen here!), and so on.

Due to their small spreadout numbers adivasis appear to be of peripheral importance to the political system, unfortunately even in the Panchayat bodies. Unlike in other parts of the district, in ITDP areas evidence of political mobilisation of the adivasis for participation in fora such as Gram Sansads, beneficiary and monitoring committees is difficult to come by. Since they do not participate regularly in the processes of the Panchayat system, other than swelling the ranks at political rallies and voting at election time, they are consigned to the margins of the political system.

Ignorance

The adivasi's ignorance of the legal and administrative system, the market, and the public facilities that government has set up for the people creates the myth of the 'stupid adivasi'. This ignorance actually stems from the adivasis' low income levels, few opportunities for formal or informal education, lack of any attempt and inability of local Panchayat and political leadership to educate them on vital points of interest (for e.g. the availability of grains in the ration shop), and even deliberate suppression or obfuscation of critical information (such as the details of sanctioned estimate of a road construction or water tank excavation scheme) by officials — both elected and appointed. Records elicit that the adivasis in this region have taken to the agricultural mode of existence over a period of about 200 years. Although conversant with the tangled environs of the forest, they are yet to fully acquire the skills of agriculture or come to grips with the structures of 'mainstream' society — formal and informal. Their ignorance sustains their exploitation and marginalisation at the hands of the 'others'.

Voicelessness

By and large, poverty, lack of education, ignorance, and political marginalisation has resulted in the voicelessness of the adivasis. A feeling has grown among them that outside their immediate tribal group their voice is not heard, neither in the decision-making bodies of local self-governance nor in the supposedly cozier confines of non-adivasi social organisations and institutions.

Panchayats

The most disturbing aspect of these vulnerable villages is the failure of the Panchayat bodies — at times, of all three tiers — to appreciate their condition. Why and how has this transpired?

The advasis live in small groups in villages scattered over undulating, forested terrain. This is in marked contrast to the way non-adivasi villages are situated in the better off eastern blocks of the district. For instance, Binpur-II, perhaps the most vulnerable block, has 401 populated villages with an average population size of 268 per village, whereas Daspur-II, the most prosperous block in the district, has only 87 villages with an average population of 2369 persons per village! As mentioned earlier, a study based on Census 2001 data reveals that in Paschim Medinipur district 4721 of 7581 populated villages, or 62.28 per cent of the total, have a population of less than 500 persons; of these 414 have a population of less than 50 and 2615 villages have a population below 250 persons. The study also elicits that the smaller the population size of a village, the greater is the concentration of Scheduled Tribe persons. The pattern of investment of development funds shows that most of the investments have been made in the larger villages and the least in the smallest villages — whether adivasi or non-adivasi. *This is in keeping with the logic of democracy but not in keeping with the objectives of either local self-government or development administration that are meant to target foremost the poorest of the poor.*

Panchayat bodies not only *do not* prioritise and allocate funds on the basis of need, but also practice an egalitarianism that does not address the problems of the most vulnerable. By and large, and not just in this district, development funds are equally divided on the basis of the number of *sansads*, or Gram Panchayats at the Panchayat Samiti level. It matters little if a particular scheme such as

IAY is required in a particular area, it will inevitably get its quota of houses. This results in inadequate utilisation of development funds on the one hand, and neglect of the needy on the other.

Decision-making in the existing 'system' hurts the adivasis the most. There is inordinate delay in deciding upon the schemes, their location and their beneficiaries at almost all three levels throughout the district. Despite constant reminders and persuasion it has not been possible to ensure that Panchayat bodies prepare a shelf of schemes in advance so that when funds are received no time is lost in implementing them. Increasingly one begins to wonder whether this inability of selecting schemes and beneficiaries in advance arises from administrative incapacity or deliberate political calculation. Increasingly one feels that panchayat bodies *do not* decide in advance because it would tie them down without any bargaining space with potential beneficiaries. *One wonders if this is sound pol-itics, but one has no doubt that this is unsound administration that costs the State hundreds of crores in funds unspent while denying basic amenities to lakhs of people.*

A substantial number of Pradhans of Gram Panchayats and Sabhapatis of Panchayat Samitis are holding their post for the first time. Several of them are junior members of their political party; they may not even have been particularly active in their party organ-isations or held important responsibilities therein. Often they are puppets in the hands of their political party leadership at the district and sub-district levels. Almost each decision taken with respect to selection and implementation of schemes are scrutinised by the party leadership at the local or superior levels. In such a scenario delay in decision-making is inevitable. This constant supervision of each minute detail over the heads of elected Panchayat office-bearers also prevents both, the individuals and institutions, from growing into responsible public functionaries. Further, *how can people perceive Panchayat bodies as credible institutions of local self-government when all decisions are known to be made not in the Gram Panchayat, Panchayat Samiti office or the concerned Sthayi Samiti, but in the local office of the political party?*

It is known that certain political parties take considerable pains to organise regular training programmes for Panchayat members of all tiers belonging to their party. Over the years such in-house training meant to develop the capacity of Panchayat representatives and holders of elected office in the Panchayat bodies has become diluted in content and diminished in frequency. This has also had a debilitating effect on the functioning of Panchayat bodies in this district.

The Panchayat Samitis and Gram Panchayats in the three blocks of Binpur-II, Binpur-I and Jamboni have been in the hands of parties other than the ruling party/coalition in the state. Binpur-II continues to be so. These Panchayat Samitis and Gram Panchayats have suffered from two types of neglect: (*a*) of the type mentioned earlier in this section; and (*b*) of step-motherly, antagonistic or outright hostile treatment by the Panchayat Samiti of the Gram Panchayats on the one hand, and by the Zilla Parishad of the Panchayat Samitis or Gram Panchayats on the other. This could take the form of discrimination in disbursement of funds, delay in processing recommendations or cases that are to be sanctioned at the district level, preventing the posting of adequate administrative personnel, etc.

In almost all the blocks a vicious nexus has developed between Panchayat functionaries, government officials and contractors (significantly, even in the Jhargram area the vast majority of contractors are non-adivasis). Often these contractors motivate and guide Panchayat officials in decision-making pertaining to various schemes. They have been known to accompany them in deputations and meetings with block, sub-divisional and district authorities. This has happened primarily because schemes are often not implemented according to financial rules and contracts are awarded without publishing a notice inviting tenders.

Leakage of development funds at the implementation stage is also a common phenomenon in these areas. In this regard, members of the nexus mentioned, jointly or separately, extract a commission from each scheme, from contractors and even from beneficiaries. The extent of leakage in most construction schemes ranges from 20 per cent to 40 per cent; in certain types of schemes it is higher. For instance, it may be difficult to believe but in the IAY the range of leakage is from 20 per cent to 50 per cent!

Office-bearers of Panchayats rarely visit the remoter areas, where the most backward villages are located — unless it is to attend or inaugurate a function. Not only do they not tour they do not even come to the Panchayat office regularly. In these blocks although Panchayat Samiti offices are normally open, but poorly attended, many Gram Panchayat offices do not open regularly; since elected officials remain absent, the Panchayat officials follow suit. The suffrage of the area also takes this state of affairs to be a given. The consequence of this situation is a state of divorce between the Panchayats and the people whom they are meant to serve. The state of quite a few Gram Panchayats in the remoter areas is, ironically, like the three celebrated monkeys: they sit serenely and see no evil, say no evil, and hear no evil!

People's Organisations

In the most backward blocks of the district, other than the formal structures of governance, very few People's Organisations and NGOs are active. Therefore, although there is considerable need and potential for social mobilisation the mainstream organisations are not quite as active as they could be. *Consequently, activists of LWE groups are moving into the vacant space.*

To chase away the darkness in the areas under scrutiny the first need is to target the most backward villages with specific programmes and funds. This task cannot be accomplished unless the Panchayat bodies take responsibility for the most vulnerable — with support from the agencies of the State government. Further, unless women, farmers, basket-makers, *kendu* leaf collectors, sal leaf plate makers, the youth — all the diverse sub-groups within this society — are made aware of their role, rights and responsibilities and organised for concerted social action, their exploitation, marginalisation and alienation will continue. Until the adivasis perceive that they have a stake in this society and a valued place in this system, the problems being faced in the western and north-western parts of Paschim Medinipur district can also not be expected to abate.

◎

Note

1. At the outset it is clarified that this account is neither comprehensive nor complete. It is like the notorious tip of the iceberg, revealing a fraction of the problems but indicating the insidious nature and magnitude thereof. The note does not include a status of the government machinery, which may be explored separately.
   [This assessment, written in March 2005, has been reproduced without any changes except in the title.]

Appendix

◎

Paschim Medinipur: District Profile

Midnapore, the largest district of West Bengal, located in the south-western side of West Bengal, was divided into two parts on 1 January 2002 — Purba Medinipur and Paschim Medinipur. Paschim Medinipur, where the old district headquarters are located in the town of Midnapore, is bounded by Purulia and Bankura district in the north, Hooghly and Purba Medinipur in the east, states of Jharkhand and Odisha in the west, and Purba Medinipur district in the south.

Paschim Medinipur district consists of four sub-divisions, 29 blocks and eight municipalities. The names of the blocks and municipalities (sub-division wise) are as follows:

Midnapore Sadar Sub-division	Kharagpur Sub-division
Blocks	*Blocks*
• Midnapore Sadar • Salboni • Keshpur • Garhbeta-I • Garhbeta-II • Garhbeta-III	• Kharagpur-I • Kharagpur-II • Keshiary • Debra • Pingla • Dantan-I • Dantan-II • Sabang • Mohanpur • Narayangarh
Municipality • Midnapore	*Municipality* • Kharagpur

Jhargram Sub-division	Ghatal Sub-division
Blocks	*Blocks*
• Jhargram	• Ghatal
• Binpur-I	• Chandrakona-I
• Binpur-II	• Chandrakona-II
• Jamboni	• Daspur-I
• Sankrail	• Daspur-II
• Gopiballavpur-I	
• Gopiballavpur-II	*Municipalities*
• Nayagram	• Ghatal
	• Chandrakona
Municipality	• Khirpai
• Jhargram	• Kharar
	• Ramjibanpur

The district has huge resources of forestry. Based on the forest resources, industries such as paper mills, saw mills, furniture-making and other allied units have been developed. In agriculture, paddy is the main product, from which rice mills, mini rice mills and solvent extraction units from rice bran oil have been developed. Potato is produced mainly in Midnapore and Ghatal sub-divisions. There is potential for the development of diverse products using coir and *babui* rope in Jhargram sub-division. Large portions of fallow land are scattered across the district. Attempts have been made to set up agro-industry parks and hand over the ownership to unemployed educated youth on a long-term lease basis, to enable them to earn their livelihood. Several thousand SHGs have also been formed in the district.

The district lies between latitudes 21°47′N to 23°00′N and longitudes 86°40′E to 87°52′E. The climate here is tropical, moist and sub-humid. The distribution of rainfall is irregular and uneven. Hard and rugged rock lateritic topography characterises the western part of the district, while the eastern side comprises nearly flat alluvial plains. The main rivers of this district are Kangsabati, Silai, Subarnarekha, Keleghai, and their tributaries. The north-western and western parts of the district are mainly covered with forest. A large portion of the western part of Paschim Medinipur district is drought-prone, whereas the eastern part is flood-prone. A few blocks under Kharagpur sub-division are sometimes also ravaged by cyclones.

The district is predominantly agricultural and stress has been given on agriculture production. Paddy, potato, green vegetables, and cashew-nuts are the main crops. In addition, several other crops such as oilseeds and some pulses are grown here. There is considerable scope for development of horticulture, especially of fruits such as mango, papaya, guava, citrus, custard apple, jackfruit and banana, in the laterite areas. Sericulture is another agro-commercial activity.

The National Highway no. 6 runs through this district. Kharagpur is the main industrial town. The south-eastern railways with the divisional headquarters at Kharagpur, is an asset. A network of state and other highways connect various parts of the district. There are some small-scale industrial clusters in and around Jhargram and Garhbeta, while certain cottage and handloom industries are found in various blocks of the district.

Some basic data of the district:

Demographic features

Details	Paschim Medinipur
Population (Census 2001 provisional)	5218399
Male	2659904
Female	2558495
Scheduled Caste	18.07 per cent
Scheduled Tribe	14.89 per cent
Total Literacy Rate (percentage)	60.69 per cent
Male Literacy Rate (percentage)	70.13 per cent
Female Literacy Rate (percentage)	50.81 per cent
Decadal Growth Rate	+ 15.68 per cent
Density of Population/sq. km	561.4
Sex Ratio (number of females per thousand male)	962
Area (in sq km)	9295.28
Mouzas	8735

(Continued)

(Continued)

Inhabited	7498
Uninhabited	1237
Net area under cultivation (in hectare)	594183

Source: Census 2001, Government of India.

Administrative Set-up (2004)

Details	Paschim Medinipur
Sub-divisions	4
Police Stations	27
Block/Panchayat Samiti	29
Municipalities	8
Wards	131
Gram Panchayats	290
Gram Sansads	3491

Information on Pre-schooling (2004)

Details	Paschim Medinipur
Number of AWCs	4441
Number of children covered (3+ to 4+ years)	182401

Educational Units (2004)

Details	Paschim Medinipur
Number of Circles	65
Government-aided Primary Schools	4645
Special Schools for Child Labour	36
PU/Rural Libraries	142
Upper Primary Schools	747
PTTI	3
Colleges	19
Teachers' Training Institutes	3

Medical College & Hospital	1
Medical College (Homeo)	1
Indian Institue of Technology (Kharagpur)	1
Industrial Training Institutes	2
Polytechnics	1
University	1
Alternative Schooling (2004)	
Number of SSKs	2496
Number of *Sahayikas*	5559
Enrollment in SSK	116199

Source: Integrated Child Development Scheme (ICDS) Administrative Report, Paschim Medinipur, 2004.

About the Author

◎

Chandan Sinha is currently Principal Secretary, Departments of Environment and Forest, West Bengal. A graduate in English Literature from St Stephen's College, University of Delhi, he has master's degrees in Public Administration from the University of South Carolina (1987) and the Maxwell School, Syracuse University (2006). He joined the Indian Administrative Service in 1989, and was the District Magistrate and Collector of Cooch Behar and Paschim Medinipur districts for about four years. He has served in various departments of the Government of West Bengal, namely Departments of Panchayat & Rural Development, Power & Non-conventional Energy, and the Health & Family Welfare. He also held the post of Deputy Director in the faculty of Lal Bahadur Shastri National Academy of Administration, Mussoorie (1996–2001).

Actively engaged in research and writing, he has published articles in various journals, and is the author of *Public Sector Reforms in India: New Role of the District Officer* (2007).

Index

◎

For Product Safety Concerns and Information please contact our EU
representative GPSR@taylorandfrancis.com
Taylor & Francis Verlag GmbH, Kaufingerstraße 24, 80331 München, Germany

www.ingramcontent.com/pod-product-compliance
Lightning Source LLC
Chambersburg PA
CBHW060140280326
41932CB00012B/1579